Common Bonds

Anti-Bias Teaching in a Diverse Society

3rd Edition

Edited by

Deborah A. Byrnes, Utah State University, Logan, UT

and

Gary Kiger, Utah State University, Logan, UT

ACEI

ASSOCIATION FOR CHILDHOOD EDUCATION INTERNATIONAL

17904 Georgia Ave., Ste. 215, Olney, MD 20832 • 800-423-3563 • www.acei.org

Bruce Herzig, ACEI Editor
Anne Bauer, ACEI Editor
Deborah Jordan Kravitz, Design and Production

Library of Congress Cataloging-in-Publication Data

Common bonds : anti-bias teaching in a diverse society / edited by Deborah A. Byrnes and Gary Kiger.— 3rd ed.
p. cm.
Addressing race, ethnicity, and culture in the classroom / Deborah A. Byrnes — Living with our deepest differences : religious diversity in the classroom / Charles C. Haynes — Ability differences in the classroom : teaching and learning in inclusive classrooms / Mara Sapon-Shevin — Class differences : economic in equality in the classroom / Ellen Davidson and Nancy Schniedewind — Language Diversity in the Classroom / Deborah A. Byrnes, Lisa Pray, and Diana Cortez — Creating gender equitable classroom environments / Janice Koch — Sexual diversity issues in schools / Deborah Byrnes — Integrating anti-bias education / James J. Barta and Corinne Mount Pleasant-Jetté — Tooling the Toolbox : checklist of skills for teaching in diverse classrooms and communities / Judith Puncochar.
Includes bibliographical references.
ISBN 0-87173-167-3 (pbk.)
1. Multicultural education—United States. I. Byrnes, Deborah A. II. Kiger, Gary. III. Title.

LC1099.3.C64 2005
370.117—dc22

2005018431

Table of Contents

1-6-05 ACEI 22.00

Introduction

Gary Kiger and Deborah A. Byrnes

Since the publication of the last edition of this book, in 1996, two profound changes have occurred that significantly affect public education in the United States. The first is passage of the No Child Left Behind legislation and the second is the post-9/11 reactions of society. The challenges for classroom teachers in our diverse schools have never been greater. The unfunded mandates under No Child Left Behind, combined with a resurgence of political values associated with religious conservatism in a culture of fear in a post-9/11 world, place severe strains on teachers who work to create classroom climates of acceptance through anti-bias teaching.

The No Child Left Behind Act of 2001 sought to improve public education for America's children. The legislation mandated accountability among schools for students' academic achievement in math and reading, as measured through testing. The uplifting rhetoric of the No Child Left Behind (NCLB) promises focused on equality of expectation: poor children attending poorly funded schools would have the same education expectations placed on them as rich students attending well-funded schools, children with disabilities would have achievement expectations on par with their peers without disabilities, and children whose first language was not English would have achievement expectations comparable to their native-English-speaking schoolmates. Learning standards are the same for all students. By emphasizing testing without taking into account ability differences among students, NCLB's sanctioning of schools that do not make "adequate yearly progress" is most likely to affect schools that serve primarily low-income students, students with special needs, and children whose first language is not English. As former U.S. Secretary of Education Richard Riley wrote, "Indeed, raising standards without closing resource gaps may have the perverse effect of exacerbating achievement gaps and of setting up many children for failure" (cited in Mathis, 2002). Moreover, with the NCLB emphasis on high-stakes testing and the underfunding of mandated provisions of the law, schools often respond by plowing resources into "teaching to the tests" efforts, rather than much-needed educational services to students who most need them. Amrein and Berliner (2002) note:

If the intended goal of high-stakes testing policy is to increase student learning, then that policy is not working. While a state's high-stakes test may show increased scores, there is little support in these data that such increases are anything but the result of test preparation and/or the exclusion of students from the testing process.

The post-9/11 social and political responses have turned the cultural focus in the United States inward. The public calls to patriotism have the potential for inciting intolerance. Some Americans harbor suspicion and fear of people who are perceived as different from cultural notions of true "Americans"; this fear can lead to prejudice, discrimination, and xenophobia. To the extent that terrorism has been linked to Middle Eastern countries and the Islamic faith, such social and political discussions often turn on religious themes. For many faiths, religious beliefs involve ultimate values that are not readily compromised or negotiated. So, tolerance in society or in the microcosm of our schools can be difficult to teach as a value when it bumps up against the certainty of religious faith. This intolerance can gain expression through prejudice and discrimination against children of different faiths, against children who are gay or lesbian, or against families that do not share a particular social and political agenda.

Purpose and Organization of This Book

The purpose of this book is to examine the growing diversity in schools in a constructive, empowering way. The authors contributing to this new edition write about various forms of cultural diversity, and suggest ways that teachers can build inclusive classroom environments. The common theme that emerges is that while diversity poses difficulties, teachers can create an environment in which differences are recognized and accepted while simultaneously reinforcing a common set of norms and values that bind students together. The authors also suggest ways for enabling students to discard existing stereotypes and actively question and reject attitudes and actions not congruent with a pluralistic society. These are the goals of anti-bias teaching in a diverse society.

Each of the seven topical chapters deals with a different form of diversity in schools: racial/ethnic, religious, ability, socioeconomic class, linguistic, gender, and sexual orientation. Chapter 1, by Deborah A. Byrnes, "Addressing Race, Ethnicity, and Culture in the Classroom," examines ways in which teachers can work toward racial and ethnic equity, social justice, and democratic goals in their classrooms. She suggests two broad strategies. First, teachers should create "multicultural, anti-bias learning environments" that would include, for example, curricular materials that explore a range of racial and ethnic cultural content. The other approach is to teach schoolchildren to act assertively against prejudice and discrimination. Teachers have an opportunity to be role models by responding to issues of prejudice or discrimination that arise in student interactions, news reports, or school materials. Although schools alone cannot eliminate racism in society, teachers can do much, Byrnes argues, to help children understand and accept racial and ethnic differences.

Chapter 2, "Living With Our Deepest Differences: Religious Diversity in the Classroom," by Charles C. Haynes, focuses on the limitations and possibilities when dealing with religious issues. Haynes contrasts teaching religion with teaching *about* religion; the latter is encouraged, while the former is unconstitutional. Because religious beliefs involve ultimate values not easily compromised, it is not surprising that religious issues have engendered bitter debates about the place of religion in public education. While certain religious interest groups have sought to influence textbook selection and curriculum development in schools, it is equally true, Haynes maintains, that teachers and textbooks too often have neglected religion entirely as a topic of study and discussion. Haynes makes a compelling argument that religious differences can be respected and addressed in the classroom if democratic, constitutional principles guide the approach.

Mara Sapon-Shevin, in "Ability Differences in the Classroom: Teaching and Learning in Inclusive Classrooms" (Chapter 3), explores ability differences. She compares and contrasts the different kinds of abilities that characterize students; physical, perceptual, and cognitive abilities are among the various dimensions schools use to differentiate pupils. Sapon-Shevin summarizes the arguments commonly heard for isolating students on the basis of ability: bright children may be "held back" by "slower learners" and special needs children cannot face the challenges of the regular classroom. She then reports the negative effects of separating children based on narrow notions of ability. Sapon-Shevin stresses the need to rethink our operating definitions of "ability" and to appreciate the research findings on the positive effects of current inclusive classroom environments.

In Chapter 4, "Class Differences: Economic Inequality in the Classroom," Ellen Davidson and Nancy Schniedewind focus on the effects of a student's socioeconomic status on his/her experiences at school. A child's class background often correlates with the parents' attitudes about learning, classroom discipline, and academic achievement. Also, a pupil's class background can influence interactions he/she has with peers and teachers (who are, by and large, drawn from the middle class). For example, peers can use class differences to ridicule one another. By not being sensitive to a child's family's lack of economic resources, teachers can unintentionally plan assignments that highlight class differences. Davidson and Schniedewind show how addressing class differences in a constructive fashion involves more than being sensitive to differential wealth among students; it also involves addressing moral judgments based on class differences that are made about children and their parents.

Linguistic diversity is the topic of Chapter 5, "Language Diversity in the Classroom." Deborah A. Byrnes, Lisa Pray, and Diana Cortez, in exploring the relationship between language and culture, maintain that language differences and language learning cannot be understood without appreciating the culture in which a language is embedded. They examine ways teachers can apply what they know (about language and culture) and enlist the assistance of classmates to teach English in a nonstigmatizing way to English language learners. Byrnes, Pray, and Cortez also discuss the importance of exploring with pupils attitudes about language and language differences.

In Chapter 6, "Creating Gender-Equitable Classroom Environments," Janice Koch examines the meaning of gender equity and discusses common patterns of gender bias that lead to inequitable school environments. Societal gender roles often are mirrored in classrooms, thereby creating environments where males are reinforced for some behaviors and females for others. Koch discusses studies identifying differences in teacher expectations, teacher-student interactions, reinforcement patterns, and disciplining strategies based on gender. Being a science educator herself, Koch particularly notes the disenfranchisement of female students in science classes. Readers are asked to examine their own classrooms to see if the potential of any student, male or female, is limited by gendered expectations. Koch concludes her chapter by sharing how patterns of gender inequity in the classroom can be changed.

In the final topical chapter (Chapter 7), Deborah Byrnes addresses "Sexual Diversity Issues in Schools." In this chapter, the only topical chapter that is completely new to the 3rd edition of *Common Bonds*, Byrnes discusses a diversity issue that often is ignored in schools. Common myths regarding sexual orientation are shared and Byrnes gives suggestions for how educators can appropriately address heterosexism and homophobia in their schools and community. The need to create school environments that are safe and nurturing for all students, regardless of sexual orientation, is the central theme of this chapter.

Chapter 8 is an integrative work that explores the application of anti-bias teaching strategies to subject areas across the curriculum. James J. Barta and Corinne Mount Pleasant-Jetté, in "Integrating Anti-bias Education," provide specific activities for classroom teachers in each of several major subject areas. Barta and Mount Pleasant-Jetté point out that anti-bias teaching should not be viewed as something "added on" to the existing curriculum. Rather, anti-bias teaching can be inextricably linked to the presentation of subject-area material in math, language arts, science, art, music, or social studies.

The concluding chapter, "Tooling the Toolbox: Checklist of Skills for Teaching in Diverse Classrooms and Communities," by Judith Puncochar, builds on the content of previous chapters in the book. In this chapter, Puncochar encourages teachers to consider how their personal beliefs and expectations influence their ability to effectively teach in increasingly diverse communities. In addition, readers are encouraged to assess how well their classrooms and schools support cultural and human diversity. This useful checklist summarizes issues teachers need to bear in mind as they create inclusive classroom environments where common bonds are discovered and differences respected.

References

Amrein, A. L., & Berliner, D. C. (2002, March 28). High-stakes testing, uncertainty, and student learning. *Education Policy Analysis Archives*, *10*(18). Retrieved November 23, 2004, from http://epaa.asu.edu/epaa/v10n18/.

Mathis, W. J. (2002). No child left behind: Costs and benefits. *Phi Delta Kappan, 84*(9), 679-686. Retrieved November 23, 2004, from www.pdkintl.org/kappan/k0305mat.htm.

Chapter 1
Addressing Race, Ethnicity, and Culture in the Classroom

Deborah A. Byrnes

We live in an increasingly ethnically, racially, and culturally diverse society. Yet, schools often do little to prepare children to live harmoniously and equitably with such diversity. This chapter will address the need for educators (most specifically, the classroom teacher) to take strong positions in opposition to prejudice and discrimination in schools and society, and to actively educate for attitudes compatible with a racially, ethnically, and culturally diverse democratic society.

Teachers often believe that children, particularly young ones, are too protected and naive to have developed any understanding of, or judgments about, race and ethnicity. Some educators also believe that discussing such topics brings children's attention to differences that otherwise would go unnoticed. They may hope that if nothing is said, children will grow up thinking that race and ethnicity make no difference. Consequently, they often avoid discussions about race and ethnicity. While these teachers may be well-meaning, their beliefs actually work against children growing up free of racial and ethnic prejudice. Such beliefs ignore the evidence that: 1) children start developing attitudes about race and ethnicity at a very young age (Sheets & Hollins, 1999); 2) prejudice and discrimination based on race and ethnicity remains a major social problem (Gollnick & Chinn, 2004; Tatum, 1997); 3) not talking about race and ethnicity makes children easy targets of stereotypes, almost from birth (Pine & Hilliard, 1990); and 4) children's understanding and acceptance of differences among various racial and ethnic groups, and their active opposition to instances of racial and ethnic prejudice, is essential if we are to create a society where there is equality for all (Davidson & Davidson, 1994).

If all racial and ethnic groups are to be treated equitably, everyone involved with educating children must take an active role in achieving that goal. Although this chapter deals most specifically with the role of the classroom teacher, the information contained here is relevant to all those concerned with creating multicultural, anti-bias learning environments. Changing schools alone will not rid society of prejudice and bigotry; schools can, however, make a valuable contribution to the resolution of this pervasive and difficult social problem.

This chapter is divided into three sections. In the first section, recommendations are made for creating multicultural and anti-bias classrooms and schools. The second section is a case study that demonstrates how one teacher has incorporated many of the recommendations made in section one. The third section of the paper includes resources on anti-bias education that will be of help to the classroom teacher.

CREATING MULTICULTURAL AND ANTI-BIAS CLASSROOMS

To integrate multicultural and anti-bias education into all areas of the school curriculum, it is important that teachers engage in self-reflection, professional development, and personal growth. This section outlines ways teachers can work with children that are effective in reducing racial and ethnic prejudice. Additionally, the author makes recommendations for ways teachers can work with other adults to facilitate the development of multicultural, anti-bias learning environments.

Education That Is Multicultural and Anti-bias

All curricula should be anti-bias and multicultural. Unfortunately, multicultural education too often has been interpreted as the addition of teaching units about different cultures and minority heroes to be taught during special weeks or seasons of the year (Banks, 1997). In the United States, for example, Native Americans are studied at Thanksgiving time, African American culture around the birthday of Martin Luther King, Jr., and Mexican Americans on Cinco de Mayo. The rest of the year, in many schools, minority cultures are relatively ignored, reinforcing students' notions that non-European groups are not really an integral part of American society.

When multicultural education *is* incorporated into a school's curriculum through the use of separate units, the rest of the school's curriculum often remains unchanged. All other subjects continue to be presented in the usual way, often in a manner that ignores minority cultures and racially based issues of power and privilege (e.g., such subjects as history, literature, science, art, and music are taught only from a Euro-American perspective).

The study and appreciation of different racial and ethnic groups must be integrated daily into all areas of the curriculum. No matter how homogeneous or assimilated one's students are, a teacher has a responsibility to teach children about the perspectives of minority ethnic and racial groups as well as the dominant group. Two excellent sources for improving one's own understanding about multiculturalism in the United States are: *A Different Mirror: A History of Multicultural America* (Takaki, 1993) and *Lies My Teacher Told Me: Everything Your American History Textbook Got Wrong* (Loewen, 1995). Inherent in these books is the message that multicultural education must go beyond the presentation of cultural artifacts, such as art, food, and clothing, or the celebration of special holidays or famous people. Such approaches are often patronizing and deflect attention away from the significant contributions and achievements of the many cultures that make up the United States.

A multicultural curriculum should help students to understand and appreciate the multicultural history of the United States. It also should lead students to question why so many minority groups have experienced prejudice and discrimination in the past. As students learn more about how power and privilege have been used to oppress people in the past, they can be more thoughtful about current human rights violations that occur. Wise teachers will help children learn that while Americans have made impressive gains in terms of civil and human rights, much work remains to be done. A thoughtful anti-bias, multicultural program enables students to look at issues and events from several points of view and from ethnic groups' perspectives, and it encourages students to make decisions and take actions in their lives that will reduce prejudice and discrimination in the future. For example, historical study of westward expansion in the United States should be studied from the perspectives of both the settlers and the Native Americans who already lived on the so-called "frontier." A more inclusive and accurate history of the United States will help young students to better understand ethnic and racial conflicts that continue today.

Assessing Materials. If educators are to integrate multicultural, anti-bias education into the entire school curriculum, they must carefully evaluate their teaching materials. All too often, the resources that are readily available to teachers (e.g., textbooks, films, resource units) are strongly biased toward the Euro-American perspective (Tunnel & Ammon, 1996).

In the process of sharing only the Euro-American perspective, the contributions of people of color are devalued and students may infer that Euro-Americans are superior. For example, many United States history books begin only after the arrival of Europeans and then focus almost exclusively on the contributions of Euro-Americans. Non-European groups are rarely adequately acknowledged for their contributions in making the United States the country it is today.

While textbooks are changing for the better, many teachers are still left to their own devices to present a more multicultural perspective of the United States. For example, curriculum materials that cover the explorer Christopher Columbus infrequently present the Native American perspective. A teacher wanting to discuss the treatment of the Taino or Arawak people is essentially on her or his own to find such material (Tunnel & Ammon, 1996).

Teachers must make a close assessment of available materials to determine if changes are needed. Visual aids should show a diversity of racial and ethnic groups in nonstereotypical portrayals. Children's books should be studied to see what percentage are about people of color and what messages are conveyed within the text and illustrations. It is important to remember that even children's books that have received prestigious awards may portray racial/ethnic minorities unfavorably, such as the Newbery award-winners *The Matchlock Gun* (Edmonds, 1942), *Smoky, the Cowhorse* (James, 1927), and *The Slave Dancer* (Fox, 1974). These books are available in almost all school libraries (Gillespie, Clements, Powell, & Swearinger, 1992). While more recent books usually have less overt problems, a surprising number of children's books about various cultures lack authenticity and teach or reinforce racial and ethnic stereotypes. Because it can be difficult to evaluate the authenticity of books that are not about your own culture, relying on professional reviews, such as those found in *Using Multiethnic Literature in the K-8 Classroom* (Harris, 1997), can be very helpful.

Textbooks should be checked to see if they integrate the perspectives of minority groups into the subject being discussed. For example, do they discuss the perspectives and contributions of Mexican Americans when studying the history of the southwestern region of the United States? Is Islam discussed only in terms of violence and intolerance, with no exploration of its broader commonalities with Christianity and Judaism (Wingfield & Karaman, 1995)? Recognizing the inherent bias in many of the materials available for educators is essential if changes are to occur. If more appropriate materials cannot be found, the biased materials should be used to generate discussions on bias, stereotyping, and discrimination.

Teaching About Prejudice and Discrimination. As part of establishing and integrating multicultural curricula into a school's education program, prejudice and discrimination must be studied and discussed. Children should be encouraged to recognize that differences exist among and within various cultural, ethnic, and racial groups, but it is not the differences, *per se*, that create problems in society. Problems are created when one or more groups make serious value judgments about these differences. Education that is multicultural should not ignore the realities of these judgments. It is only through the recognition of such value conflicts that students can realistically hope to create change. Teachers and students should not view "colorblindness" (i.e., ignoring or not noticing race or ethnicity) as the ideal. Encouraging students to be "colorblind" ignores and denies the importance of race and cultural experiences with respect to each person's identity (Tatum, 1997). Color differences exist, and we should not have to deny them for someone to be "okay." It is not the differences in race or ethnicity that we should ignore; it is the stereotypes and harmful prejudgments about such differences that we must teach students to recognize and work against.

It is important for students to understand that many people have suffered and continue to suffer as the result of irrational beliefs and actions (prejudice and discrimination). It is not enough that they understand there is injustice in the world; students also must learn that they can make a difference. By being aware of and sensitive to instances of prejudice and discrimination, students can actively work against prejudice and discrimination in themselves as well as in others. As a beginning step, a student might be encouraged to make a personal commitment to make friends with peers from different racial and ethnic groups and to read books that are about racial, cultural, or ethnic groups other than his or her own. Children also should be assisted in developing appropriate responses to instances of prejudice and discrimination (Byrnes, 1988). For example, letting a person who tells a bigoted joke know that you are offended or assertively telling a peer that he or she is engaging in stereotyping are important actions that a student can learn to take. Writing letters and voicing concerns about issues of prejudice and discrimination in one's school and community are also appropriate, even for young children.

It also is important, when addressing past and present instances of prejudice and discrimination, that Euro-American children not be made to feel *personally* responsible for what others have done. If discussions are not handled sensitively, Euro-American children may end up feeling personally blamed for many of the racial injustices that are discussed and may respond defensively. Euro-Americans should not be stereotyped as racist, any more than it should be assumed that all people of any group have any specific characteristic. Euro-American individuals throughout history have fought against injustice, prejudice, and discrimination (e.g., Eleanor Roosevelt, Harry S. Truman, Gloria Steinem, Robert Coles). Help your Euro-American students identify with these role models.

Self-Awareness

To help children develop understanding of and respect for racial and ethnic differences and become actively anti-discriminatory, teachers must look closely at themselves to see if they are good models. Educators must examine their own knowledge, attitudes, behaviors, and expectations. Multicultural, anti-bias education is often difficult to implement because classroom teachers have had little preparatory training or experience. For example, teachers may have little knowledge of other cultures or their values, contributions, and experiences, because these topics have not been part of their own schooling or teacher-preparation programs. Likewise, many teachers may have little understanding of the relationship between race or ethnicity and power, and the injustices that prejudice and discrimination create (Duarte & Reed, 2004; Wardle, 1996). These deficiencies tend to be passed on to students and may result in teachers being unaware of the racial and ethnic biases that exist in their own education settings (Mallory & New, 1994; Tatum 1997). For example, one reason children of certain ethnic and racial groups tend to be over-identified for special education services and underrepresented in programs for gifted and talented students is because teachers do not recognize and value cultural differences in how individual students learn; nor do they recognize unorthodox talents. Only through self-education and self-monitoring can teachers avoid passing on the Euro-American ethnocentrism that is pervasive in the U.S. society and education system.

Seek Out Knowledge. Opportunities to gain insights into other cultures and to learn about the relationships between race, culture, and power should be seized whenever possible. This could be through university classes in ethnic or multicultural studies, inservice workshops, lectures, cultural events, books, or most important, direct contact and interaction with people of other cultures. Involvement in groups whose main purpose is to protect the rights of others (e.g., National Association for the Advancement of Colored People, American Civil Liberties Union, Children's Defense Fund, Anti-Defamation League) is another way to become more knowledgeable about social-injustice concerns.

Examine One's Own Cultural Values and Expectations. Teachers also must examine their own cultural values and expectations. Every teacher (as well as every student) brings his or her own cultural background to the classroom. Because most teachers and teacher educators in the United States are Euro-American, schools tend to benefit Euro-American students, whose cultural patterns and styles often are consistent with those of the majority of teachers (Anderson, 1988; Pine & Hilliard, 1990).

Recognizing the differences in values and behavioral styles between different groups, and understanding how these differences may inadvertently influence our attitudes and, consequently, our behavior toward certain students, is essential. Teachers must check to see if they have an "ideal student" image that mirrors their own style and background. A teacher holding such an image may categorize students who are different in learning style, language, or behavior as less able or disadvantaged (Twitchin & Demuth, 1985). Such labels often affect the expectations a teacher has for a student and, consequently, can have serious ramifications for student achievement (Hilliard, 1989). Demanding less in terms of scholarship, waiting less time for responses, criticizing students more, praising less, calling on students less often, and being less willing to give students the benefit of the doubt are just some of the often subtle ways educators may respond to students whom they believe are low in academic ability (Hilliard, 1989; Sadker & Sadker, 1986). To make things worse, a child can pick up on a teacher's differing expectations for himself or herself as compared to those for classmates, and the effects may be incorporated into the attitudes a student holds for himself or herself and others (Twitching & Demuth, 1985).

When white teachers are not aware of the privileges they have as a result of their race, they may not understand how students of color and their parents experience life in their schools and communities. Such lack of awareness can act as a blinder to the prejudice and discrimination that still exists in society (Kailin, 2002). McIntosh (1990) identifies a range of daily privileges that people of color cannot count on in the way that a white person can. She notes, for example, that as a white American, she can go shopping pretty much anywhere, well assured that security staff will not follow her. She can turn on the television or read the paper and see a wide range of people of her race. If she were to move, she could be confident that she could purchase or rent any house within her budget. She can feel confident that her children in almost any class will study materials that testify to the existence and contributions of her race. She or her children can act badly without having such behavior attributed to her race.

It is important to remember that most teachers are unaware of the degree to which they or others are treating certain groups of students differently than others (Sadker & Sadker, 1986). Thus, it is essential that teachers not assume their classrooms are free of bias simply because they personally abhor discrimination. All educators need to examine their classrooms closely for subtle behaviors that may be based on culturally biased images, expectations, and privileges.

Be Actively Anti-Prejudice and Anti-Discrimination. Educators have a responsibility to be models for their students. If we wish students to have tolerance for differences and to actively counter bigotry, then we must examine ourselves for these same qualities. Educators must, in their teaching and personal actions, demonstrate sensitivity to and respect for cultural differences and a commitment toward creating a pluralistic democracy that fights prejudice and discrimination. We must ask ourselves: Are we willing to confront racial or ethnic discrimination when it occurs? Do we let others know that we find ethnocentric comments and actions unacceptable? Do our students see us as actively addressing instances of stereotyping and bias? Do students perceive us as being sincerely interested in and respectful of the contributions made by the many ethnic and racial groups represented in their country? Do we show children our commitment by talking to them about why discrimination occurs and how we can prevent it from happening?

As we examine our own attitudes and behavior, it is important to recognize that respect does not imply being value-neutral. For example, in everyday life, an individual can respect and defend another group's customs (e.g., clothing, music, food, interaction style) without liking the specific practices or seeing them as options for himself or herself. One goal of anti-bias education is to move children away from ethnocentrism so that such differences are not perceived as wrong and inferior, but rather as interesting manifestations of a group's culture and heritage. As teachers, we don't have to like rap or bluegrass music, quiet and meditative meals or boisterous dinnertime conversation, modest dress or wild and colorful clothing, but we do need to see these variations as "cultural differences" and not expressions of "cultural inferiority." Children will learn much about the world from the responses to differences that we model for them.

Creating Environments That Reduce Prejudice

In addition to integrating a multicultural perspective across the curriculum and being a positive model for students, a teacher can do much to create environments that foster respect and understanding for differences and discourage prejudice and discrimination. The following strategies have been shown to be helpful in creating more positive attitudes toward persons of other racial and/or ethnic groups.

Cooperative Interactions. One of the most effective means by which students become more accepting of others is in the use of cooperative-learning groups (Johnson & Johnson, 2002; Pate, 1995). Research on cooperative grouping shows increased academic achievement as well as improved interracial relations (Pine & Hilliard, 1990). Cooperative learning involves the heterogeneous grouping (by ability as well as by culture and gender) of students, who then work together to meet a group goal. There are several ways to structure such learning groups (see, for example, Slavin, 1994, or Stahl, 1992). Regardless of the particular structure chosen (e.g., Student Teams-Achievement Divisions [STAD], Teams-Games-Tournaments [TGT], Team-Assisted Individualization [TAI], Jigsaw), cooperative-learning groups always should take place in ongoing, supportive environments where all participants have equal status. Maintaining such a supportive environment requires that teachers monitor interactions within cooperative groups to ensure that some individuals are not being left out and to provide timely support for processing nonproductive group interactions.

In schools where the population is homogeneous, such grouping for cross-racial and cross-ethnic interactions is difficult, if not impossible. However, any opportunity to have students engage in cooperative interactions with members of other groups should be seized. Such encounters should incorporate the basic components of cooperative education. Members in groups should have equal status, and the work or play should take place in an ongoing, supportive, caring environment and be oriented toward a group goal. One suggestion for achieving such an environment is by creating sport teams and drama-production groups that combine students from different communities and schools. This sort of cooperative interaction does not truly take place if members of racial and ethnic groups are simply asked to visit the school and talk about their culture. Mere exposure to knowledge about another culture and impersonal, non-cooperative interactions do little, if anything, to break down prejudice (Lynch, 1987).

Enhancing Self-Esteem. Creating classroom environments that promote the development of genuine self-esteem is another way educators can work against the formation of prejudices (Byrnes, 1988). Some studies have identified a relationship between an individual's self-esteem and the degree of prejudice (Pate, 1995, p. 27). Children who have high self-esteem are less likely to hold prejudices than children who have low self-esteem. (This is not to say that the relationship is necessarily causal.) Campbell and Foddis (2003), however, caution us not to confuse pseudo self-esteem with genuine self-esteem. Pseudo self-esteem is based on external sources, such as being approved by others, having high social status, and liking one's physical appearance. Genuine self-esteem involves feeling competent to take on life's challenges and holding a conviction that one is deserving of respect, love, and joy. Genuine self-esteem is not developed when teachers overpraise students' work and encourage them to feel "special" regardless of what they do.

Research tells us that, in general, children have higher self-esteem in school environments that foster security, acceptance, independence, and responsibility and where warmth, authentic praise, and appropriate limits are consistently present (Curry & Johnson, 1990). Curry and Johnson, who share numerous strategies for fostering self-esteem in school environments, emphasize that to help children develop a genuine sense of human value, we cannot rely on isolated "you are a winner" type of activities. Equitable, nurturing, and challenging learning conditions that support self-esteem need to be present schoolwide. Efforts to develop such environments should be part of any program designed to reduce racial and ethnic bias among students.

Developing Cognitive Sophistication. Research evidence suggests that children may become less prejudiced when they develop higher levels of cognitive sophistication. Individuals who are dogmatic, and think in terms of sharp, dichotomous terms, are more likely to be prejudiced and act in discriminatory ways (see review in Pettigrew, 1981). If children learn to identify overgeneralizations and stereotypes and attend to meaningful social behaviors rather than biases, they may become less prejudiced (Pate, 1995). Thus, teachers should provide many opportunities for children to learn about prejudice and discrimination and to identify the faulty thought processes that underlie and perpetuate them. Students should learn to be on guard for stereotypes and inappropriate uses of generalizations and categorical thinking in their own and in others' thinking.

Killoran (2004) shares how teachers newly sensitized to integrating anti-bias curriculum into their classrooms can find an amazing number of opportunities to integrate discussions on prejudice and discrimination into the curriculum. For example, an astute teacher of 3rd- and 4th-graders read the book *Harry Potter* aloud to her class and used the story to discuss name calling and prejudice. Not only did her students talk about how Hermione, a mud-blood (not a pure-blood wizard), was treated; they also discussed how race and gender were addressed in Rowling's books. Subsequently, her students began noticing how other authors presented or didn't present people of color and women and girls in their writing.

Notably, the research on cognitive approaches and prejudice strongly suggests that factual information is not sufficient to reduce prejudice (Avery, Bird, Johnstone, Sullivan, & Thalhammer, 1992; Pate, 1995). Lectures on prejudice and stereotyping will do little to help children be less prejudicial. We must go beyond content coverage of such topics as cultural diversity, human rights, tolerance, and prejudice and consider how we can engage children in rethinking their existing viewpoints and address any misinformation they may possess. We must involve students in discussions that help them to justify, express, and reconsider their views in light of new information (Wade, 1994). These are the abilities of a cognitively sophisticated individual.

Increasing Empathy for Others. Increasing students' understanding of and respect for the feelings of others who are racially or ethnically different also has been shown to be helpful in reducing prejudice (Pate, 1988, 1995). Activities that have a strong affective component, which elicits empathy, can help students see the world from the point of view of those from other cultural groups. Books, plays, movies, short stories, and simulations can be particularly helpful in helping students understand and empathize with the plight and struggle of individuals confronted with discrimination and prejudice (Byrnes, 1988). Slater (2002), however, cautions that in order for media to be influential in building empathy and changing attitudes, homophily needs to be present. "Homophily," the affinity for someone like oneself, occurs with the positive identification of self to the lead character. If students cannot relate to the main character or they find the character unlikable, they are much less likely to care about what happens to that person. Be careful in your selections so that the resources used do not unwittingly perpetuate stereotypes instead of promoting empathy.

Working With Others for Change

Teachers who are committed to multicultural, anti-bias education also must work for change beyond their own classrooms. This can be done in many ways. Encouraging your entire school to develop a strong multicultural, anti-bias policy is an important step. Teachers are most effective in combating prejudice and discrimination when such efforts are long-term and are supported by school-wide policies and practices (Davidson & Davidson, 1994; Lynch, 1987). Talk with other teachers and administrators about what the school as a whole can do to create a learning environment that recognizes and supports the multicultural society in which we live. Part of this effort should be toward developing a school anti-racism policy explicitly stating that racial stereotyping, harassment, and abuse will not be tolerated (Pine & Hilliard, 1990). An examination of practices that may lead to certain racial and ethnic group members being tracked into special education or remedial classes also should be undertaken.

Involve Parents. It is also important to involve parents and other community members in your efforts to help children develop greater understanding of the benefits, as well as the challenges, of living in a culturally diverse society (Derman-Sparks and the A.B.C. Task Force, 1989). Certainly, parents should be involved in the development of any school-wide policy. At the classroom level, you can keep parents informed of your multicultural, anti-bias curriculum emphasis through parent/teacher meetings and newsletters. It is important to help parents understand that helping children develop respectful, tolerant attitudes towards others who are different from themselves is essential, as children will be living and working in an increasingly pluralistic, democratic society. School-sponsored programs and activities designed to promote cross-cultural understanding are doubly advantageous if organized by a group of diverse parents themselves.

Diversifying the Faculty. Any educator who is trying to emphasize multiculturalism should also take a closer look at the make-up of the school's faculty (Sleeter, 1990). Messages about the worth of all individuals, regardless of race or ethnicity, are hollow if students see only Euro-American teachers and administrators in their schools. Diversity among the staff is essential, as it provides an important lesson in equity to students, helps children develop respect for and understanding of people from racial and ethnic groups other than their own, and provides role models for students of color (Pine & Hilliard, 1990, p. 597). While many teachers have limited input into faculty hiring decisions, teachers should use what influence they do have to ensure the consideration and hiring of teachers who are members of minority groups.

Theory Into Practice

In this chapter, we have discussed the importance of education that is multicultural and strongly anti-bias. The following case study demonstrates how one teacher has utilized many of the teaching strategies and processes shared in this chapter in her own classroom. The case study illustrates how respect for racial/ethnic differences and a deep concern for fairness and social equality can be developed in incidental moments of teaching as well as in more formal curriculum approaches and strategies. Amy Hafter, the teacher in the case study, does not shy away from addressing difficult topics with her students. She recognizes that her students are not "colorblind" and that they pick up messages about race and ethnicity in their daily lives. In her democratically oriented classroom, Amy uses such strategies as cooperative, interracial/interethnic group experiences; activities and questions that promote self-esteem, empathy, and higher level thinking skills; and literature choices that encourage students to understand and respect other cultures. She serves as a model to her students; she actively fights discrimination and is strongly committed to equity and social justice. She wants to instill in her students the importance of working toward a society where all people are respected and treated fairly regardless of their race or ethnicity.

CASE STUDY

When Amy Hafter began a new appointment as a 4th-grade teacher, she became aware of just how much she needed to address issues of prejudice and discrimination with her students. On the second day of school, one of her students called another a "nigger." Amy was dismayed and anguished over this racial slur being used so easily by a 9-year-old. Consequently, she has made "respecting differences" a clear and consistent part of her teaching. According to Amy, "The more I thought about it, the more I realized that prejudice and discrimination starts when children are young. We have to address it then."

At the time of this study, Amy taught 4th-graders in a low-income community in Hayward, California. It was her fourth year of teaching, and her third year at this particular school. She had 29 students, 20 of whom were male. Her students were from many different ethnic/racial groups. In order of size, from largest to smallest, there were Euro-American, African American, Latino, Afghan American, and Native American groups of students. No single group represented a majority. Only a few of her students were first-generation immigrants. All of her students had a good facility with English.

I was impressed by what I saw on my numerous visits to Amy's classroom. Her students demonstrated respect for one another, concern for the way individuals were treated, and interest in cultures other than their own; they worked cooperatively. While observing Amy's classroom, I saw principles of multicultural and anti-bias education being integrated creatively and successfully. Here is how one teacher has worked to prepare children to live peacefully and thoughtfully in a pluralistic society.

There were no desks in Amy's classroom. She chose, instead, to use large tables that fit into her cooperative-learning philosophy. Students kept their materials in tote trays under the table. Every few weeks when the groups were changed (always by random assignment), students simply took their tote trays with them to their new tables. Amy feels strongly that students gain academically, socially, and emotionally from working in cooperative groups. She also believes that such groups are an essential element for any program designed to help children accept and respect differences. Observing the groups, I was pleased to note that a new student, purportedly the child of Gypsies, was treated respectfully within her group even after giving a totally illogical response to a group math activity. The students in her group, although some of them were obviously a bit surprised by her answer, accepted her response without teasing or making derogatory comments. This was a good example of one of the basic premises of cooperative groups that Amy teaches her students: You cannot make a person feel uncomfortable about working in the group with you. If you do, you lose the right to work in the group.

Amy enhances her students' self-esteem, another important component of any prejudice-reducing program, by helping them to learn that their ideas are valuable and should be heard. She wants them to expect respect from her and from their classmates. Amy tries never to "shoot down" an opinion. In this way, she is modeling respect for other viewpoints and encouraging her students to think about issues and take risks. If a student shows disrespect for someone else's ideas, he or she usually is sent out of the classroom. This rarely happens, except among new students. As soon as she can slip away, Amy asks the student why he or she thinks he or she was asked to leave. The student is asked to reflect on why his or her behavior was hurtful and inappropriate and what behavior would be more appropriate. It doesn't take long for students to realize that the idea of respecting each other's viewpoints is taken seriously in this classroom. They also learn that their own viewpoints, in turn, will be respected. As Amy noted, "The students who have been with me all year [about two-thirds of the class] also help a lot in socializing the new ones."

Amy frequently spends time processing group interactions with her students. After a group cooperative project has been completed, students often are asked to talk about how well their group worked together. Did students respect each other's ideas? Was everyone given the opportunity to contribute? How were disagreements resolved? Students are discouraged from using individuals' names in their comments. For example, the comment, "Two members kept making jokes, so it was hard to get everyone's ideas written down" is acceptable; "John and Sue kept us from getting done" is not. The students learn not to label their classmates; they learn to define situations in ways that help them resolve conflicts. Students discuss how it feels when people don't cooperate and they are encouraged to address such situations in their groups.

Any situation that involves an individual or group being discriminated against is discussed at length with the whole class. For example, when one student recited a rhyme that used racist language, Amy talked with the student individually and she also set aside time for the entire class to discuss why such rhymes are hurtful. Amy tries to get her students to discuss the issue as a group and adds her own views or clarifying points after they have listened to one another. In the above case she asked her students, "How did you feel when you heard it?" One student answered, "Mad! Because to call someone a 'nigger' means you think they're inferior and dumb." The students did an admirable job of educating one another. Amy reinforced their reasoning ability by praising their group-discussion skills and their sensitivity to one another's feelings. Her students' growing understanding of the nature of prejudice and discrimination was evident in such responses as:

When T called me a "nigger" it really made me mad. It didn't use to make me as mad when I heard that word. But now I know how my African ancestors were made slaves and it's different. I know what it means.

Amy rarely passes up an informal opportunity to address the importance of respecting cultural differences or to identify instances of prejudice and discrimination toward any group. For example, in mathematics class, the students practiced their graphing skills, using M&Ms. In discussing their work, Amy talked about how M&Ms were a good example of what they had studied about people—we come in a lot of different colors on the outside but we're all the same inside. In a discussion of the popular children's film *The Land Before Time,* Amy drew parallels between the prejudice and discrimination some of the dinosaurs experienced with instances of racial and ethnic prejudice that happen in the students' worlds. At the individual level, when a student who was helping Amy after class commented that a woman with an earring in her nose looked weird, Amy used it as an opportunity to briefly comment on the cultural relativity of beauty. She pointed out that pierced ears and bleached hair might be considered just as strange by people unfamiliar with American culture.

Discussions on respecting one another, accepting and enjoying differences, and actively fighting prejudice and discrimination are also purposefully integrated into many areas of the curriculum. For example, Amy uses a literature-based reading program. The books she selects for her program reflect her purpose of helping students to develop empathy and understanding for others, regardless of the color of their skin or their cultural background. Some of the books she used with this class were: *Freedom Train*; *Roll of Thunder, Hear My Cry*; *Sing Down the Moon*; *Sign of the Beaver*; and *Gold Cadillac*. All of these books have racial/ethnic minorities as the main characters, and the plots involve important lessons regarding equality and respect for, and understanding of, cultural differences. Amy asks her students difficult questions as they read these books. For example, when they studied the book *Roll of Thunder, Hear My Cry*, the class discussed what an "Uncle Tom" is and what it means in their own lives to "kiss up" to someone who is in a position of power.

In the area of social studies, Amy avoids using the textbook whenever she can and instead uses materials that are more multicultural and less biased toward Euro-American perspectives. Amy admits this plan involves more work on her part, but she believes it is the only way to provide meaningful learning experiences that reflect the cultural composition of her students and their community. In a unit on the history of California, for example, she included a strong emphasis on the perspective of minority groups in the state. She also developed her own social studies lessons that addressed the internment of Japanese Americans during World War II. Fortunately, Amy's principal was supportive of her anti-bias curriculum.

After her students attended an excellent concert and lecture that featured African American music and history, the class integrated the new information into other topics they had been discussing. The class talked about Martin Luther King, Jr., Harriet Tubman, and others whose efforts made it possible for the students to have schools like their own, where all kinds of people could work and play together. Amy talks to her class about how strange it is when she visits her relatives in a community where everyone looks and acts the same. She shares how much more interesting she thinks it is when there are many different types of people to get to know. Amy leaves no doubt in her students' minds as to where she stands with respect to enjoying diversity and fighting against bigotry and prejudice.

When her students, over several weeks, viewed the 12-part PBS video *The Voyage of the Mimi—Part II* (a series about the search for a "lost" city of the ancient Maya civilization), Amy frequently stopped the video and discussed topics related to individual and cultural differences. For example, in one episode a character refers to the Mayans as "savages," not knowing that one of the people to whom he was talking was a descendent of the Mayans. In the film, the person is deeply offended and the other character apologizes, stating he didn't know the man was part Mayan. Amy used this event as an opportunity to ask her students why people feel hurt when their culture is criticized. She asked if the comment would have been any more appropriate if no one who was Mayan had heard it. Such discussions encourage students to think critically about prejudice and discrimination, to develop empathy for others, and to engage in non-prejudicial verbal and nonverbal behavior.

Students regularly shared current events articles that addressed important social issues and promoted frequent discussions on such issues as homelessness, capital punishment, and discrimination. One day, a student brought in an article discussing the firing of an African American school superintendent in Selma, Alabama. Amy asked her students what they thought was happening in Selma, given the information presented in the article. A discussion on racism ensued. Many of the students felt strongly that the superintendent probably was fired because he was black. They related the situation to other events of which their parents had spoken or to incidents of racial prejudice that they had observed or experienced. Amy was noncommittal with respect to her own opinion, but encouraged the students to express and support their own views. At the end of the discussion, one student summarized that we should all be able to be friends and treat each other fairly, even if we're different colors.

* * * * *

Since the above case study was written, Amy Hafter has gone on to serve as a teacher mentor for the state of California, working on issues of diversity and conflict resolution. She also has served as an educational consultant to predominantly African American and Latino schools in Chicago. She is currently an educational researcher for SRI International in California. For this edition of *Common Bonds,* I asked her to provide an update on her thinking about anti-bias education.

• *Given your more recent experiences, if you were to go back to teaching at your former school, would you do things differently than you did then?*
Amy: If I could go back, I would dedicate even more time to working with students about issues of diversity. I would talk more about the links between poverty and lack of opportunity for certain populations of kids. I would address more "isms" that kids practice without even thinking about their impact on other human beings. I would talk more about ageism, sexism, religious bigotry, ability differences, and homophobia as well as issues of class, race, and ethnicity.

I realize I facilitated many celebrations of differences, but I did not take full advantage of the opportunities to help students think about others and differences outside of the classroom. Our classroom culture was secure, but as my students grew older, I saw some of them act in racist, sexist, homophobic ways that they had agreed were unacceptable in our classroom. I would do more to ensure that my students really believe that a key component of success in the outside world is their ability to interact with diverse groups of people in a thoughtful and tolerant manner.

• ***Do you think schools are getting better at anti-bias teaching?***

Amy: It saddens me to say that I don't think schools are very focused on issues of bias and diversity. Generally, the concept is taught as "we are all the same underneath" or some such cliché—a sort of shot in the arm inoculation that may even be given by guest speakers and consultants to the school. In my daughter's elementary school, which is almost exclusively white, the school sponsored a month-long curriculum push around the themes of diversity. But the rest of the year was dedicated to pre-scripted reading and math curriculums, with seemingly no room for further discussion of diversity issues.

In a western Chicago school (K-8) where I consulted, the population of students was 85 percent Latino, approximately half from Mexico and half from Puerto Rico. The other 15 percent was almost exclusively African American. In interviews with students across grade levels, most of the kids expressed frustrations that the teachers didn't know *"who they were."* Most often, teachers called the students "Mexicans" regardless of where they were from. Some teachers acted surprised when a Latino child could not speak Spanish. Some teachers routinely spoke Spanish to the whole class as though non-Spanish-speaking students were not there. There were gangs vying for control of the local parks and an active street drug trade, but the kids told me the teachers didn't seem to care. In my three years in that school, not once did I see a lesson devoted to honoring or understanding differences.

In some of the 100 percent African American schools where I consulted, I saw too many of the teachers, most of whom were African American themselves, telling students that they were "lazy," "a drain on society," and that they would "never amount to anything." The teachers, some of whom had grown up in the same neighborhoods as these students, told me that the kids were generally unruly, unprepared to learn, dirty, and that "the parents just don't care." Kids in the school, even in the earliest grades, told me that many of the teachers had no respect for the students. Attempts to talk with the students about prejudices and misconceptions within the school or out in the world seemed nonexistent.

As a last example, a parent in one of my former communities shared with me that her daughter attended a school where the superintendent spoke with great pride about their district's multicultural sensitivity. She discovered this was clearly not true at her child's school. Her daughter, an adopted African American child who was scoring in the 95th percentile in mathematics, was not bringing home any math homework. At first, her mom assumed the teacher was easing the 4th-graders into math homework, so she asked her daughter when the homework would begin. Her daughter informed her, "Mom, we don't get homework in lab; only the regular kids get homework."

A stunned mother made an appointment to speak with the teacher. At the appointment, the teacher seemed equally stunned to have a white mother appear. The mother asked why her daughter, who if anything should be in an accelerated math program, was in a remedial lab. The teacher replied, "I just haven't had time to assess all of our students yet." The mother asked if any white or Asian children were automatically placed in the lab. The teacher said, coincidentally, no, but that was just circumstance. Upon viewing the test scores and cumulative records that she had in her file, the teacher became embarrassed and apologetic. Still, she was not willing to consider that her choice to place the child in a remedial setting may have been based solely on the child's skin color.

This is not to say that all the teachers I have seen are callous, non-responsive practitioners. I have been in several schools where teachers as a whole are dedicated to ensuring an inclusive, respectful, non-biased culture at the classroom and school levels. However, from my experiences, it seems more like the exception.

• **What do you see as our greatest needs in the area of anti-bias education today?**

Amy: Ours is a land full of people who represent almost every ethnic group, practice a world of religions, and have many other differences, such as different languages, socioeconomic status, and sexual orientations. We need to break down the misconceptions and fears that children and adults have of those who are not like them.

I am still an optimist. Children are the key, because they are not clouded by as many misconceptions and are often more willing than adults to accept people who are different from themselves. They need to learn from us that words really do hurt; that people need to be accepted based on their actions, not their appearances; and that the more a community (and eventually a nation) embraces these differences, the better life will be for all. In a harmonious society, people can expend their energies in more productive ways, whether for work or leisure. Respectful tolerance needs to be on the forefront for all educators in every aspect of our practice, so that kids will grow up thinking it is customary to always consider its importance before acting.

Taking it one step further, I would love to see some space devoted to tolerance on a nationally normed standardized test. I can only imagine the race for curriculum writers and school district administrators to place the teaching of tolerance and acceptance for diversity into their curriculums.

*   *   *   *   *   *   *

Amy Hafter stands as an example of the many educators who are working hard to create learning environments that prepare children to live thoughtfully and responsibly in a culturally pluralistic democracy. I thank her and her students for their contribution to this chapter.

There is no such thing as a *neutral* educational process. Education either functions as an instrument which is to facilitate the integration of the younger generation into the logic of the present system and bring about conformity to it, *or* it becomes "the practice of freedom," the means by which men and women deal critically and creatively with reality and discover how to participate in the transformation of their world. (Shaull, 1970, p. 15)

RESOURCES FOR TEACHERS

Prejudice-Reduction Activity Books and Materials

Bullard, S., Carnes, J., Hofer, M., Polk, N., & Sheets, R. H. (1997). *Starting small: Teaching tolerance in preschool and the early grades.* Montgomery, AL: Southern Poverty Law Center.

Bisson, J. (1997). *Celebrate!: An anti-bias guide to enjoying holidays in early childhood programs.* St. Paul, MN: Redleaf.

Byrnes, D. (1995). *"Teacher, they called me a_____!" Confronting prejudice and discrimination in the classroom.* New York: Anti-Defamation League of B'nai B'rith.

Derman-Sparks, L., and the A.B.C. Task Force. (1989). *Anti-bias curriculum tools for empowering young children.* Washington, DC: National Association for the Education of Young Children.

Derman-Sparks, L., Phillips, C. B., & Hilliard, A. G. (1997). *Teaching/learning anti-racism: A developmental approach.* New York: Teachers College.

Duvall, L. (1994). *Respecting our differences: A guide to getting along in a changing world.* Minneapolis, MN: Free Spirit.

Ford, C. W. (1994). *We can all get along: 50 steps you can take to help end racism at home, at work, in your community.* New York: Dell.

Hall, N. S. (1998). *Creative resources for the anti-bias classroom.* Albany, NY: Delmar.

Mazel, E. (Ed.). (1998). *And don't call me a racist!* Lexington, MA: Argonaut.

McGovern, M. (1997). *Starting small. Teaching tolerance: A project of the Southern Poverty Law Center* [video]. Montgomery, AL: Teaching Children Tolerance.

Paley, V. (2000). *White teacher* (3rd ed.). Cambridge, MA: Harvard University.

Sapon-Shevin, M. (1998). *Because we can change the world: A practical guide to building cooperative, inclusive classroom communities.* Upper Saddle River, NJ: Pearson.

Schniedewind, N., & Davidson, E. (1998). *Open minds to equality: A sourcebook of learning activities to promote race, sex, class and age equity* (2nd ed.). Englewood Cliffs, NJ: Prentice-Hall.

Thomson, B. J. (1993). *Words can hurt you: Beginning a program of anti-bias education.* Reading, MA: Addison-Wesley.

Other Anti-Bias Sources and Materials

American/Arab Anti-Discrimination Committee
4201 Connecticut Ave, NW, Suite 300
Washington, DC 20008
www.adc.org (click on education)
Anti-Defamation League
823 United Nations Plaza
New York, NY 10017
www.adl.org
Prejudice Institute
2743 Maryland Ave.
Baltimore, MD 21218
www.tolerance.org
Teaching Tolerance (biannual publication)
Southern Poverty Law Center
400 Washington Avenue
Montgomery, AL 36104
www.tolerance.org

References

Anderson, J. A. (1988). Cognitive styles and multicultural populations. *Journal of Teacher Education, 39*(1), 2-9.

Avery, P. G., Bird, K., Johnstone, S., Sullivan, J. L., & Thalhammer, K. (1992). Exploring political tolerance with adolescents. *Theory and Research in Social Education, 20*(4), 386-420.

Banks, J. A. (1997). *Teaching strategies for ethnic studies* (6th ed.). Boston: Allyn & Bacon.

Byrnes, D. (1988). Children and prejudice. *Social Education, 52,* 267-271.

Campbell, R. L., & Foddis, W. F. (2003). Is high self-esteem bad for you? *Navigator, 6*(7-8). Retrieved July 17, 2004, from www.objectivistcenter.org/navigator/articles/nav+rcampbell_wfoddis_high-self-esteem.asp.

Curry, N. E., & Johnson, C. N. (1990). *Beyond self-esteem: Developing a genuine sense of human value.* Washington, DC: National Association for the Education of Young Children.

Davidson, F. H., & Davidson, M. M. (1994). *Changing childhood prejudice: The caring work of schools.* Westport, CT: Bergin & Garvey.

Derman-Sparks, L., & the A.B.C. Task Force. (1989). *Anti-bias curriculum tools for empowering young children.* Washington, DC: National Association for the Education of Young Children.

Duarte, V., & Reed, T. (2003). Learning to teach in urban settings. *Childhood Education, 80,* 245-250.

Edmonds, W. D. (1942). *The matchlock gun.* New York: Dodd.

Fox, P. (1974). *The slave dancer.* New York: Dell.

Gillespie, C., Clements, N., Powell, J., & Swearinger, B. (1992). The portrayal of ethnic characters in

Newbery award-winning books. *Yearbook of the American Reading Forum, 12*, 109-125.

Gollnick, D. M., & Chinn, P. C. (2004). *Multicultural education in a pluralistic society* (6th ed.). Upper Saddle River, NJ: Pearson.

Harris, V. J. (Ed.). (1997). *Using multiethnic literature in the K-8 classroom.* Norwood, MA: Christopher-Gordon.

Hilliard, A. G., III. (1989). Teachers and cultural styles in a pluralistic society. *NEA Today, 7*(6), 65-69.

James, W. (1927). *Smoky, the cowhorse.* New York: Scribner's.

Johnson, D. W., & Johnson, R. T. (2002). Ensuring diversity is positive: Cooperative community, constructive conflict, and civic values. In J. S. Thousand, R. A. Villa, and A. I. Nevin (Eds.), *Creativity and collaborative learning: The practical guide to empowering students, teachers, and families* (2nd ed., pp. 197-208). Baltimore: Paul H. Brookes.

Kailin, J. (2002). *Antiracist education.* New York: Rowman & Littlefield.

Killoran, I. (2004). Rethink, revise, react: Using an anti-bias curriculum to move beyond the usual. *Childhood Education, 80,* 149-156.

Loewen, J. W. (1995). *Lies my teacher told me: Everything your American history textbook got wrong.* New York: Simon & Schuster.

Lynch, J. (1987). *Prejudice reduction and the schools.* New York: Nichols.

Mallory, B. L., & New, R. S. (1994). *Diversity and developmentally appropriate practice.* New York: Teachers College Press.

McIntosh, P. (1990). White privilege: Unpacking the invisible knapsack. *Independent School, 90*(4), 31, 5 p.

Pate, G. S. (1988). Research on reducing prejudice. *Social Education, 52,* 287-289.

Pate, G. S. (1995). *Prejudice reduction and the finding of research.* (ERIC Document Reproduction Services No. ED 383 803)

Pettigrew, T. (1981). The mental health impact. In B. P. Bowser & R. G. Hunt (Eds.), *Impacts of racism on white Americans* (pp. 97-118). Beverly Hills, CA: Sage.

Pine, G. J., & Hilliard, A. G., III. (1990). Rx for racism: Imperatives for America's schools. *Phi Delta Kappan, 71*(8), 593-600.

Sadker, M., & Sadker, D. (1986). Sexism in the classroom: From grade school to graduate school. *Phi Delta Kappan, 67*(7), 512-515.

Shaull, R. (1970). Foreword. In P. Freire, *Pedagogy of the oppressed* (pp. 9-15). New York: Herder & Herder.

Sheets, H., & Hollins, E. R. (Eds.). (1999). *Racial and ethnic identity in school practices: Aspects of human development.* Mahwah, NJ: Lawrence Erlbaum.

Slater, M. D. (2002). *Using stories to prompt attitude and behavior change.* Retrieved July 19, 2004, from www.comminit.com/st2003/sld-9168.html

Slavin, R. E. (1994). *Cooperative learning: Theory, research, and practice* (2nd ed.). Upper Saddle River, NJ: Pearson.

Sleeter, C. E. (1990). Staff development for desegregated schooling. *Phi Delta Kappan, 72,* 33-40.

Stahl, R. J. (Ed.). (1992). *Cooperative learning in social studies: A handbook for teachers.* Menlo Park, CA: Addison-Wesley.

Takaki, R. (1993). *A different mirror: A history of multicultural America.* Boston: Little, Brown.

Tatum, B. D. (1997). *"Why are all the black kids sitting together in the cafeteria?" And other conversations about race.* New York: Basic Books.

Tunnel, M. O., & Ammon, R. (1996). The story of ourselves: Fostering multiple historical perspectives. *Social Education, 60*(4), 212-215.

Twitchin, J., & Demuth C. (compiled by). (1985). *Multi-cultural education: Views from the classroom.* London: British Broadcasting Corporation.

Wade, R. (1994). Conceptual change in elementary social studies: A case study of fourth graders' understanding of human rights. *Theory and Research in Social Education, 22*(1), 74-95.

Wardle, F. (1996). Proposal: An anti-bias and ecological model for multicultural education. *Childhood Education, 72,* 152-156.

Wingfield, M., & Karaman, B. (1995). Arab stereotypes and American educators. *Social Studies and the Young Learner, 7*(4), 7-10.

Chapter 2
Living With Our Deepest Differences: Religious Diversity in the Classroom

| Charles C. Haynes |

Bitter conflicts over the role of religion in the classroom deeply divide the United States and pose a significant threat to the future of public education. Highly charged disputes and lawsuits about prayer, religious clubs, religious holidays, and other religion-in-schools issues are only the most visible signs of a pervasive alienation from public education felt in many religious communities throughout the United States. Not since the 19th century "Bible wars" have so many citizens been so strongly convinced that public schools contradict their values, ignore their traditions, and exclude their voices (al-Hibri, Elshtain, & Haynes, 2001; Flowers, 1988; Glenn, 1988; Nord, 1995).

Tragically, citizens in communities throughout the United States ignore this threat and continue to shout past one another about "school prayer," "secular humanism," "cultural bias," "religious holidays," "values education," and the many other controversies that have made the public school classroom a battleground for conflicting religious values and world views. Caught in the crossfire are classroom teachers, who are told to "educate for citizenship" and "teach appreciation for diversity" while growing divisions pit one group against another in the public square.

The religious differences so prevalent in the battle over public schools are now exacerbated by exploding pluralism in the United States. In California, which receives nearly one-third of the immigration to the United States, minority group members constitute a majority in public school enrollment. The student body of a single high school in Miami Beach represents 67 nationalities. A teacher in northern Virginia reports that 15 languages are spoken in her class and that her students often must serve as translators at parent-teacher conferences.[1]

In school districts across the country, teachers confront daily what other citizens choose to ignore: religious diversity in the United States presents the nation and the schools with unprecedented challenges. The language of pluralism may no longer be confined to the "Protestant, Catholic, Jewish" discussion prevalent in the 1950s. Religious pluralism today includes believers from all the world's faiths as well as increasing numbers of people who indicate no religious preference at all. Islam, to mention just one highly significant example, will soon be, if it is not already, the second largest faith in the United States after Christianity. New populations of Muslims, as well as Buddhists and many other religious and ethnic groups, are entering U.S. schools in significant numbers (Eck, 2001).

All these developments—religious and ethnic divisions, loss of faith in public education, and exploding pluralism—summon us to rethink the role of religion in the classroom. At issue is a simple, yet profoundly important, question: How will we live with our deepest differences? Our answer to that question may well determine the future of public education and the health of the body politic in the third century of the U.S. experiment in constitutional freedom.

ENDING THE SILENCE ABOUT RELIGION

If we are to live with our differences, we must acknowledge the importance of religious diversity even as we seek common ground. Efforts by school officials to ignore differences by excluding religion from the curriculum, or by acting as though religious divisions do not exist (or do not matter), succeed only in producing false unity and false toleration. Elizabeth Kristol (1989) argues:

A healthy pluralism may in fact be characterized by the mutual respect that arises from a simmering of conflicting viewpoints and diverse senses of identity. . . . True tolerance means looking differences squarely in the eye and admitting the appalling fact that when other people seem to differ from us, this is because they actually believe their view of the world to be true. (p. A19)

Respect for differences and authentic toleration will be possible only when schools end what has been a virtual silence about religion and begin to take religion and religious liberty seriously. There is much irony in the fact that the public school, the very locus of the "culture wars," is the least likely place to find a discussion of the role of religion in history and society (Davis, Ponder, Burlbaw, Gorza-Lubek, & Moss, 1986; Haynes, 1985; Nord, 1995; Vitz, 1986). Ignoring religion and religious diversity has neither avoided controversy nor encouraged toleration—witness the ongoing court battles and endless fights over textbooks.

Silence about religion has only served to impoverish our curriculum and deny our students a full education. More serious still, we have given students the dangerously false message that religions operate only on the margins of human life and are largely irrelevant to human history and culture. Such misapprehension about religion promotes misunderstanding and intolerance, leaving students prey to distorted notions of how human beings have struggled with questions of meaning and value throughout the ages.

The neglect of religion in the U.S. curriculum may be traced, in part at least, to the fear of controversy and widespread misunderstanding surrounding the United States Supreme Court rulings of the early 1960s, which declared state-sponsored religious practices in the public schools to be unconstitutional. What most educators do not understand (or choose to ignore) is that in those same rulings, the Court clearly indicated that teaching *about* religion is not only constitutional, but also necessary for a good education.

Fortunately, recent efforts to find consensus on the place of religion in the classroom have begun to affect the curriculum (Haynes & Thomas, 2002). State standards, particularly in the social studies, are mandating more discussion of religion in the public schools. Teaching *about* religion across the curriculum is beginning to improve: textbooks are changing, new supplementary materials are available, and more opportunities for teacher education are offered each year (Douglass, 2000; Henderson, 2003). Despite these gains, much work remains to be done if study about religion is to be taken seriously in public schools (Nord & Haynes, 1998).

A CIVIC FRAMEWORK FOR RELIGIOUS DIVERSITY

The growing consensus that study about religion is proper in public education offers teachers an unprecedented opportunity for promoting understanding and respect among people of all faiths. While this is easy to say (and for states to mandate), it is much more difficult to carry out in the classroom, especially in divided communities where some citizens are suspicious of any initiative that public schools may take in studying religion. The risks associated with not learning about one another in an age of increasing pluralism, however, are much greater than the risks associated with appropriately including religion in the curriculum.

The first requirement for any teacher wishing to deal honestly and openly with religious issues in the curriculum and classroom is to give careful attention to the Religious Liberty clauses of the First Amendment to the Constitution: "Congress shall make no law respecting an establishment of religion, or prohibiting the free exercise thereof . . ." These 16 words provide the civic framework for teaching about religion and for handling religious differences in the public school classroom.

The United States Supreme Court has interpreted the First Amendment to mean that public schools must be neutral concerning religion: they may neither promote nor inhibit religious belief or non-belief. The public school curriculum may not, therefore, include religious indoctrination in any form (including hostility to religion). Such teaching would constitute state sponsorship of religion and would violate the freedom of conscience protected by the First Amendment.

Religious indoctrination, however, is not the same as teaching *about* religion or giving a fair hearing to religious perspectives. In the 1960s school-prayer cases, which ruled against state-sponsored school prayer and Bible reading, the Court indicated that public school education may include teaching about religion. Writing for the Court in *Abington v. Schempp* (1963), Associate Justice Tom Clark stated:

[It] might well be said that one's education is not complete without a study of comparative religion or the history of religion and its relationship to the advancement of civilization. It certainly may be said that the Bible is worthy of study for its literary and historic qualities. Nothing we have said here indicates that such study of the Bible or of religion, when presented objectively as part of a secular program of education, may not be effected consistently with the First Amendment. (p. 203)

Beyond this baseline distinction between indoctrination and study about religion, certain key civic values and responsibilities flow from the First Amendment's Religious Liberty clauses. These values are so fundamental and enduring (and so vital to the classroom), they may be called the three Rs of religious liberty: rights, responsibilities, and respect.

- **Rights.** Religious liberty, or freedom of conscience, is a fundamental and inalienable right founded on the inviolable dignity of the person. In our religiously diverse classrooms, it is essential that we emphasize this basic right as a cornerstone of American citizenship. Students must have a clear understanding that the rights guaranteed by the Constitution are for citizens of all faiths, as well as for those professing none.
- **Responsibilities.** Religious liberty is a universal right that depends upon a universal responsibility to respect that right for others. Teachers must help students of all cultures and faiths to recognize the inseparable link between the preservation of their own constitutional rights and their responsibility as citizens to defend those rights for all others.
- **Respect.** Debate and disagreement among people of different faiths and world views are vital to classroom discussion and a key element of preparing children for citizenship in a democracy. If we are to live with our differences, particularly our religious differences, *how* we debate is as critical as *what* we debate. As teachers deal with religious diversity in the classroom, it is vital that they teach a strong commitment to the civic values that enable people with differing religious and philosophical perspectives to treat one another with respect and civility.

Rights, responsibilities, and respect, then, are the democratic first principles for addressing the role of religion in public schools. Teaching about religion is only one requirement of this civic framework. Teachers also must be careful to protect the religious liberty rights of students. For example, students have the right to pray alone or in groups, as long as such prayer is not disruptive of the educational process or coercive of others. Students have the right to share their faith with others, express themselves religiously in class discussions or projects, and distribute religious literature subject to time, place, and manner restrictions. In secondary schools, students have the right to form religious clubs if the school allows other non-curriculum-related clubs to exist (Haynes & Thomas, 2002).

When teaching about the many cultures and faiths of the United States and the world, teachers must simultaneously teach and model the common ground—the rights and responsibilities outlined in the American constitutional compact. Done in this way, teaching about religion and recognizing religious liberty in the classroom become excellent opportunities for teaching respect for the universal rights and mutual responsibilities within which the deep differences of belief can be negotiated.

GUIDELINES FOR TEACHING ABOUT RELIGION

The principles of religious liberty remind us that although no religious consensus is possible in the United States, it does remain possible to develop out of differences a shared understanding of religion's role in public schools and public life. In 1987, concerned about the recurring conflicts over religion in the schools, a group of educational and religious leaders met in an effort to find common ground, based on the civic values of rights, responsibilities, and respect.

All of the groups represented, from the National Education Association to the National Association of Evangelicals, expressed great dismay over the divisive battles in the schools and courts and their devastating impact on public education. All agreed that the confusion about the role of religion in public schools has left school boards, administrators, and teachers unprepared to handle religious differences and controversies.

Far too often, schools are being asked to deal with societal problems without sufficient support and cooperation from the larger community. The time had come, the group decided, to assist local schools by reaching a national consensus about the constitutionally permissible and educationally sound role of religion in public education. Such an agreement would help to ensure that religious diversity is respected in the schools and that religious perspectives and values are fairly represented in the curriculum.

After a year and a half of discussion and negotiation, participants found that the principles of religious liberty can provide a common vision for the common good. For the first time, 17 groups from across the religious and political spectrum reached agreement about the proper role of religion in the public school curriculum. The Christian Legal Society joined with the American Jewish Congress. The Islamic Society of North America and the National Council of Churches agreed with the National School Boards Association and the American Association of School Administrators.

The group's guidelines, "Religion in the Public School Curriculum: Questions and Answers,"[2] stress the important distinction between teaching *about* religion, which is permissible, and religious indoctrination, which is prohibited by the First Amendment. The participants made a strong case for the natural inclusion of teaching about religion. In answer to the question concerning *where* study about religion belongs in the curriculum, the guidelines read:

Wherever it naturally arises. On the secondary level, the social studies, literature, and the arts offer many opportunities for the inclusion of information about religions—their ideas and themes. On the elementary level, natural opportunities arise in discussions of the family and community life and in instruction about festivals and different cultures. Many educators believe that integrating study about religion into existing courses is an educationally sound way to acquaint students with the role of religion in history and society.

Religion also may be taught about in special courses or units. Some secondary schools, for example, offer such courses as world religions, the Bible as literature, and the religious literature of the West and of the East. (Haynes & Thomas, 2002, p. 91)

A year after the group issued these first guidelines in 1988, members reconvened to tackle the perennial problem of religious holidays in public schools. Despite widespread doubt that it was possible to reach consensus concerning the infamous "December dilemma," the group produced "Religious Holidays in the Public Schools: Questions and Answers."[3] That publication emphasized an academic, rather than devotional, approach in public schools. Consequently,

Teachers must be alert to the distinction between teaching about religious holidays, which is permissible, and *celebrating* religious holidays, which is not. Recognition of and information about holidays may focus on how and when they are celebrated, their origins, histories and generally agreed-upon meanings. If the approach is objective and sensitive, neither promoting nor inhibiting religion, this study can foster understanding and mutual respect for differences in belief. (Haynes & Thomas, 2002, p. 106)

Teaching about religion and religious holidays may include the use of art, drama, music, or literature with religious themes if it serves a sound education goal in the curriculum. Use of religious symbols as examples of cultural and religious heritage is also permissible as a teaching aid or resource; such symbols, however, "may be displayed only on a temporary basis as part of the academic program" (Haynes & Thomas, 2002, p. 107).

The most sensitive and controversial question concerning religious holidays in the schools is, of course, "What about Christmas?" The guidelines state:

Decisions about what to do in December should begin with the understanding that public schools may not sponsor religious devotions or celebrations; study *about* religious holidays does not extend to religious worship or practice.

Does this mean that all seasonal activities must be banned from the schools? Probably not, and in any event such an effort would be unrealistic. The resolution would seem to lie in devising holiday programs that serve an educational purpose for all students—programs that make no students feel excluded or identified with a religion not their own.

Holiday concerts in December may appropriately include music related to Christmas and Hanukkah, but religious music should not dominate. Any dramatic productions should emphasize the cultural aspects of the holidays. Nativity pageants or plays portraying the Hanukkah miracle are not appropriate in the public school setting.

In short, while recognizing the holiday season, none of the school activities in December should have the purpose, or effect, of promoting or inhibiting religion. (Haynes & Thomas, 2002, p. 108)

Questions may arise in connection with holidays at many other times during the school year. For example, some parents may ask for their children to be excused for religious reasons from activities or parties surrounding such holidays as Valentine's Day and Halloween. Such requests should be routinely granted.

But what about requests for excusal even when the holiday is being treated in an academic manner? The guidelines read: "If focused on a limited, specific discussion, such requests may be granted in order to strike a balance between the student's religious freedom and the school's interest in providing a well-rounded education" (Haynes & Thomas, 2002, p. 109). The rule of thumb should be to accommodate requests for excusal from limited portions of the curriculum if such requests are reasonable and feasible.

Parents also will ask that students be excused from school to observe religious holidays within their traditions. School policies should take into account the religious needs and requirements of students by allowing a reasonable number of excused absences, without penalties, to observe religious holidays. The guidelines note, however: "Students may be asked to complete makeup assignments or examinations in conjunction with such absences" (Haynes & Thomas, 2002, p. 109).

These consensus statements provide local communities and schools with a broad framework for developing their own policies. When schools demonstrate that they take religion and religious liberty seriously through sound policies and substantive staff development, they receive strong support in their communities and can restore trust where it has been lost.

YES, BUT HOW?

Now that widespread agreement exists that schools should teach about religion, questions remain about *how* to do it. Teachers are being asked to teach, for the first time, topics long ignored in the textbooks and controversial in the community. These teachers want and need straightforward advice on how to teach while traversing this unfamiliar and sensitive terrain. The following answers to frequently asked questions offer practical approaches for meeting the challenges and avoiding the pitfalls of teaching about religion in a religiously diverse society.

When Should Teachers Talk About Religion, and How Much Should They Say?

The best approach to discussions about religion is to place them within a historical and cultural context. Courses in history, literature, art, and music on the elementary and secondary levels, as well as discussions of family, community, and instruction about holidays and cultures, offer natural opportunities to teach about religious influences and themes.

How much is taught about the religion or religions of a particular historical period or culture, and decisions about which religions to include in the discussion, always should be determined by the academic requirements of the course. Teachers need teach only that which is essential to understanding the events or peoples under consideration.

Students should be made aware that any examination of religious traditions as part of a study of history and culture is necessarily limited. Teachers may find it helpful to inform students as to why particular religious influences and themes have been chosen for study. Students also need to know that much more could be said about the complexity and richness of religious traditions. Alert them to the fact that a wide diversity of opinion exists about religious events and ideas, not only among the various religions, but also within the traditions themselves.

How May Teachers Teach About Religion in a Way That Is Fair and Balanced?

We have already noted that teaching about religion must be done in an environment free of indoctrination. While a variety of religious perspectives may be presented, the teacher should not advocate either a religious or anti-religious perspective. When discussing religious beliefs, teachers can avoid injecting personal bias by teaching through attribution (e.g., by reporting that "most Muslims believe . . .").

It is important to remember the principle that fair and balanced study about religion must involve critical thinking about religion in history. Religion has been an integral factor in some of the most inspiring as well as the most horrific events in history. The full historical record (and various interpretations of it) must be open to analysis and discussion. In this regard, it is preferable to use primary sources where possible, enabling students to directly encounter and interpret the historical record.

The study of destructive or oppressive acts carried out in the name of a religious belief, however, should not be opportunities for attacking the integrity of the religion itself. All religious traditions have tragic chapters in which the ideals of the faith were not fully lived. These parts of the historical record can be taught without condemning a particular religion or religion in general. Attacks by teachers on religion, or on the theology or practice of any faith, do not belong in a public school classroom.

Be careful to avoid making qualitative comparisons (e.g., religion A is superior to religion B). Structural comparisons, such as pointing out that most religious traditions have scriptures and community worship, may be, however, a helpful way to organize class discussion. It also may be appropriate to compare and contrast the different perspectives religions might have on historical or current events.

What Are Some Common Pitfalls in Teaching About Religious Differences?

In an attempt to appear "tolerant" or "neutral" when teaching about religion, teachers sometimes, usually inadvertently, qualify religious truth claims as relative or reduce all religions to a common denominator—speaking of all religions as being "all the same" underneath their differences. For most religious people, however, such "toleration" distorts their faith and is anything but neutral. It matters very much to a Christian, a Jew, or a Muslim what one takes to be ultimately true. These faiths, and many others, subscribe to absolute truths derived from the sources of revelation and authority in their traditions. The idea that all faiths are ultimately the same may be compatible with some world views, but is itself a philosophical or religious position. For a teacher to advocate this position in the classroom is a form of indoctrination.

Equally questionable are teachers' attempts to "explain away" religious faith as merely social or psychological phenomena. Such opinions may leave students with the impression that all truth is relative and that there are no absolutes. Teachers may present various theories of religion and introduce students to the social, economic, and cultural context in which religions have formed and changed. It is essential, however, to first report how people of faith interpret their own practices and beliefs and how these beliefs have affected their lives historically—as well as how they affect people's lives today.

Public school teachers must strive to teach about the various approaches to truth without advocating one religious or philosophical position over another. Respect for differences is crucial if one is to understand the beliefs of the world's religious traditions. By taking care not to reduce or portray as relative the truth claims of religions, the teacher allows the student to learn how each faith understands itself.

Should Teachers Have Students Role-play Religious Practices?

Re-creating religious practices or ceremonies through role-playing activities is not appropriate in public school classrooms. Such activities, no matter how carefully planned or well-intentioned, risk undermining the integrity of the faith involved. Religious ceremonies are sacred to those who practice them. Role-playing may unwittingly mock or, at the very least, oversimplify the religious meaning or intent of the ritual. Re-creations of religious practices also could violate the consciences of students asked to participate. A better approach is to use audiovisual resources and primary source documents to introduce students to ceremonies and rituals of the world's religions.

What Should the Response Be When Students Ask the Teacher To Reveal His/Her Own Religious Beliefs?

Some teachers choose not to answer the question, stating that it is inappropriate for a teacher to inject personal beliefs into the discussion. Teachers of young children, in particular, have said they find this to be the most satisfactory response. Other teachers, not wishing to leave students guessing about their personal views, and in the interest of maintaining an open and honest classroom environment, answer the question straightforwardly and succinctly.

The teacher who decides to answer the question by telling about his or her religious background should probably not do so at the beginning of the course or the year. Such questions are perhaps best answered once the teacher has had an opportunity to demonstrate how various religious and nonreligious perspectives may be discussed with sensitivity and objectivity.

When answering questions about personal beliefs, teachers may take the opportunity to note: "These are my personal beliefs, but my role here is to present fairly and sympathetically a variety of beliefs as we study the history of the world's great cultures. I only state my personal background so that you may better evaluate what I tell you." By answering the question briefly, with little elaboration or discussion, a teacher can offer a good lesson in civic values. Students learn that people with deep convictions are able to teach and learn about others' convictions in ways that are fair and balanced.

How Should Students' Religious Views Be Handled in the Classroom?

Teachers should not solicit information about students' religious affiliations or beliefs. Nor should students be asked to explain their faith or religious practices to the class. Such requests put unfair pressure on those students who may be reluctant to act as spokespersons for their tradition. Furthermore, students may be unqualified or unprepared to represent their traditions accurately. Students do have the right, however, to express their own religious views during a class discussion or as part of a writing or art assignment, as long as their statements are relevant to the subject under consideration and meet the academic requirements of the assignment.

It is the teacher's responsibility to clearly delineate, at the beginning of the course or topic, the civic ground rules for class discussion. The first principles of rights, responsibilities, and respect ought to be in place as part of the civic framework of every class. These civic values support a classroom environment conducive to exploring a broad range of ideas and views in a way that is both respectful and nonthreatening. Students will learn that differences, even the deepest ones, can be discussed with civility, and that ridicule and prejudice have no place in schools or society.

MEETING THE CHALLENGE IN THE CLASSROOM

How should teachers go about establishing a civic framework for teaching about religion in the classroom? Martha Ball provides an answer.

Today, Martha directs the Utah Rights, Responsibilities, and Respect Project. But for many years, she was in the classroom teaching social studies to upper elementary and middle school students in Salt Lake City.

What you did *not* hear in Martha's classroom were angry arguments about religion, with name-calling and personal attacks. And you did *not* hear Martha Ball using her position as a teacher to indoctrinate students—either for or against any religion. As it happens, Martha is of the majority faith in Utah. Her students and parents viewed her as a fair-minded educator able to teach about various faiths and worldviews with balance and respect. There were at least two reasons why Martha was successful at integrating significant discussion of religion: first, she understood and applied a civic framework (as outlined in this chapter) in her classroom; second, she took advantage of educational opportunities that prepared her to teach about a variety of religions with fairness and objectivity.

Martha began each school year by asking her students to consider how the civic principles of the First Amendment enable Americans to live with their deepest differences. She ties the discussion to the three key concepts of rights, responsibilities, and respect discussed earlier.

Students learned that the First Amendment is built on the conviction that religious liberty is an inherent right of every person. At the same time, they learned that a commitment to religious liberty for oneself must be linked to a civic responsibility to guard that right for others. They discussed how religious diversity in the United States makes it vitally important that citizens recognize their civic duty to protect the rights of others, including those with whom they strongly disagree.

By taking responsibility for the rights of others, Martha's students came to understand that they weren't being asked to compromise their own deep convictions. Nor were they being asked to accept or condone the beliefs and practices of their classmates. They were committing themselves, as American citizens, to discussing their differences with civility and respect.

Martha did not impose these ideas in her classroom. Rather, she presented them as civic principles that, when upheld, enable individuals to work together across their religious differences for the common good. She engaged students in the task of translating these principles into ground rules for the classroom. After writing and talking about what kind of class they wanted—how they wanted to be treated and how they should treat others—the students arrived at an agreement on ground rules for their class.

Through this process, Martha set the stage for respectful exchange about difficult issues. Her students were able to talk about religious issues and differences because they were prepared to do so civilly. During a discussion of Utah history, for example, a student (who happened to be Mormon) said, "Well, I know my church is the one true church." A Roman Catholic student spoke up: "But I know that *my* church is the true church." When the Mormon student started to get angry, Martha asked him to recall the agreement reached by the class on the meaning of religious liberty. She reminded the students of how Roger Williams, a man of deep religious convictions, created a society where each citizen was free to choose in matters of faith. "What would Roger Williams say?" she asked the angry student. "What are your ground rules for this class?" He replied, "I guess I have to say that if I have the right to say that my church is true, then he has the right to say his is true." Martha's students learned that they have a right to express their religious views, but they also respect others' right to hold and express different views.

Martha discovered that when students commit themselves to civic ground rules she was able to teach more about religion, and the students entered into discussions with greater interest and liveliness. Throughout the school year, her students would remind one another, and Martha herself, of the First Amendment ground rules they agreed to uphold. Her classroom became a microcosm of the American experiment in religious liberty and diversity—at its best.

CONCLUSION

Ignorance and contention about the role of religion in the public school curriculum is nothing new. For more than 150 years, Americans have fought about religion in the schools—and we have yet to get it right. The Protestant hegemony that characterized the early history of public schools has been replaced in many schools with silence about religion, censorship of religious perspectives, and, in some instances, violation of students' religious liberty rights. Other schools have continued to promote the majority faith.

None of these approaches is consistent with the principles of religious liberty embodied in the First Amendment. The time finally has come to end both indoctrination and hostility by ensuring that religion is treated fully and fairly in the curriculum. Fortunately, we have, at long last, broad agreement across the religious and political spectrum that this should be done. In 1995, 20 leading religious and education groups (including the Christian Coalition and People for the American Way) agreed on the following description of religious liberty in public education:

Public schools may not inculcate nor inhibit religion. They must be places where religion and religious conviction are treated with fairness and respect. Public schools uphold the First Amendment when they protect the religious liberty rights of students of all faiths, or none. Schools demonstrate fairness when they ensure that the curriculum includes study *about* religion, where appropriate, as an important part of a complete education.[4]

Our challenge now is to put this agreement to work in classrooms by guarding students' religious liberty rights and by teaching about religion in ways that are constitutionally and educationally sound. By so doing, we prepare our children to live with even their deepest differences, and we help to sustain the boldest and most successful experiment in religious liberty in the history of humankind.

RESOURCES FOR EDUCATORS

Religion in American Life—A Series for Young Adults

All public school libraries should have this series of scholarly works on religion in the United States, written for young readers in middle and high school. Edited by Yale University professors Jon Butler and Harry Stout and published by Oxford University Press, *Religion in American Life* is a 17-volume series authored by some of the nation's leading scholars in the field of religious studies. For more information, visit Oxford University Press at www.oup-usa.org.

Additional Books for Young Readers on Religious Traditions

Among other recent books written for young people about the world's religions, two are especially appropriate for use in public schools: *A World of Faith* by Peggy Stack, available from Signature Books, is helpful for introducing elementary-age students to religious diversity in America. Mary Pope Osborne's *One World, Many Religions,* published by Alfred A. Knopf, is a lively account of the world's major faith traditions that is suitable for students in the upper elementary grades through high school.

On Common Ground—A CD-ROM on World Religions

A groundbreaking resource for students and teachers is *On Common Ground: World Religions in America*, a CD-ROM produced by Columbia University Press. This multimedia resource uses text, primary sources, photographs, music, film, and the spoken word to bring alive the religious diversity of the United States. Prepared by Harvard University professor Diana Eck, the CD-ROM draws on the Pluralism Project, a Harvard-based study that documents America's religious landscape.

Calendar of Religious Holidays

Every teacher, especially in the elementary grades, would do well to have a calendar of religious holidays and ethnic festivals. Holidays and festivals can be valuable opportunities for introducing information about religions and cultures throughout the school year. Such calendars also alert teachers to their students' religious traditions and to observances that may result in student absences. The National Conference of Christians and Jews (71 Fifth Ave., New York, NY 10003) publishes a three-year calendar marking key religious and ethnic holidays.

America's Religions: An Educator's Guide to Beliefs and Practices

Teacher Ideas Press publishes a guide by Benjamin Hubbard, John Hatfield, and James Santucci about the beliefs and practices of a number of the world's religions. Designed specifically for teachers, the guide examines each religious group in terms of its origins, beliefs, sacred scriptures, practices, main subgroups, common misunderstandings and stereotypes, and classroom concerns.

Finding Common Ground: A Guide to Religious Liberty in Public Schools

The First Amendment Center makes available a comprehensive guide to resources for teaching about religion and for protecting religious-liberty rights of students. All of the guidelines have been endorsed by a broad range of educational and religious organizations. For more information or to download the guide, visit www.firstamendmentcenter.org.

References

Al-Hibri, A. Y., Elshtain, J. B., & Haynes, C. C. (2001). *Religion in American public life: Living with our deepest differences.* New York: W. W. Norton & Co.

Davis, O. L., Jr., Ponder, G., Burlbaw, L. M., Gorza-Lubek, M., & Moss, A. (1986). *Looking at history: A review of major U.S. history textbooks.* Washington, DC: People for the American Way.

Douglass, S. L. (2000). *Teaching about religion in national and state social studies standards.* Nashville, TN: First Amendment Center and Council on Islamic Education.

Eck, D. L. (2001). *A new religious America.* San Francisco: HarperCollins

Flowers, R. (1988). They got our attention, didn't they?: The Tennessee and Alabama schoolbook cases. *Religion and Public Education, 15,* 262-285.

Glenn, C. L. (1988). *The myth of the common school.* Amherst, MA: University of Massachusetts Press.

Haynes, C. C. (1985). *Teaching about religious freedom in American secondary schools.* Silver Spring, MD: Americans United Research Foundation.

Haynes, C. C., & Thomas, O. (2002). *Finding common ground: A guide to religious liberty in public schools.* Nashville, TN: First Amendment Center.

Henderson, S. (2003). *Teaching about religion in public schools: Where do we go from here?* Nashville, TN: First Amendment Center & Pew Forum on Religion and Public Life.

Kristol, E. (1989, September 25). False tolerance, false unity. *New York Times,* p. A19.

Nord, W. (1995). *Religion and American education: Rethinking a national dilemma.* Chapel Hill, NC: The University of North Carolina Press.

Nord, W., & Haynes, C. C. (1998). *Taking religion seriously across the curriculum.* Alexandria, VA: Association for Supervision and Curriculum Development.

School District of Abington Township, Pennsylvania et al. v. Schempp et al., 374 U.S. 203 (1963).

Vitz, P. (1986). *Censorship: Evidence of bias in our children's textbooks.* Ann Arbor, MI: Servant Publications.

Notes

[1] These are two of the many challenges of pluralism described by teachers in the workshops and seminars sponsored by the First Amendment Center.

[2] "Religion in the Public School Curriculum: Questions and Answers" is found in the publication *Finding Common Ground: A Guide to Religious Liberty in Public Schools.* This publication is available from the First Amendment Center at 1207 18th Ave. S., Nashville, TN 37212 or online at www.firstamendmentcenter.org. The sponsors of the guidelines are: American Academy of Religion, American Federation of Teachers, Americans United Research Foundation, Baptist Joint Committee, American Association of School Administrators, American Jewish Congress, Association for Supervision and Curriculum Development, Christian Legal Society, The Church of Jesus Christ of Latter-day Saints, National Association of Evangelicals, National Council of Churches of Christ in the USA, National Council for the Social Studies, National School Boards Association, The Islamic Society of North America, National Conference of Christians and Jews, National Council on Religion and Public Education, and the National Education Association.

[3] "Religious Holidays in the Public Schools: Questions and Answers" also may be obtained through the First Amendment Center (see footnote 2). The quotes that follow are from this document, now included as a chapter in *Finding Common Ground* (Haynes & Thomas, 2002).

[4] Free copies of the full text of "Religious Liberty, Public Education, and the Future of American Democracy" may be obtained from the First Amendment Center (see footnote 2). The sponsors of this statement are: American Association of School Administrators, American Center for Law and Justice, American Federation of Teachers, Association for Supervision and Curriculum Development, Carnegie Foundation for the Advancement of Teaching, Central Conference of American Rabbis, Christian Coalition, Christian Educators Association International, Christian Legal Society, Citizens for Excellence in Education, The Freedom Forum First Amendment Center at Vanderbilt University, National Association of Evangelicals, National Association of Secondary School Principals, National Congress of Parents and Teachers, National Council of Churches of Christ in the U.S.A., National Education Association, National School Boards Association, People for the American Way, and Union of American Hebrew Congregations.

Chapter 3
Ability Differences in the Classroom:
Teaching and Learning in Inclusive Classrooms

| Mara Sapon-Shevin |

Although we may talk about classrooms as "the kindergarten" or "the 3rd grade," and may *assume* similarities in the skills and interests of chronologically similar students, the reality is that all classrooms are heterogeneous. Typical classrooms have *always* served (or ill-served) students who varied along any number of continua, including performance or ability, either by ignoring those differences or through elaborate tracking and grouping strategies. Now, however, many schools are moving towards more *purposive* heterogeneity; teachers recognize the value of teaching children to interact comfortably with a wide range of people and so work to create classrooms and practices that acknowledge differences among students in the classroom and respond to them thoughtfully and creatively (Sapon-Shevin, 1999, 2001, 2003).

This philosophy, known as full inclusion (Kluth, Straut, & Biklen, 2003; Rainforth & Kugelmass, 2003; Villa, Thousand, Stainback, & Stainback, 2000), represents a commitment to creating schools and classrooms in which all children, without regard to individual needs or disabilities, are educated together. Rather than trying to "fix" children so that they can be fit back into relatively untouched "regular classrooms" (a process often referred to as "mainstreaming"), inclusion aims to substantially alter general education classrooms to make them more responsive to heterogeneous groups of learners. Inclusive classrooms embody the belief that diversity is a positive force in children's and teachers' lives and should be embraced, rather than ignored or minimized.

Inclusive classrooms attempt to honor and respond to the many kinds of diversity that children bring to the classroom. Differences in race, ethnicity, gender, family background, language, sexual orientation, and religion—as well as differences in ability/performance— are not dismissed in the name of standardization, but rather are appreciated and become part of the curriculum itself. Inclusive classrooms also must address differences in what is typically called "ability." Although one can never accurately predict any child's full potential or ultimate performance, children do differ in their *current* skills, knowledge, and competence. In traditional classrooms, these differences may lead to children being assigned to different reading or math groups, or being identified as "learning disabled" or "gifted." In reality, all children have abilities and strengths, as well as areas in which they require more intensive instruction. As educators, we must make decisions about how to respond to these differences in educationally and ethically appropriate ways.

The task of responding appropriately to students' learning and performance differences has been severely challenged by the recent focus on high-stakes testing and standardization. Many schools and legislatures are moving towards judging students (and teachers) according to predetermined standard benchmarks that cannot be modified or individualized, making responsive teaching difficult. Nonetheless, considerable progress has been made in attempts to teach inclusively while also meeting high standards (Kluth, Straut, & Biklen, 2003; Rainforth & Kugelmass, 2003). In the current standardization climate, teachers need support as they attempt to meet all children's individual needs while still maintaining high standards and a cohesive classroom community.

What are the challenges of teaching in classrooms that educate children who read well alongside those who do not read at all, or children who learn quickly and easily with traditional methods alongside those who need intensive instruction or alternative strategies? How do we discriminate appropriate differentiation, based on high expectations, from tracking and "dumbing down," based on stereotypes or prejudicial labeling? The following exploration of these topics first examines some of the myths about ability differences and ability grouping that often perpetuate rigid, dysfunctional ways of teaching and instructional organization. Next, the author contrasts such beliefs with the realities of heterogeneity and mixed-ability groups, and explores some more appropriate ways to organize classrooms and instruction. A list of resources for implementing inclusive teaching concludes the chapter.

MYTHS ABOUT ABILITY AND ABILITY GROUPING

Myth 1: There Is Such a Thing As Ability

Many educators believe that each child has some fixed ability level that defines the best he or she can possibly do. Thus, we talk about children "not working up to ability" and, conversely, "overachieving" (that is, doing better than we predicted they would). Using these putative differences as a basis, we label children as "smart," "average," or "slow." For children whose differences appear more salient, we use the terms "gifted" or "handicapped." We often adjust our curricula and expectations accordingly. In actuality, all people, including all children, vary along a number of dimensions, and it is generally not helpful to talk about ability as if it were a fixed, immutable potential for achievement. How well any child does is a function of many variables, including the nature of the curriculum, the child's self-concept, the flexibility and support of those who surround the child, and the child's interest in the task. Therefore, if conditions were right, *we could all do better!* As Hunt (1961) noted:

It is highly unlikely that any society has developed a system of child rearing and education that maximizes the potential of the individuals which compose it. Probably no individual has ever lived whose full potential for happy intellectual interest and growth has been achieved. (p. 346)

Therefore, in some ways, we are all *underachievers*, and it makes sense for teachers to find ways to help all children achieve more and to create classrooms that nurture and support diversity. The work by Armstrong (1993) and Gardner (1983) on multiple intelligences helps us recognize the many ways to "be smart," and understand that a single continuum of "ability" makes little pedagogical sense.

Myth 2: Students Learn Better in Homogeneous Groups

Some teachers still believe that by narrowing the range of abilities in the classroom, children will learn better because tasks will be more appropriate. Actually, despite the fact that many teachers continue to group students by ability, research findings overwhelmingly suggest that homogeneous grouping does not consistently help anyone learn more or better (Massachusetts Advocacy Center, 1990; Thousand, Villa, & Nevin, 2002). In fact, organizing children into high-, average-, and low-ability groups actually *creates* differences in what children learn by exposing them to different kinds of material. Although some children in high-ability groups may benefit from such arrangements, those who lose the most are the children placed in average- and low-ability groups. Such grouping practices tend to compound racial, ethnic, and economic differences in schools, as poor children and children of color are least likely to be served in enriched, gifted, or high-ability tracks. These children are more likely to end up in vocational or low-ability groups (Oakes & Lipton, 1999).

Ability grouping also takes a serious toll on children's self concepts and on their opportunities to form meaningful relationships across groups. Children in the "slow group," the "low reading group," or what gets labeled as the "dumb class" are often painfully aware of the limited expectations adults have for them. Children so identified often face teasing and ridicule from their peers. Similarly, children who are put in top groups or removed to gifted classes are often labeled as "brains" or "nerds" and may find themselves socially isolated. Grouping children creates distance among them and tends to amplify and solidify whatever actual differences originally existed (Sapon-Shevin, 1994, 1999).

Myth 3: Teaching Is Easier in Homogeneous Groups

Teachers who have always organized instruction around three reading groups, or around a high-math group and a low-math group, find homogeneous grouping comfortable and familiar. However, teachers who group homogeneously also complain about a lack of time to meet individual needs and about the low motivation and involvement levels of some students. By grouping heterogeneously for instruction, especially using models like cooperative learning and peer tutoring (in which children learn to help one another), teachers often find that teaching becomes more enjoyable (Putnam, 1994; Sapon-Shevin, 1999; Sapon-Shevin, Ayres, & Duncan, 2002; Thousand, Villa, & Nevin, 2002). When heterogeneous teaching models are working well, children receive the benefit of peer instruction and motivation; the teacher's role shifts from management to instruction. Many teachers report their students being livelier and more involved, and that they enjoyed more challenging and exciting teaching experiences.

Myth 4: Children Are Cruel and Cannot Accept Differences

All of us have seen children teased and tormented because of their differences. We have all heard children call one another "four-eyes," "metal mouth," "dummy," or "fatso." Children also have a tremendous capacity to become supportive and nurturing friends of classmates who are different from themselves. Yet children cannot develop such understanding, appreciation, and social skills if they are kept isolated from peers who are different. Mere contact is not enough to promote positive responses to differences; teachers must systematically address student differences and structure learning activities that encourage positive social interaction. The social climate of the classroom must be a *first* priority, not something to be "squeezed in" if time remains. Although children can be cruel, they can be systematically taught to be caring, empathic, and supportive of one another (Sapon-Shevin, 1999).

Myth 5: Parents Support Homogeneous Grouping and Tracking

Because many cultural messages tell us that differences are bad and that people who are different must live and be educated separately, it is no wonder that many parents accept the practices of homogeneous grouping and the segregation of children who are different. Increasingly, however, parents of children labeled as "handicapped" are challenging the practice of placing their children in separate, isolated schools or classrooms. These parents want their children to grow up as part of the community in which they live, and this means going to school and playing with chronological peers. Many parents of "typical" children also have come to support integration or full inclusion within schools (Thousand, Villa, & Nevin, 2002). This is particularly true as they see their children becoming comfortable with, and knowledgeable about, disabilities and differences. Even parents who initially expressed concern that the presence of children with educational challenges would "dilute" the quality of their own child's education have noted that, when conscientiously implemented, inclusive, regular classrooms do not lose any of their "rigor"; rather, they become more flexible, accommodating learning environments for all children.

Parents whose children have been labeled "gifted" are often conflicted. Some parents feel (rightfully) that their child's unique needs cannot be met in the typical, workbook-oriented, lock-step classroom and that removal to a special class is the only solution. They are concerned that their "high-achieving" child will be bored or held back by less intelligent classmates. Other parents, however, worry about separating their child from his or her "regular" classmates; they do not want their child to feel stigmatized or overly different from other children (Sapon-Shevin, 1994). If not all of their own children are labeled "gifted," they also worry about creating schisms within their own family. Many of these concerns, however, are a function of the inadequacy of many regular classrooms, rather than inherent flaws in the principles of multi-level, multi-modality classrooms. If and when parents can be shown "regular" classrooms that meet the individual needs of each child within an inclusive, accepting classroom community, the potential for parental support of heterogeneous grouping will be enhanced (Kluth, Straut, & Biklen, 2003).

TEACHING AND LEARNING IN INCLUSIVE CLASSROOMS

In order for teachers to teach and students to learn in heterogeneous classrooms, considerable attention must be given to classroom organization, curriculum design, and community building. What kinds of teaching strategies are most appropriate and successful in heterogeneous classrooms? How can students learn to accept and understand one another's differences?

Cooperative Learning

Cooperative learning is one of the optimal ways to teach children with different abilities in the same classroom. Cooperative-learning instruction involves children working together, helping each other to learn. Much of the early work in cooperative learning referred to the importance of heterogeneous grouping as a principle. More recently, the concept of heterogeneity has been expanded to address specific strategies for incorporating *all* children within cooperative learning, including those previously segregated in special classes or separate programs (Putnam, 1994; Sapon-Shevin, 1990; Sapon-Shevin, Ayres, & Duncan, 2002; Thousand et al., 2002).

Of the many structured systems of cooperative learning, one method, called Jigsaw (Aronson, 1978), involves dividing the material to be learned into five or six parts and assigning students to heterogeneous five- or six-member teams. Each student is responsible for learning and then teaching his or her portion of the material to the whole team. Members of different groups who have been assigned the same portion of material meet in "expert groups" to study and discuss their section. Because each group member is responsible for all the material, all students must help each other learn; no one can sit back without participating.

The Jigsaw method can be used to teach many things: one 2nd-grade teacher divides the class into groups of five and gives each group member two of the week's 10 spelling words to teach to the rest of the group. A 5th-grade teacher required group members to learn and then teach different parts of a unit on South Africa. Group members specialized in the music, art, food, geography, or history of the region. Paula Boilard, a band teacher, divided her jazz band into groups who became "experts" in the rhythm, dynamics, articulation, and melody of a new piece. By learning the rhythm for all the instruments, each member gained a much better sense of how the whole piece fit together. The band's harmony was increased in many ways!

In another method for organizing the classroom for cooperative learning, sometimes called

"Learning Together" (Johnson & Johnson, 1999), the teacher assigns heterogeneous groups of students to produce a single product as a group. The teacher arranges the classroom to facilitate peer interaction, provides appropriate materials, constructs and explains the task so that it requires group cooperation, observes the students' interactions, and intervenes as necessary. Students might be placed with a partner, for example, and asked to do a complex math problem. Each member must be able to explain the answer; they cannot just say, "Because Mike said the answer is 34." Therefore, higher level students must work with and teach lower level students. Larger groups, consisting of four or five students, might be asked to produce a skit, with different group members assigned to the writing, directing, and acting; or the students write a cooperative report.

This method places considerable emphasis on teaching group members appropriate social skills to facilitate smooth interaction and cooperation. This can be done in various ways. Sometimes, one student in the group functions as the observer, recording the various facilitative behaviors of the group members. He or she might note, for example, how often each member talks, encourages others, asks questions, or clarifies. At the end of the session, the observer shares this information with the group, so that all students can begin to understand which behaviors help a group succeed and how these behaviors can be developed.

An alternative way to build appropriate group social skills is to assign special tasks to each group member. If the group's task, for example, is to generate a list of ways the school could recycle waste products, one group member might be assigned the role of recorder (writing down what people say), one the role of encourager (making sure that everyone contributes), one the role of clarifier (making sure that everyone agrees with and understands what has been written), and one the role of reporter (sharing with the large group what has been recorded). These roles might be clearly described for the students on different cards, and the teacher could engage students in lessons on how to do each task: "What are some ways you could encourage other people in your group?" or "What are some clarifying questions you could ask your group members?"

Teachers can encourage class-wide cooperation in less formal ways as well. One 4th-grade teacher implemented what she called the "family rule." Students were seated in clusters of four desks; the rule was that no one in the group could ask the teacher a question unless he or she had first checked with everyone else in the group. Consequently, the teacher received relief from answering an endless stream of questions. The students not only took active responsibility for helping their classmates find the right page, figure out the worksheet instructions, and spell difficult words, but also began to see each other as resources in many other ways. The teacher reported that children who were worried or upset about other issues (e.g., lost lunch money, a bully on the playground, a sick puppy at home) began to turn to one another for comfort and support.

Teachers also encourage support and cooperation by putting children in charge of more aspects of the classroom. In some classrooms, students take roll, do the lunch count, decorate bulletin boards, make decisions about scheduling concerns, and orient classroom visitors. By providing ample opportunities for children to exercise leadership and make choices, a teacher can help children to see one another as more than "the worst reader" or "the best math student."

Unfortunately, for many teachers, cooperative learning has been reduced to something they "do with" (sometimes "to") students for a brief period of the day or week. Formulaic, regimented systems of cooperative learning often predominate, taking away the impetus for a fully cooperative classroom experience. We need to examine every aspect of the classroom—what we teach, how we teach it, how we organize and manage students, how we respond to questions, how we solve problems, and how we talk about concerns. Within this framework of Socially Conscious Cooperative Learning (Schniedewind & Sapon-Shevin, 1998), children learn and live a philosophy of mutual care and interpersonal responsibility.

Peer Tutoring

Another way to address different skill levels within a class is to arrange for children to be resources for one another, through peer tutoring or peer teaching (Thousand et al., 2002; Thousand, Villa, & Nevin, 2002). Such programs can be arranged at many different levels, both within classrooms and across grade levels. In one school, every 6th-grader has a 1st-grade math "buddy" with whom he or she works, three times a week. This system provides extensive one-on-one instruction for the 1st-graders, and the 6th-grade teacher has reported that even the "weakest" math students in her class are showing a renewed interest in and enthusiasm for mathematics. She has seen some of the 6th-graders doing extra work to prepare for their teaching, so they would "be sure to get it right." In other schools, 1st-graders read regularly to appreciative 2nd-graders, and 6th-graders help integrate children with special needs. Teachers report that when students are involved in the process of integration, incidents of teasing virtually disappear and any infractions are dealt with by the other students. "Don't make fun of Jim, he has cerebral palsy; he talks fine and we understand him," is a representative remark made by the students to correct their peers.

Patty Feld, a teacher in a small rural school, organizes her students to help one another. Several times a week, the children participate in what she calls SHOA (Students Helping One Another). For a designated time period, children work together in pairs, with one child being responsible for helping the other. Half the time, Patty decides what the pair will work on; at other times, the student being helped is allowed to decide what kind of help he or she wants. All students read books at their own level. In weekly book-sharing time, students tell each other about what they are reading and learning. All the students benefit from one another's learning because they get to hear about books they might not be able to read, and reading-level differences are minimized by the cooperative sharing.

Teachers can arrange for students to help one another and become educational resources and sources of support in other ways. One teacher, who had a CD player and was anxious to ensure that all students learned to operate it properly, taught one little boy all about the machine. He learned what all the buttons did, how to adjust the volume, and how to operate the machine gently. He taught two other children during the day and checked them out on the process. Each of these children then taught two more, until the whole class knew the correct procedures. The new equipment was carefully attended at all times, and some of the classroom dynamics shifted by structuring situations where "high achievers" learned from nonreaders.

Another 5th-grade teacher kept four students in at recess to learn a difficult craft project. The teacher then asked each of these students to work with his or her table mates to complete the project. Students began to see one another in a new light, regarding children who were not typically considered "stars" with newfound respect. This teacher wondered why she hadn't always taught the activity this way, instead of trying to supervise 25 children, who were struggling with gluing and assembling, at the same time.

In order for peer teaching or peer tutoring to positively affect some of the typical status hierarchies within classrooms, teachers must be careful that all children get a chance to be the teacher or the leader, and that no one is stuck permanently in the role of receiving help. In inclusive classrooms where the range of skills and interests is wider than usual, it is especially important that relationships be reciprocal (Van Der Klift & Kunc, 2002).

One way to ensure this reciprocity is to broaden the kinds of activities and projects that children do throughout the school year. One teacher created a Classroom Yellow Pages that listed children's names, their areas of "expertise," and the ways in which they were willing to provide assistance to classmates. The guide included such entries as:

LaDonna Smith: jump-rope songs and jingles; willing to teach double-dutch jumping and crossing over to anyone interested.

Miguel Hernandez: baseball card collector; can show interested people how to start a collection, special cards to look for, and how to figure batting averages and other statistics.

By encouraging students to look beyond some of the typical school subjects by which to evaluate themselves and each other, the teacher created new areas of interest, promoted peer interaction, and broke existing stereotypes about "who was smart and who wasn't." Study of the multiple intelligences theory (Armstrong, 1993; Gardner, 1983) can help us to think more broadly about abilities and differences so that all students are valued for their strengths and supported in their areas of challenge.

Multi-level Teaching

In order to teach a wide range of students within one classroom, teachers need to rethink not only how they teach, but also what they teach. Instead of assuming that all students will be engaged in identical learning experiences for the same unit and evaluated according to the same criteria, the curriculum can be conceptualized as broad and inclusive. If the class is doing a unit on space, for example, the teacher can organize space activities and projects on many different levels. Children who have exceptional reading and research skills might be asked to write a report on the origins of the galaxy. Other children might be asked to draw and label the major planets in the solar system. A child with limited language skills might be required to be able to point to pictures of the sun, the moon, and the earth in different arrangements. Every student would share their completed projects with the whole group, so that everyone benefits from the diversity of activities.

In one classroom that contained both students identified as "gifted" and students labeled as "mentally retarded," the teacher set up a school sandwich store. The students took teachers' orders for Friday's lunch and delivered their sandwiches on that day. All of the class members were involved in the project, but at different levels. Depending on their math skills, some children calculated prices according to ingredient costs, some figured out state and "classroom tax," and others did the actual shopping. Students whose educational objectives included functional skills, such as meal preparation, worked to make the sandwiches. Other students generated publicity and issued a monthly business report. By constructing a project like this, the teacher was able to engage all students in a collaborative project and still meet each individual's educational needs (Rainforth & Kugelmass, 2003).

Teachers need to continually challenge the traditional curriculum and ask themselves: What does each child need to know? What aspects of this unit can be modified or adapted? Can students participate in the same activity with different levels of evaluation and involvement, or does an alternate, related activity need to be provided (Thousand et al., 2002)?

By asking these questions, teachers may find that they can achieve more flexibility for the whole class, and that modifications made with a particular student in mind can benefit many students. Patty Feld implements multilevel instruction by teaching across modalities. By including reading, writing, drawing and movement in her lessons, she is able to address the age and skill differences present in a particular group of students. In a unit on dinosaurs, for example, students wrote a play based on research, built three-dimensional dioramas, created an animal pantomime activity, and crafted a dinosaur fact rap. Classroom posters read, "We encourage our friends"; Patty tells students that questions are always okay. She not only encourages question asking, but also turns those questions back to the group. She says she has learned to ask open-ended questions that do not have right or wrong answers, and to wait for multiple replies. Often, a child who has not immediately jumped into the discussion makes a contribution at a later time that enriches the conversation. Students who witness such exchanges realize that there are many ways to be smart.

Another teacher assigned one student each day to take a set of notes for the class (a carbon copy of personal notes), in order to meet the needs of a deaf student who could not take notes. The teacher later found that these notes were also helpful to students with learning problems who could not both listen and take notes, students whose handwriting left them with very inadequate notes, and students who were absent and needed to catch up. Another teacher, on the advice of the learning-disabilities teacher, began writing key words on the board and teaching them before beginning a new lesson. She found that all students benefited from this pre-teaching motivation and organization. Another teacher, in helping one student get himself organized by teaching him to use an assignment notebook and to check with peers for assignments, found that many students in her class could benefit from a similar system to keep themselves on task and on track. Such classroom modifications and adaptations benefit children's learning and also demonstrate that all students are valued. The message is clear: We do not abandon people who are having difficulties.

Teaching Social Skills

In order for cooperative learning and peer tutoring to be effective, teachers may need to address social skills. Teachers may want to provide direct instruction in ways to praise, offer encouragement, and resolve conflicts.

One way of teaching such skills is by engaging students in a unit on giving and receiving help. Students can explore and practice ways of offering help (saying "Can I help you?" rather than "Let me do that; you're too short-dumb-slow"); as well as ways of accepting and declining help gracefully (saying "No thanks, I'm doing fine," rather than "What do you think I am, dumb or something?"). All people need practice in these nuances.

Teachers can help students reflect on questions such as the following:

- What are three things I do really well?
- What are three things I have trouble doing?
- What are some ways I can provide help to people?
- What are some things I need help with, and what kind of help would I like?

The answers to these questions will show students, and the teacher, that everyone has skills and abilities, and everyone needs help in certain areas. Karen may be a whiz as a reader, but she may need help fitting into playground games. Carmen may struggle with her math, but she is great at remembering things and getting people and activities organized. Classrooms can become communities of mutual support if teachers promote respect for differences and provide multiple opportunities for students to see each other in many ways.

Patty Feld finds heterogeneous groups to be "a lot more like life," and she enjoys the interplay among different children. Patty addresses differences with her students directly. When some of the children wanted to play basketball, she engaged the students in a discussion of how they might pick the teams so that it would be more fair and more fun for all. They also discussed ways of encouraging each other to play better. Students who were more skilled in the sport spent part of each gym period working with students whose skills were more limited.

Issues of friendship and exclusion also can be addressed directly. I worked with four teachers in using Vivian Paley's book *You Can't Say You Can't Play* (1992). The book details how Paley, a kindergarten teacher, proposed a rule that children could not exclude one another, and documents the subsequent discussions and implementation. These four teachers—a kindergarten, a 1st-grade, a 2nd-grade, and a 4th-grade teacher—implemented Paley's rule in their own classrooms and watched carefully as children wrestled with issues of how to include a diverse group of peers in play and work activities. By making issues of inclusion a topic for discussion and observation, and a focus of classroom concern, the teachers substantially altered their classroom climates and taught children new ways to think about reaching out and embracing others (Sapon-Shevin, Dobblelaere, Corrigan, Goodman, & Mastin, 1998).

When children are working closely together, conflicts inevitably will arise that they must learn to resolve. One teacher set aside a walk-in closet where children in conflict can take themselves—not be sent to—when they are having a conflict and need some time and space to work it out. Another teacher initiated what she calls the Problem Pail. Any students having a conflict can write what happened on a slip of paper and put it in the pail. Twice a week, the teacher gathers the class together and fishes "problems" out of the pail. Each person involved in the conflict gets a chance, without interruption, to tell what happened. Then, the whole class generates possible solutions or strategies for resolving the problem. The teacher often finds that the problems have already been worked out. The students sometimes come to the pail and remove a slip of paper because it no longer applies. With tattling removed as an option, some problems simply dissipate because it is too much trouble to write them down. Her class also keeps charts of problem solutions—a classroom compendium of solutions to conflict. When similar issues arise, the teacher is able to ask, "What did we do the last time something like this came up?" Students often refer to these charts on their own.

Teaching About Differences

Some teachers mistakenly assume that if they do not talk about the ways in which children in their classes differ—do not comment on the fact that one child reads more slowly, that another talks with difficulty, or that still another finishes math problems before anyone else— they will somehow avoid the comparisons and competitive evaluations in which children often engage. In truth, the opposite is more likely. When teachers do not directly address differences in skills and abilities, students receive the message that certain things simply cannot be talked about and their discomfort is likely to increase. How, then, should teachers handle the differences in their classrooms?

First, teachers need to be careful not to send negative messages about differences. Star charts on the wall that indicate who is doing well and who is doing poorly are not conducive to creating a classroom community that respects diversity. Most forms of competition in the classroom—spelling bees, awards for the "best team," and voting on the best essay—should be eliminated. Such competition is damaging not only to the student who does poorly ("We don't want Michael on our math team; we had him last week"), but also to students who consistently do well ("She thinks she's so smart just 'cause she got done faster than everyone else"). A good rule of thumb is this: If a visitor to the classroom can tell from the bulletin boards, the seating arrangement, or wall charts who is doing "better" and who is "in trouble," then it is certain that the children themselves are also painfully aware of those differences and comparisons. Respect for differences is more likely to develop if all children contribute something to bulletin boards, students choose which of their completed assignments they would like to display, and room arrangements are flexible and inclusive. Avoiding negative comparisons, however, is only the first step, and it is far from enough. Teachers must find multiple opportunities to talk about and honor children's differences. When one kindergarten class integrated a student with seizures and severe speech and motor difficulties, the teacher engaged the children in an active discussion of the girl's limitations and how they could include her. The children themselves figured out ways that their classmate could participate in games, which aspects of the reading lesson she might be able to do, and how they could include her in social activities throughout the day and on the weekend.

When children see that individual differences are supported in a noncompetitive classroom environment, they are free to celebrate the successes of their classmates without comparison (Sapon-Shevin, 1999). In one classroom I entered, a student rushed up to me and said, "Craig just got a new reading book and he can read real stories now!" Although the child who shared Craig's accomplishment with me had been reading for many years, he was able to recognize and appreciate Craig's important milestone. Confident in his own success and supported for his own accomplishments, he understood that every child in the room was working on their individual goals in order to learn.

Teachers with heterogeneous classrooms who attempt to individualize instruction to meet children's needs at first will be asked, "How come Noah doesn't do the same math we do?" or "When will I get to work on the computer like Nicole does?" How a teacher responds to such questions will do much to set the tone of the classroom. Generally speaking, honest, forthright answers seem best: "Noah works in a different book because he's working on addition, and he's not ready for multiplication yet" or "Let's find a time when you can work with Nicole on the computer." Most who teach in inclusive classrooms report that, after a short period of time, children accept the fact that other children may be working on different levels or materials, and they often assist other students when they can. When both needing and giving help are treated as common, natural occurrences, children will more likely be accommodating of one another's challenges and appreciative of their accomplishments.

Promoting positive responses to diversity also means interrupting inappropriate responses swiftly and directly: "It's not right to call other people 'stupid'—what else could you say to Karen?" Teachers who tolerate name-calling and put-downs give children the clear message that such behavior is acceptable, or even inevitable. At a recent conference of GLSEN (The Gay, Lesbian, Straight Educators Network), I learned and adopted the phrase "zero indifference," a commitment to noticing and challenging inappropriate teasing, bullying, and harassment in the classroom. A teacher who says, "What can you do? Children are just like that" indicates that he/she does not feel able or inclined to address the social climate of his or her classroom. It is important that all educators carefully consider their own values regarding differences and what they want to convey to students (Sapon-Shevin, 2003).

Many excellent curricula for teaching about differences exist, some of which are included in the resource list at the end of this chapter. Students certainly need to know about the ways in which they differ in terms of skills, abilities, and interests. It is equally important, however, for students to discover the ways in which they are alike. Stressing differences without talking about similarities can give students the idea that they have no common ground upon which to build relationships. When teachers are discussing student differences—who is good at what, who has trouble, and so forth—they also must talk about the fact that all students are in school to learn, all persons have things they do well and things they do less well, and everyone does better with encouragement and support (Hall, 1999; Levin, 1994). It is also important not to ground discussions of differences in the language of disability. Recently, a 3rd-grade teacher of a very inclusive classroom approached me for advice. She was complimenting one of her students who has Down syndrome about her excellent achievement on a recent test when a boy in the "gifted" program wandered by, heard the conversation with the other student, and said, "Big deal—I got a 100!" The teacher asked me what she should explain to the "gifted" boy about Down syndrome and developmental delays. "Nothing," I responded. "This is not about Down syndrome—this is about being a nice, caring human being. And caring humans don't say hurtful or diminishing things to other humans." It's important that we don't diminish or limit our lessons about right treatment of others to a set of rules about "How to treat the disabled." To do so limits our scope and effectiveness.

THINKING ABOUT INCLUSIVE CLASSROOMS

To create inclusive classrooms, teachers must think about what they teach, how they teach, and how they structure interactions among students. Transmitting consistent messages about the positive nature of diversity and the need for inclusiveness means that all aspects of classroom life must reflect that commitment.

The Curriculum

Think critically about the kinds of display materials in the room. Do these materials model the belief that we all belong and all can contribute? Just as teachers will want to include books, posters, and information about people of color and of various ethnic backgrounds in their classrooms, materials about people with differences and disabilities also should be included and integrated into all aspects of the curriculum. A unit on the five senses, for example, can include information on vision and hearing impairments. A unit on fairy tales can include a discussion of characters who feel different, such as the Ugly Duckling or Rumpelstiltskin, and a discussion of labeling and stereotyping. A unit on architecture can include information about physical accessibility to buildings and barrier-free designs. All students' accomplishments should be included in classroom displays and all students' contributions should be valued.

Our Language

How do we talk about differences? Do we imply that it is better to be "all the same," or do we attach value to diversity? How do teachers refer to the resource room, how and how much do they explain why some children are chosen for the gifted program, and how do they respond to children who are struggling or failing? Teachers can ask students: "What should we do when someone in our class makes a mistake?" or "If you were struggling with something, what kind of support would you want?" Children can learn to be critical of stereotypes and misinformation about differences and disabilities. One teacher asked students to bring in cartoons containing words like "idiot" and "imbecile." The teacher used them to lead a discussion about "smartness" and "stupidity" and how we should respond to such derogatory words and concepts. Learning to monitor our own and others' language is an important step in creating inclusive classroom communities.

Our Own Relationships With People Who Are Different

Does the teacher model respect for, and inclusion of, people who are different within his or her own life? It is hard for a teacher to convey the importance of including people who think or learn differently if this commitment is not represented in his or her own life. Some teachers who tolerate teasing and the exclusion of children who are different are still working through their own past experiences with inclusion and exclusion. Gaining some clarity about the damaging ways in which we all were excluded periodically (or consistently) can be an important first step in increasing students' sensitivity. As we work to get ourselves, as teachers, surrounded by the networks of support we need, we can be more effective in helping our students do the same.

CONCLUSION

For classrooms to be inclusive, modeling respect and appreciation for all children, the areas identified in this chapter must inform all aspects of classroom life. Children learn what they live. If they are segregated by ability and skill for most of the day, an hour's lesson on respecting diversity is not likely to have a major impact. The typical school day or year provides multiple opportunities to problem-solve issues of inclusiveness. When one 5th-grade class wanted to plan refreshments for a party and accommodate the needs of a vegetarian child, a child who kept kosher, and a child who was Muslim, the children brainstormed food choices that would allow everyone to eat comfortably. When a child using a wheelchair was not strong enough to lift himself out of his chair, the whole class became involved in a fitness and muscle-building unit that revolved around improving upper-body strength. Classrooms such as these send a consistent message: We are a community; we are all in this together; we will take responsibility for one another; we won't abandon people because of their difference or difficulties.

RESOURCES

Many excellent resources are available for both teaching children about differences, and structuring cooperative, inclusive classroom teaching.

Resource Guides for Cooperative Learning and Inclusive Teaching

These books may help teachers organize instruction and curriculum to promote positive peer interactions and the inclusion of children of various ability levels.

Aronson, E. (1978). *The jigsaw classroom.* Beverly Hills, CA: Sage.

Cohen, E. G. (1994). *Designing groupwork: Strategies for the heterogeneous classroom.* New York: Teachers College Press.

Gibbs, J. (2001). *Tribes: A new way of learning and being together.* Windsor, CA: Center Source Publications.

Johnson, D., & Johnson, R. (1999). *Learning together and alone.* Englewood Cliffs, NJ: Prentice-Hall.

Kagan, S. (1985). *Cooperative learning: Resources for teachers.* Riverside, CA: University of California, School of Education.

Schniedewind, N., & Davidson, E. (1987). *Cooperative learning, cooperative lives: A sourcebook of learning activities for building a peaceful world.* Dubuque, IA: William C. Brown.

Sharan, Y., & Sharan, S. (1992). *Expanding cooperative learning through group investigation.* New York: Teachers College Press.

Thousand, J. S., Villa, R. A., & Nevin, A. I. (Eds.). (2002). *Creativity and collaborative learning: The practical guide to empowering students, teachers and families.* Baltimore: Paul Brookes.

Tovey, R. (1995). Awareness programs help change students' attitudes towards their disabled peers. *Harvard Educational Newsletter, 11*(6), 7-8.

Resources for Creative Conflict Resolution and Class Climate

These books bring up issues of management, discipline, and conflict resolution, all of which may require a different, more thoughtful approach in classrooms that are purposively heterogeneous.

Drew, N. (1987). *Learning the skills of peacemaking: An activity guide for elementary-age children on communicating, cooperating, resolving conflict.* Rolling Hills Estates, CA: Jalmar Press.

Fletcher, R. (1986). *Teaching peace: Skills for living in a global society.* New York: Harper and Row.

Kreidler, W. J. (1984). *Creative conflict resolution.* Glenview, IL: Scott, Foresman.

Levin, D. E. (1994). *Teaching young children in violent times: Building a peaceable classroom.* Cambridge, MA: Educators for Social Responsibility.

Prutzman, P., Burger, M. L., Bodenhamer, G., & Stern, L. (1978). *The friendly classroom for a small planet: A handbook on creative approaches to living and problem solving for children.* Wayne, NJ: Avery Publishing.

Ramsey, P. G. (1991). *Making friends in school: Promoting peer relationships in early childhood.* New York: Teachers College Press.

Sapon-Shevin, M. (1999). *Because we can change the world: A practical guide to building cooperative, inclusive classroom communities.* Boston: Allyn and Bacon.

Resources on Cooperative Play and Games

These books can help teachers find ways to organize recreation and play so that children who are at different levels of skill all can have fun. These books contain suggestions for games and play that are inclusive and promote positive social interaction.

Fluegelman, A. (1976). *The new games book*. Garden City, NY: Dolphin.

Orlick, T. (1978). *The cooperative sports and games book: Challenge without competition*. New York: Pantheon.

Sobel, J. (1983). *Everybody wins: Non-competitive games for young children*. New York: Walker and Company.

Weinstein, M., & Goodman, J. (1980). *Playfair: Everybody's guide to noncompetitive play*. San Luis Obispo, CA: Impact Publishers.

Strategies for Promoting Full Inclusion Within Schools

These books describe the movement known as "full inclusion," which advocates reorganizing and restructuring schools so that all children, including those with disabilities, are included. They include many strategies for thinking about school reform and classroom organization.

Perske, R. (1988). *Circle of friends: People with disabilities and their friends enrich the lives of one another*. Nashville, TN: Abingdon Press.

Putnam, J. W. (1994). *Cooperative learning activities and strategies for inclusion: Celebrating diversity in the classroom*. Baltimore: Paul Brookes.

Sapon-Shevin, M. (1999). *Because we can change the world: A practical guide to building cooperative, inclusive classroom communities*. Boston: Allyn and Bacon.

Stainback, S., & Stainback, W. (Eds.). (1996). *Inclusion: A guide for educators*. Baltimore: Paul Brookes.

Stainback, W., & Stainback, S. (Eds.). (1990). *Support networks for inclusive schooling: Interdependent integrated education*. Baltimore: Paul Brookes.

Thousand, J. S., Villa, R. A., & Nevin, A. I. (Eds.). (2002). *Creativity and collaborative learning: The practical guide to empowering students, teachers and families*. Baltimore: Paul Brookes.

Villa, R. A., Thousand, J. S., Stainback, W., & Stainback, S. (Eds.). (2002). *Restructuring for caring and effective education: Piecing the puzzle together*. Baltimore: Paul Brookes.

Teaching About Differences: Curriculum Guides

These resources offer strategies for talking and teaching about individual differences, including, but not limited to, disabilities.

Derman-Sparks, L., & the A.B.C. Task Force. (1989). *Anti-bias curriculum: Tools for empowering young children*. Washington, DC: National Association for the Education of Young Children.

Neugebauer, B. (Ed.). (1992). *Alike and different: Exploring our humanity with young children*. Washington, DC: National Association for the Education of Young Children.

Schniedewind, N., & Davidson, E. (1998). *Open minds to equality: A sourcebook of learning activities to affirm diversity and promote equity*. Englewood Cliffs, NJ: Prentice-Hall.

Children's Books About Differences

Many excellent children's books model diversity and inclusiveness. In addition to books that directly address disability/difference issues, more general books that address the multiple differences that exist in classrooms and society can be helpful in beginning a discussion with children.

Andreae, G. (2000). *Giraffes can't dance*. London: Orchard Books.

Ashley, B. (1991). *Cleversticks*. New York: Crown Publishers.

Carroll, J., & Smith, C. (2001). *Billy the punk*. New York: Random House.

Combs, B. (2000). *ABC: A family alphabet book*. Ridley Park, PA: Two Lives Publishing.

Combs, B. (2000). *123: A family counting book.* Ridley Park, PA: Two Lives Publishing.

dePaola, T. (1983). *Now one foot, now the other.* New York: Putnam.

Fierstein, H. (2002). *The sissy duckling.* New York: Simon and Schuster Books

Hazen, B. S. (1985). *Why are people different? A book about prejudice.* New York: Golden Books.

Heine, H. (1986). *Friends.* New York: Aladdin Books.

Henkes, K. (1991). *Chrysanthemum.* New York: Trumpet Book Club.

Hoose, P., & Hoose, H. (1998). *Hey, little ant.* Berkeley, CA: Tricycle Press.

Jimenez, K. P. (2000). *Are you a boy or a girl?* Toronto, Canada: Green Dragon Press.

Kasza, K. (1987). *The wolf's chicken stew.* New York: G.P. Putnam's Sons.

Knight, M. B. (1993). *Who belongs here? An American story.* Gardiner, ME: Tilbury House Publishers.

Laguna, S. (2002). *Too loud Lilly.* New York: Scholastic Group.

Munson, D. (2000). *Enemy pie.* San Francisco: Chronicle Books.

Pinkwater, D. (1977). *The big orange splot.* New York: Scholastic Press.

Seskin, S., & Shamblin, A. (2002). *Don't laugh at me.* Berkeley, CA: Tricycle Press.

Wild, M., & Argent, K. (1998). *Miss Lily's fabulous pink feather boa.* Toronto: Penguin Books.

References

Armstrong, T. (1993). *Seven kinds of smart: Identifying and developing your many intelligences.* New York: NAL-Dutton.

Aronson, E. (1978). *The jigsaw classroom.* Beverly Hills, CA: Sage Publications.

Gardner, H. (1983). *Frames of mind: The theory of multiple intelligences.* New York: Basic Books.

Hall, N. S. (1999). *Creative resources for the anti-bias classroom.* Albany, NY: Delmar Publishers.

Hunt, J. M. (1961). *Intelligence and experience.* New York: Ronald Press.

Johnson, D., & Johnson, R. (1999). *Learning together and alone: Cooperative, competitive and individualistic learning.* Boston: Allyn and Bacon.

Kluth, P., Straut, D. M., & Biklen, D. P. (2003). *Access to academics for all students: Critical approaches to inclusive curriculum, instruction, and policy.* Mahwah, NJ: Lawrence Erlbaum Associates.

Levin, D. (1994). *Teaching young children in violent times: Building a peaceable classroom.* Cambridge, MA: Educators for Social Responsibility.

Massachusetts Advocacy Center. (1990). *Locked in/locked out: Tracking and placement practices in Boston public schools.* Boston: Author.

Oakes, J., & Lipton, M. (1999). *Teaching to change the world.* Boston: McGraw Hill.

Paley, V. G. (1992). *You can't say you can't play.* Cambridge, MA: Harvard University Press.

Putnam, J. W. (1994). *Cooperative learning activities and strategies for inclusion: Celebrating diversity in the classroom.* Baltimore: Paul H. Brookes.

Putnam, J. (1997). *Cooperative learning in diverse classrooms.* Columbus, OH: Merrill.

Rainforth, B., & Kugelmass, J. W. (2003). *Curriculum and instruction for all learners: Blending systematic and constructivist approaches in inclusive elementary schools.* Baltimore: Paul H. Brookes.

Sapon-Shevin, M. (1990). Student support through cooperative learning. In W. Stainback & S. Stainback (Eds.), *Support networks for inclusive schooling: Interdependent integrated education* (pp. 65-79). Baltimore: Paul Brookes.

Sapon-Shevin, M. (1994). *Playing favorites: Gifted education and the disruption of community.* Albany, NY: State University of New York Press.

Sapon-Shevin, M. (1999). *Because we can change the world: A practical guide to building cooperative, inclusive school communities.* Boston: Allyn and Bacon.

Sapon-Shevin, M. (2001). Making inclusion visible: Honoring the process and the struggle. *Democracy and Education, 14*(1), 24-27.

Sapon-Shevin, M. (2003). Inclusion: A matter of social justice. *Educational Leadership, 61*(2), 25-29.

Sapon-Shevin, M., Ayres, B., & Duncan, J. (2002). Cooperative learning and inclusion. In J. S. Thousand, R. A. Villa, & A. I. Nevin (Eds.), *Creativity and collaborative learning: A practical guide to empowering students, teachers and families* (2nd ed., pp. 209-222). Baltimore: Paul Brookes.

Sapon-Shevin, M., Dobblelaere, A., Corrigan, C. R., Goodman, K., & Mastin, M. C. (1998). Promoting inclusive behavior in inclusive classrooms: "You can't say you can't play." In L. H. Meyer, H. S. Park, M. Grenot-Scheyer, I. S. Schwartz, & B. Harry (Eds.), *Making friends: The influences of culture and development* (pp. 105-132). Baltimore: Paul H. Brookes.

Schniedewind, N., & Sapon-Shevin, M. (1998). Professional development for socially conscious cooperative learning. In C. M. Brody & N. Davidson (Eds.), *Professional development and cooperative learning: Issues and approaches* (pp. 203-219). Albany, NY: SUNY Press.

Thousand, J. S., Villa, R. A., & Nevin, A. I. (Eds.). (2002). *Creativity and collaborative learning: A practical guide to empowering students, teachers and families* (2nd ed.). Baltimore: Paul Brookes.

Van der Klift, E., & Kunc, N. (2002). Beyond benevolence: Supporting genuine friendships in inclusive schools. In J. S. Thousand, R. A. Villa, & A. I. Nevin (Eds.), *Creativity and collaborative learning: A practical guide to empowering students, teachers and families* (2nd ed., pp. 21-28). Baltimore: Paul Brookes.

Villa, R. A., Thousand, J. S., Stainback, W., & Stainback, S. (Eds.). (2000). *Restructuring for caring and effective education: Piecing the puzzle together* (2nd ed.). Baltimore: Paul Brookes.

Chapter 4
Class Differences: Economic Inequality in the Classroom

Ellen Davidson and Nancy Schniedewind

The disparities in wealth and income that currently exist in [the United States] have not been seen in over a hundred years. Today the richest 1% own more wealth than the bottom 95%, and the CEOs of large corporations earn more than 500 times what their average employees make. The nation's wealthiest families, 1/100th of one percent of the population, receive almost as much income as the poorest 20 million families in America. (Sanders, 2003, p. 1)

*T*he gap between rich and poor is increasing steadily in the United States. While the richest one percent of the U.S. population saw its financial wealth grow 109 percent from 1983 to 2001, the bottom two-fifths watched as its wealth fell 46 percent (Kostigen, 2004). In addition, recent federal education legislation and initiatives, such as the No Child Left Behind Act (NCLB) and voucher proposals, will further increase class inequality in U.S. schools and society, despite their stated intentions of providing more opportunities for low-income students.

Schools typically do little to help young people understand how economic inequality affects them and how it affects other students in different circumstances—their understanding of their place in the world, their interactions with others and their ability to learn (Knapp & Woolverton, 2004). We seldom help students understand what they might do to change that inequality, nor do we help them develop the skills needed to do so. Yet education about class, and taking action to change class inequality, is necessary if we hope to provide equitable educational opportunities for all and if we hope to maintain a democratic society.

Many Americans, especially those with sufficient income to live comfortably, do not think or talk much about class. The prevailing ideology that all Americans have an equal chance to succeed—and those who don't "make it" have only themselves to blame—prevents people from examining economic inequality. Similarly, educators seldom are encouraged to reflect on the ways class bias affects them, their students, and schools. We may have gone to a workshop or taken a course on dealing with racism or sexism in education, but how often have we been offered a workshop on classism? We can go into a good children's bookstore and request books that portray children of different races and ethnicities and find many excellent options. Currently, we also can find books for children that actively address, and address well, issues of race and gender. But what happens if we ask for books that portray families from a range of socioeconomic classes or ones that actually address class as an issue the way race or gender are addressed? While teachers may point to class background as a source of a student's learning or behavior problem, they often do not fully understand the societal and institutional role in this problem—the discrimination that may accompany class difference and that requires collective efforts to address and change. We hope that the ideas in this chapter will help bring about that understanding.

"Class" relates to a person's position in society, as determined by money, education, occupation, power, and access to resources and opportunities. Class background correlates with many factors, including those related to schooling, such as expectations of the education system, support for various teaching approaches, and attitudes toward discipline. "Classism" is the differential treatment of groups of people because of their class background and the reinforcement of those differences through values and practices of institutions, such as schools. Schools, however, can and should be democratic institutions that provide all students with an equal chance for success. This chapter examines how class differences are perpetuated and how we can work to transform them.

WHY ADDRESS CLASSISM IN EDUCATION?

There are many complex causes for the problems in schools that arise from the effects of class difference. Stereotypes of, and prejudices about, people from different class backgrounds affect the thinking and behavior of both teachers and students. Classism becomes entrenched when such class prejudices and stereotypes are reflected by people and institutions in authority, such as teachers and schools, and perpetuated by cultural attitudes and values. Sometimes those in schools are conscious of the role they play in this perpetuation; more often, it is inadvertent. On the other hand, schools do not differentiate when they should—such as when students' socioeconomic backgrounds affect their educational needs.

Class differences do affect learning. Since most schools promote the values and practices of middle and upper class people, children from those classes tend to do better in school than those of poor or working class people, because they have already imbibed the ideas and behaviors of that dominant culture (Delpit, 1995). Children from homes of lower economic status are likely to have fewer opportunities to develop many of the skills needed to succeed in school. Their parents often are less able to offer help on homework, provide many books in the home, pay for expensive trips, or afford community-based educational and extracurricular opportunities. What is particularly important is that students themselves do not usually see these inhibitors or stimulants to academic success as contributing to their academic performance. Poorer students typically come to blame themselves and regard themselves as dumb, while privileged students develop a personal confidence in their competence unconnected to its source in class privilege.

The effects of class on children's education are evident in the day-to-day experiences of children in classrooms across the United States. Structural arrangements within the class structure of U.S. society perpetuate inequality in education. For example, housing and schools are highly segregated by class and race (Wilson, 1996), thus also segregating neighborhood schools by class and race. The most highly trained and effective teachers are most likely to teach in middle class and upper middle-class school districts; teachers, like students, face subtle sorting by class background among schools in a district and within programs in schools (Hacker, 1992; Knapp & Woolverton, 2004). According to the Education Trust (Jerald, 2002), students in high-poverty secondary schools have 34 percent of their courses taught by teachers without at least a minor in the subject area, compared to 15 percent of the courses taught in low-poverty schools. Between 1996 to 2000, poor middle and secondary students experienced a marked rise in uncertified mathematics teachers from 14 percent to 22 percent, whereas non-poor students experienced a rise of only 1 percent (Jerald, 2002).

Moreover, schools that serve lower income children often are characterized by unimaginative curricula, buildings in disrepair, violence, lack of parental involvement, little in the way of technological equipment, and a distinct lack of extracurricular programs (Kozol, 1991; Wilson, 1996). At first glance, it might appear that computers can be found in schools all across the United States. Upon closer examination, however, access to computers, and especially access to the Internet, is heavily correlated with class (Barton, 2003; Smerdon, 2000).

The effects of classism on positive social interaction are also evident in schools. As children move into the upper elementary grades, and especially into middle school or junior high, they often find it harder and harder to cross class lines in social interactions, either in school or in the community. Barriers arise based on what students have, what neighborhood they live in, how their family lives, what they wear, what music they enjoy, their vocabulary, and who their friends are. Classism thwarts learning, inhibits positive social interaction among students, and ultimately reinforces societal inequalities.

Americans tend to believe that schooling can help people transcend their class status. While this is true for some individuals, thus giving anecdotal support to this image, schools overall serve to reinforce distinctions of class, race, and gender. In fact, they reproduce the class structure by providing different materials, institutional practices, and teacher interaction patterns for students of different class backgrounds (Oakes, 1986, 1994). Schooling for lower class students is more likely to train them for routine and manual labor, while that provided to upper- and middle-class students involves more creativity and self-management. The instruction available to lower class students is typically less challenging, more repetitive, and more concerned with social control than that provided for students of higher class backgrounds. A correlation between social class and educational outcomes emerges, with lower class students having lower levels of educational attainment, as reflected in years of schooling and drop-out rates, as well as educational achievement, as indicated by grades and test scores. The reverse is true for upper class students (Knapp & Woolverton, 2004).

Not surprisingly, college enrollment rates for current secondary school students correlate heavily with their parents' level of education. Eighty-two percent of high school students whose parents attended college go on to college themselves, 54 percent of those whose parents completed high school go on to college, and only 36 percent of those whose parents did not complete high school go on to college (National Center for Education Statistics, 2001). Breaking this cycle and giving access to more first-generation college students will take direct confrontation of classism in America.

This differential treatment affects student self-perception and consciousness as well. When upper- and middle-class students receive innovative, progressive instruction, they come to see themselves as naturally capable of thinking critically and taking leadership. When poor and working-class students receive routine instruction and authoritarian modes of discipline, they become conformist and accepting of routine in order to get by in school. Thus, both groups are prepared for the types of jobs waiting for them in a class-based society.

Lower class students typically experience a limiting pedagogy, one that includes a traditional approach to discipline, teacher control of learning tasks, and reliance on seat work and worksheets. Knapp and Woolverton put it well: "This approach to pedagogy teaches students that little is expected of them (except, perhaps compliance), they are not highly valued, they cannot be trusted to guide their own learning or conduct themselves responsibly in the classroom and they must accept low-level positions in a rigidly controlled hierarchy" (Knapp & Woolverton, 2004, p. 674).

Teachers often have opportunities to attend workshops that help them better understand race and gender. It is rare, however, to find workshops that help teachers examine class and classism. This is especially unfortunate, because research on the effects of class could broaden educators' understanding.

For example, teachers could learn that class affects educational success "right from the starting gate"—in other words, right before kindergarten. Poor children begin kindergarten with lower cognitive skills than their advantaged peers.

Before even entering kindergarten, the average cognitive score of children in the highest socio-economic status (SES) group are 60 percent above the scores of the lowest SES group. . . . Of the many categories of factors considered—including race/ethnicity, family educational expectations, access to quality child care, home reading, computer use, and television habits—*SES accounts for more of the unique variation in cognitive scores than any other factor by far.* (Lee & Burkham, 2002, p. 3)

These children then enter schools with fewer resources and less well-trained teachers; thus, the gap is magnified.

Contributing to the early gap are hunger, nutrition, and lead poisoning, factors that affect children both before entering school and once in school (ETS, 2003). Lead poisoning has serious ramifications for children's learning, behavior, and overall development. Children who are poor are three times more likely to have dangerously high lead levels than children who are not poor (Caufield, 2003). In addition, children who are poor have access to less good nutrition than middle class children. This affects both how they feel in school and their ability to learn (Barton, 2003).

The gap is maintained not only by such school-based factors as teacher preparation, teacher experience, technology-assisted instruction, and school safety, but also by such factors in the home learning environment as parent availability, reading to children, television watching, and student mobility (ETS, 2003). For example, a family moving creates an unstable academic environment for children. The percent of low-income students who are frequent school changers is triple that of middle-income students. Families who rent, by and large, move more often than those who own their own homes. The effect of this mobility on school achievement is significant. Forty-one percent of frequent school changers are behind in reading and 33 percent are behind in mathematics; of those who have not changed schools, 26 percent are behind in reading and 17 percent are behind in mathematics (Barton, 2003).

Class differences also influence the effects of summer vacations on the achievement gap. While poor and middle class students make *approximately the same gains* during the school year (Entwisle, Alexander, & Olson, 2001), low-income children lose ground over the summer while their wealthier peers gain ground. Thus, children begin the next school year in September with a greater disparity in achievement than they had in June. With an average loss of three months per school year, the accumulation of this gap becomes an 18-month gap by the end of 6th grade and a two-year gap by middle school (McGill-Franzen & Allington, 2001).

Finally, recent federal policies reinforce institutional class discrimination. No Child Left Behind was introduced as a way to help *all* children succeed in school, yet the reality is quite the opposite. Low-income children are dropping out of school because they have not been prepared to pass their state's high-stakes tests or, more insidiously, they are being encouraged to drop out of school so their scores will not hurt their school's overall score.

Noted author Alfie Kohn has written critically about the many dangers of NCLB (Kohn, 2004). For example, the requirement that every single student score at or above the proficient level by 2014 is prompting schools to encourage students to drop out, because some students' success is so much in doubt. NCLB essentially creates a "diversity penalty"; the more subgroups of students a school has, the less likely it will be to make adequate yearly progress with every group. Teachers and administrators are more likely to want to remove troubling children from classrooms so their scores do not count towards school averages and passing rates. Schools also are more inclined to retain children so that they will reach the age of 16 and drop out before their scores count towards the school passing rate (Kohn, 2004).

The original intent of NCLB was to provide financial assistance to schools that had disadvantaged students and that were showing improvement. Since sufficient funds have not been allocated, schools now must contend with the stringent requirements without the resources necessary to meet them. As Paul Houston writes, "Let us be sensitive to the hard bigotry of high expectations for all while some are left at a disadvantage. . . . It is one thing to expect people to pull themselves up by their own bootstraps, but first you need to make sure they are wearing boots" (cited in McKenzie, 2003, p. 2).

Most educators are discouraged by these patterns, since we hope that our teaching can be a vehicle for class mobility. One way that hope can be realized is by better understanding classism and working to change it, and helping our students to do the same.

HEIGHTENING TEACHER AWARENESS ABOUT CLASS

Teachers are typically middle class; their values, part of the hidden curriculum, can affect the self-esteem of students from lower socioeconomic classes. Many teachers come from middle-class families; for many, their own social-class identities don't prepare them to deal with students whose social class backgrounds are different from their own (deMarrais & LeCompte, 1999).

Discrimination by teachers, while typically unintentional, can be overt. We have not been encouraged to look at institutionalized practices that support inequality, particularly class bias. Therefore, when we start examining classism seriously, we may face surprising or unsettling realizations. We may come to realize, for example, that we have been unintentionally perpetuating inequality in our classrooms or our lives. While rarely easy to accept, such realizations can be hopeful; once aware of a problem, we can change it.

We must begin by assessing how our own class backgrounds affect our views and our ability to understand people who were raised under different circumstances. For example, it might be difficult for teachers from middle-class backgrounds, who grew up never worrying about having enough to eat or a roof over their heads, to understand and teach children who have such anxieties. Similarly, many teachers may have difficulty identifying and empathizing with the overwhelming self-doubt of working-class students.

In any case, awareness of our own class backgrounds must become a lens through which we deliberately examine our actions and beliefs. We are often unaware of the subtle ways our own biases affect the classroom, such as the unintentional homogeneous composition of reading groups or our differing reactions to students' clothing. We can educate ourselves about the life experiences of those from other socioeconomic backgrounds and about classism in our society by reading, talking to others, and reflecting upon what we see and hear. We can learn to be inclusive in how we work with our students, rather than perceiving a particular, usually middle-class, way of doing things as the only right way. (See interviews with teachers and suggested readings at the end of this chapter.)

In thinking about how to make changes, we might ask ourselves some questions. How does class bias affect learning in our schools? Do teachers have different academic expectations for children from different class backgrounds? Do teachers assume that some students will eventually go to college and others won't? Such expectations are subtly communicated to students and affect their own expectations. Ray Rist, in his classic study, explored primary teachers' assumptions about their students' economic status and how those assumptions affected time spent with, and expectations of, various groups of children. Anecdotal reports passed on to subsequent teachers resulted in the subtle tracking that began in kindergarten and continued throughout the years (Rist, 1970). Expectations matter! In fact, research shows that learners who are perceived to be from lower class backgrounds, regardless of race, tend to be perceived more negatively and as less competent than they are, while those from more upper-class backgrounds tend to be perceived more positively (Knapp & Woolverton, 2004; Percell, 1993).

One way to begin is by examining ways that classroom teachers can gain insights into their daily practice. What questions might they ask themselves? For example, are children allowed to bring in things that cost money for sharing? If so, in what price range? A teacher conscious of how socioeconomic class can affect the classroom would structure sharing in creative ways that do not depend on money (e.g., sharing things children have made, sharing stories or music from their own cultures, sharing a skill they have learned from a grandparent, or sharing experiences they have had). Do we use examples of major consumer products in our lessons, reinforcing the idea that "normal" people have the desire and means to buy them? Do teachers ask students to write about summer vacations, thereby assuming that all students travel with their families or attend summer camp? Or do they structure such assignments to be inclusive and affirming to students who do not have the privilege of such outings?[1]

Assignments that are structured to include use of materials from home are one way that unintentional classism is perpetuated. For example, when children work in small cooperative groups to make three-dimensional maps, those children from economically more advantaged homes usually have access to more interesting materials. When involved in any sort of academic design contest (e.g., creating a package that will protect an egg when it is dropped from the school roof or creating and then racing rubber band vehicles), children with more resources at home have an unintended and unfair advantage. In a school more conscious of these issues, the whole class can collect a variety of materials that would be available for everyone to share.

A school could raise the money needed for field trips and school outings to ensure that *everyone* can afford to go. In many low-income neighborhoods, no single family can afford to pay a great deal for school trips or other opportunities, but many families, whether or not they have children themselves, would be pleased to contribute by participating in school fundraisers (e.g., by purchasing small items such as candy or candles). If the school is in a neighborhood where few people can afford to participate in such fundraisers, then teachers can call upon local businesses to sponsor trips. Parents or older students can help write mini-grants for such sponsorship. Some schools in mixed-income neighborhoods have a "brown envelope" program. Students are periodically given plain brown envelopes. Families, or others, can send in small monetary contributions in cash. The envelopes are unlabeled and no one knows who has brought in money, nor how much.

Teachers can examine the messages about "class" in textbooks and children's literature. Do texts focus on "famous people," usually those of privileged-class status, or are the accomplishments and hard work of poor and working-class people given equal focus and respect?[2] Do texts honor well-known individuals, or do they also honor anonymous groups of people, such as those in labor unions, who worked collaboratively to bring about change? Look at the messages in storybooks. Do people who work hard always succeed? What message does this send to children whose parents are struggling hard and not making it? Do texts and stories implicitly blame poor people for their situation, or do they help children understand how some people have unequal opportunities because of their class background?

Educators can create opportunities to explore class issues with their colleagues. An excellent activity to raise teachers' consciousness about class is a version of the Horatio Alger activity. This can be done at a faculty meeting or teacher workshop. Teachers meet in small groups, with each group directed to create a list of 10 characteristics that they think *collectively* (when considered together) give a reasonable picture of someone's socioeconomic class. Groups brainstorm and argue about possibilities and then decide how critical they think each characteristic is, whether it is worth one or two points, moving forward or back. At this point, the lists can be shared for comparison. A further step, appropriate for some groups, is to play out each list with the participants lining up and walking the lists.[3]

How do teachers deal with the class bias that emerges in social interaction among students? To tolerate name-calling or put-downs based on class bias (e.g., "What do you do, shop at Goodwill?") is to condone them. A strongly enforced norm of "no put-downs" is always in order. Do teachers themselves sometimes make assumptions about their students' class backgrounds, based on superficial facts that may be misleading?

We also can ask ourselves questions about classism in the wider school community. If schools have reading or other academic tracks, do most students in lower tracks come from lower income levels? Do most of the students in special programs for the gifted come from a privileged background? In classrooms, we have the opportunity to help children from different class backgrounds get to know each other by grouping students who might ordinarily, and sometimes inadvertently, distance themselves from each other. Teachers can promote both greater academic learning and a deeper inter-class understanding by using cooperatively structured/heterogeneous learning groups and teaching students about class bias to prevent reinforcement of old stereotypes. Students can learn to respect and affirm cultural diversity, creating an inclusive, rather than exclusive, atmosphere.

As we begin to answer some of these questions, we find many ways we can begin to deal with classism. One way is to constantly reflect upon our own assumptions and biases, and then adjust our day-by-day teaching to meet the needs of students from diverse socioeconomic backgrounds. Another is to educate students about class bias and provide opportunities for change in their classrooms and schools. As we reflect on and analyze that which occurs in our own lives and classrooms, we may be led to pursue more comprehensive changes as well. For example, we may ask how competitive norms and practices in schools and society contribute to the values and expectations that lead to class bias. Well-thought-out use of cooperatively structured learning in classrooms can improve academic learning for all and help students reflect on how competition supports inequality and cooperation contributes to equality (Schniedewind & Davidson, 1987).

HELPING STUDENTS UNDERSTAND AND CHANGE CLASSISM

Teachers can intentionally teach students about economic inequality and how to effect change in attitudes and practices that reinforce classism. In their own classrooms and schools, students can examine how class bias may be perpetuated and they can work cooperatively to remove classroom-based barriers to equal learning, respect, and opportunities for all. Students must become empowered to make changes within their control and develop a broader perspective on wider-reaching societal changes they will be able to help facilitate as they grow older. One sequential process for teaching students to understand and change many forms of inequality is laid out in *Open Minds to Equality: Learning Activities To Promote Race, Sex, Class and Age Equity* (Schniedewind & Davidson, 1999). Here, we describe those steps in regard to educating children about classism. Details about most of the activities described in the following section can be found in *Open Minds*.

Initially, it is crucial to build a supportive atmosphere in the classroom, one in which all children feel accepted and valued, both by the teacher and other students. At the beginning of the year, we should provide students activities for getting to know each other and developing trust. Before we initiate such activities, however, we must examine them for possible class bias and make needed modifications. Students should learn skills for working together. Some students may come to our classrooms with well-developed skills in cooperation, while others may need a great deal of guidance. These skills must be taught, just as reading or math skills are taught. When students feel secure, accepted, and respected by their teachers and peers, and feel empowered to share their ideas and work cooperatively with others, they can deal most effectively with an issue like economic inequality, which brings out many strong emotions.

It is also important to create a norm that affirms discussion of class issues. Discrimination against people because of the amount of money they have is a facet of classism. The media bombards Americans with the message that if you are poor, it is your own fault, while those who prosper can take all the credit for themselves. Students of a low socioeconomic status may have absorbed this message. Similarly, more privileged students may have acquired a self-righteous sense of superiority. Students may not recognize such feelings in themselves. If they are aware of these feelings, they may not be comfortable talking openly about them, especially in a mixed-class group. Therefore, we should set a tone in the classroom that encourages discussions of these issues. The following statement can be adjusted to fit specific classroom situations.

All of us come from different family situations. For some, money isn't a problem but for others, having enough money for basic necessities is always a worry. Many of us fall in between. Some of us come from homes where our parents have had a great deal of education and others come from homes where a college education has not been possible. Some of us come from families who have easily been able to get what they want and make things happen the way they want it to. Other members of our class come from families who haven't had these advantages and don't have this kind of power. We will work hard to create a classroom where we understand, respect, and value each other, whatever our family situation, and learn what we can do to help create a society where everybody has enough of what they need to live.

As students become more comfortable talking about class issues, it is the teacher's responsibility to maintain guidelines for interpersonal communication and an ethic of care that protects their vulnerability. Teachers must be careful not to make assumptions about income, access to resources, or values. They should, instead, teach students to gather data from which to work. Such activities can make excellent interdisciplinary lessons in mathematics and social studies. Students can be asked to anonymously complete sentence stems about what they usually receive for birthday presents or what they do in their free time. Students can make drawings about what they hope to be when they grow up or what they would change about society if they could. Aggregate responses can be made into charts, bar graphs, pictographs, or circle graphs, and analyzed mathematically and socially.

Students need such accurate information about people of diverse class backgrounds and opportunities if they are to "walk in someone else's shoes" and see the world from a different perspective. Role-playing a hypothetical situation in which a student is going to be left out of an event because of insufficient funds can be, with a good follow-up discussion, an effective way to develop empathy with a student in that situation. Then, students can discuss times in their own lives when they, or other children, faced problems because of money shortages. The class can investigate further by comparing how economically advantaged and disadvantaged students dealt differently with the role-play situation, and brainstorm strategies they could try in real life to deal more equitably with such a situation. Role-playing real-life situations also can help students with diverse class-based experiences to empathize with each other and speak out about issues generated by class inequality (Lyman, 2001).

Defining and discussing economic inequality and its consequences is important to students' growing awareness. They can learn about stereotypes based on class bias by working together to finish an open-ended story about the reaction of classmates to a student whose family might be evicted from their apartment. They can identify the stereotypes and prejudices and write a different ending. After sharing endings, the students can discuss why some people stereotype others and what everyone loses by doing so. They also can share examples of class-based stereotypes that may have affected them personally as well as ways to combat such discrimination.

Children can learn to understand and identify institutional discrimination when shown the effects of prejudices and stereotypes practiced by those with more power than others or by such institutions as schools, families, the government, and businesses. Concrete examples may help. A student could read aloud a letter from a working-class high school student, expressing her disappointment at not being able to go on to college, or fulfill her dream of becoming a doctor, because she must work to help support her younger siblings. After talking about that student's feelings, the class can discuss personal examples of having to give up something important to them because of the cost. Students can discuss such questions as: Why did a lack of money have to end her hope of becoming a doctor? How should education programs select students to become doctors? How should they support them? How do all Americans lose by the current situation of difficult access to a medical education? Such discussions give students new ways of understanding discrimination that is based on economic inequality.

Next, students are ready to examine how classism denies particular groups of people resources while supporting the success and achievement of others. They can learn to recognize the process of "blaming the victim." Students can examine how inequality can result from a system of institutional discrimination that distributes resources, opportunities, and power unequally, rather than from the deficiencies of *individuals*. Through experiential activities, students can feel what it is like to be expected to achieve without having access to equal resources and opportunities. In one such activity, the class may be divided into five groups, each group expected to make a mobile related to a topic being studied. Groups are given *unequal* resources for the project, but are evaluated by a *common* standard. After this experience, the students can share how they feel. They can discuss situations in which people are expected to do equally well without having the same resources, power, and money.

Students may come to see how the privileges enjoyed by groups of higher economic status are directly connected to the lack of privilege for those of lower socioeconomic status. They also can learn about opportunities that privileged individuals and groups have to foster change. In a simulated situation, two students, who will represent the most privileged demographic in the United States, are served ice-cream sundaes; most of the rest of the students, representing middle-class America, each receive an apple; and 25 percent, representing the poorest segment of the population, each get only a raisin. The situation can be played out in a number of ways. A long discussion usually follows. Students first focus on how they felt and how they thought others felt. They discuss the choices they made and the choices they had but did not act upon. Was food shared? What questions did they ask themselves? What did they ask each other? A follow-up discussion could examine how this simulated situation reflects the current economic and food-distribution situation in the United States, how those with plenty of food are connected to the hungry, and what can be done to change the structure of economic inequality.

A comparable experiential activity about the distribution of wealth in the United States involves having students sit on chairs, each chair representing 10 percent of the wealth in the United States and each occupant representing 10 percent of the population. As the activity plays out, one person will be stretched out on 3 or 4 chairs and 4 or 5 people will be piled on one chairs, with others in between. Processing questions based on the visual and physical impact of the activity prompts valuable insights (Kellogg, 2001).

Once students understand class discrimination better, they can examine their own environment—classroom, school, home, communications media, and their community—for class bias. Occasionally remind students that the intent is not to criticize, but rather to discover examples of inequality and understand that a great deal of discrimination is unintentional; only when people become aware of abusive attitudes can they change them.

Students can examine their schoolbooks in any subject area for classism. They can count how many people represented in the texts are middle or upper class compared to those of lower socioeconomic classes, and determine if people from different classes are presented in different ways. Similarly, students can learn to pinpoint examples of class bias in other books they read and consider how books influence their own views about class. When students work in groups and compare findings, they can discuss what classes of people most stories address, try to determine the author's opinion of them, and explore how students of different class backgrounds might feel when reading about characters whose lives are unlike their own.

Similarly, students can examine the communications media. Groups can be assigned to watch television commercials and newspaper advertisements to determine representation of people from different classes and what products they advertise. By analyzing television entertainment, they can determine the class and qualities of those portrayed and compare television families' economic situations to real conditions. Students also can analyze packaged products to determine how stereotypes of middle-class people are perpetuated as compared to those of lower class people. What messages are being sent about superiority and inferiority? What effect do stereotypes have on real people?

Students can work to foster change by learning about people who struggle for economic equality, such as exploited factory workers who organize strikes. They can discover examples of more egalitarian living, working, and learning situations in other countries, such as free access to medical education in Norway.

Students can act to make a difference. By engaging in collaborative efforts to make change, they develop a sense of personal and collective power. Providing them practice in assertively standing up for their beliefs helps students build the skills and confidence to foster change. Students then can develop ways to educate others about class bias. After their textbook analysis, for example, students can write to publishers about the class bias they discovered and request that changes be made. Or they may identify books that are not class-biased and share that list with other classes. The class can discuss a story, such as *Scooter* by Vera Williams (see "Books for Students" at the end of this chapter), in order to challenge class bias. Students can even write their own stories that counteract stereotypes of low-income people. Suggest creating a problem in their story that a family might face because of unequal opportunities and resources, and then developing a creative solution that might include people making changes in the conditions that caused the problem. After peer review, students can present their stories to other classes in the form of skits, filmstrips, story boards, and/or displays on bulletin boards. They can create books for their school library that can be borrowed by students from other classes.

Students can re-create television ads to make them class-fair, and write letters to product packaging companies with descriptions of preferable class-fair examples. Students can display their visual presentations on class bias in ways that will encourage others to think and ask questions. Change can be contagious.

CREATING NORMS AND PRACTICES TO AFFIRM CLASS DIFFERENCES

Educators can examine classroom and school procedures that are class-biased and work to create alternatives that validate children of all class backgrounds. In any role—as teacher, administrator, or parents—working individually or together, we can proactively act to challenge class-based norms and create inclusive practices that empower all young people.

By examining resources that might not get distributed to children equally, teachers can help students to develop ways to make their classrooms more equitable. How can we create a classroom where everyone has access to books? How can we help students who do not have the advantage of parents who read to them? One solution is to have students of mixed-ability levels read to each other in school, thereby encouraging many students to be eager readers. Telling or reading stories to each other in school enriches children's sense of the breadth of literacy and affirms a range of lifestyles and cultures. All children can learn to value reading aloud and being read to.

If family economic situations make it difficult for some children to order from book clubs, the class may devise creative ways for raising money to enable all children to get a reasonable number of books. A car wash, bake sale, or raffle could be an effective means of raising money. Local businesses can donate items for the raffles. Students can have fun with such a project while making book purchasing more equitable.

Also, teachers can find more equitable ways of charging families for field trips. An ice skating trip with free admission but with a $4 fee per child to rent skates is only truly free for those children who own ice skates. By asking each family to contribute 50 cents, the trip can be made financially accessible for all students.

Better-educated parents usually find it easier to help their children with schoolwork. How can teachers handle this discrepancy in a way that is helpful and affirming to all children and all families? Can we set up tutoring systems through which parents with particular skills also help other children? Can we organize cooperative groups in which children from different backgrounds work together and get help from any or all of their parents? How about restructuring some school assignments so that parents with skills not traditionally recognized by schools may have those skills affirmed and be able to help?

One 2nd-grade teacher in an economically diverse school talked about her realization that her middle-class children were making greater gains in mathematics because their parents were more able to play the assigned homework math games. She had taught these games to parents during math open house nights, but many of her working class parents hold several jobs and were not able to attend. Many of these parents also couldn't read English well enough to follow the directions. Believing that *all* her students deserved opportunities for fun and educational experiences outside of the classroom, she followed through to ensure that each child in the class would have someone who could consistently and accurately play math games with him/her. She taught the games to the teachers in the after-school programs her students were attending so that children could play them during after-school homework club. She looked up older children in her students' neighborhoods and taught them how to play the games so they could help their younger neighbors.

Academic tracking, most pronounced in secondary school, often makes its way into elementary schools as well. While educators used to think this practice served students and teachers well, tracking consistently has been shown to be counterproductive to student learning at all ability levels (Bellenca & Schwartz, 1993; Oakes, 1986, 1994). Perhaps more important, tracking also reinforces classism. Educators who raise critical questions about homogeneous grouping and tracking and work to institute educationally sound alternatives, such as cooperative learning, make important contributions to changing classism in schools (Petersen, 2001). For these efforts to be effective, however, administrators, teachers, students, and parents need to learn how heterogeneous grouping benefits all students through increases in academic achievement and improvements in social skills for students at all levels. Schools need parental and community support in order for these changes to last and truly serve all students.

Teachers can also be role models for students by being advocates for class equity. A 4th-grade teacher in a predominantly middle-class school noted that someone had written a letter to the editor in the local newspaper that used the term "trailer trash." She wrote her own letter to the editor objecting to the use of that term, and brought the two letters into her class and facilitated a discussion about them with her students. After the discussion, a quiet student came up to her and thanked her for writing the letter, explaining that she lived in a trailer park and was hurt by that kind of language. After that, the student became much more actively engaged in the class.

Administrators, too, have an important role to play in building a school community that embraces children of all class backgrounds. A Boston principal tells a story of one family from her school offering to buy ceiling fans for all the classrooms in the school. While she was pleased at the thought of the classrooms being more comfortable in warm weather, she didn't want to perpetuate a dynamic in the school of a wealthy family being the sole contributors to such a project. Instead, she thanked this family and encouraged them to be part of a drive to raise money for the fans. This family was able to give a larger donation than the other families, but it was done anonymously and the fans were purchased with a fund supported by many school families.

Another principal wanted to increase her school library at a faster rate than could be supported by the city. She found a local business willing to sponsor a "birthday books" program. In this program, a representative from the business meets with the school librarian on a monthly basis to choose an appropriate book for each child with a birthday in the upcoming month. The business purchases those books and presents them at a monthly assembly. Each birthday child can take home the book at first and then it becomes part of the school library. When representatives of the business have *their* birthdays, they, too, receive special books, take them home, and then donate them to the school library. The principal reports that children who have graduated from the school often come back to see *their* birthday books from the years they attended the school.

TEACHERS TALK ABOUT CLASS

My immediate response when someone says "class" is to get my back against the nearest wall and come out with this: "What do you mean by class?" Because I think it is a complicated issue. . . . Class gets boiled down to issues of parents' income, issues of parents' education, but it's more complex. . . . I prefer talking about "access." I ask myself, "Is this a family that has had access? Access to schooling choices? Making health care choices? Advocating politically? Can this family come into a school situation and have impact on the school? Can they get what they need and want?" There's certainly something that's typical of *middle-class kids* in school and atypical of kids who are poor kids, kids for whom the United States is a new country—language issues play into it. So it's not as simple as income or parent education.—Judy Richards[4]

Dealing with day-to-day class issues in the classroom is complex. Judy Richards and Alma Wright, two experienced teachers, actively address class issues in their classroom cultures and daily teaching. Their clear beliefs about how best to work with a diverse socioeconomic population can help us better understand how individual teachers can handle these issues. In addition to an overall framework, each has developed many specific strategies. By comparing and contrasting their views, we can get a more complete picture.

Judy Richards teaches 3rd and 4th grades in an alternative public school in Cambridge, Massachusetts. She is white and comes from a working-class background. Her class is approximately one-third Haitian (generally lower income), one-third white middle class or professional, and one-third African American or white working class.

Alma Wright has taught 1st and 2nd grades for more than 30 years at the Trotter School in Boston. Alma reports that the African American and Latino students at the school are primarily working class or poor; many students of color from professional homes in Boston go to private schools or participate in a program that buses them out to predominantly white suburban schools. She goes on to say that most of the African American and Latino children live in housing projects and come from single-parent homes. The white children in her class are primarily from middle-class homes with professional parents. Many white children from working-class homes attend parochial schools.[5] Alma herself is African American and from a low-income background.

Judy and Alma point out that in order to create a classroom that is as free from classism as possible and that affirms all children without regard to their class backgrounds, teachers must be aware of class issues and consistently look at how their actions affect children of varied classes. This means examining expectations, both covert and overt, and being careful not to make assumptions about lifestyles and beliefs. Alma's and Judy's examples point to the myriad ways that class inequality can intersect with inequality that is based on race and/or culture.

Values

Judy views schools as places where middle-class values and culture are constantly reaffirmed. Middle-class families support and perpetuate school values; thus, children from these homes receive affirmation from their teachers, because their home values are similar to the school's values. In contrast, teachers often judge and condemn poor and working-class families when their values and choices are different from those espoused by the school.

Judy asks herself, and asks us, to think about how our beliefs may cause us to judge those with values different from our own. She asks, "How often do we judge parental behavior as a righteous choice or not righteous choice? How is that tied into our behaviors with our students? What message do students get from our judgments?" Judy believes that middle-class teachers often inadvertently make judgments that criticize working-class parents for their choices—for example, buying name-brand clothing rather than discount clothing, or choosing to buy an elaborate game system rather than using that money for books.

Another area where Judy sees teachers making judgments is in the use of language and insistence on standard English. She says that judgments about the class implications in language—grammar, vocabulary, and syntax—come up repeatedly in the classroom. Judy recounts a time when she heard a student say to a teacher, "Miss, I ain't got no pencil." Instead of providing or not providing the pencil, the teacher used this as an opportunity to ridicule the student's language and emphasize that home language was not appropriate at school. By defining some language as "only-for-home language," Judy believes school becomes a place where the student does not feel accepted or respected. She believes that this approach reinforces these borders between home and school in a way that alienates children, rather than helping them cross those boundaries.

Reading plays a crucial role in the interconnection between social class and school achievement. Judy believes that having books at home is directly related to class, not race. She talks of knowing both white kids and black kids who come from homes where parents are not readers. Judy asks, "How do you encourage more reading in homes that don't do it, without implying that not doing so means there is something wrong with the family?"

For Judy, this concern is bound up in her belief that it is absolutely crucial to actively affirm the culture of her students. Many of her Haitian students come from homes where families do not read but where there exists a rich storytelling tradition. This is also true for some of the white students in her school whose parents are only beginning readers themselves but come from regions of the United States where storytelling is an integral part of the culture. She believes that it is important to place a great deal of value on storytelling, acknowledging that passing on stories orally is also a valuable literary tradition. "You give both validity and honor to another kind of literacy," Judy said. "You broaden your sense of literacy to include the verbal piece as well as the written piece." She wants her middle-class students to realize that alternative practices have equal status. "Having a mother who isn't a reader isn't viewed as deficient. The fact that she isn't a reader isn't what's highlighted. The fact that she is a good storyteller is really important."

Alma provides her own classroom lending library. She says all her students have books at home, but not necessarily the books middle-class teachers expect. The parents of children in her class buy books at the grocery store, and they buy coloring books. This approach needs to be appreciated and affirmed by classroom teachers. Alma also gives every child a gift of two books each year. In addition, the school has a "home reading program" in which children who read each night for eight weeks get a free book to keep.

Being Inclusive

Judy says that "not condemning" a particular lifestyle is definitely not enough; teachers must actively affirm a diversity of lifestyles. Judy's classroom is inclusive rather than selective. She invites parents to participate actively in her classroom, providing varied opportunities that appeal to different parents. A core group of parents regularly volunteers to help with the Friday morning problem-solving sessions. These are almost entirely white, middle-class parents. Judy attributes this homogeneity primarily to the fact that these parents have professional jobs that allow them flexibility in scheduling. She also recognizes that her Friday mornings are high-powered in a particular way that is attractive to well-educated, middle-class parents who have confidence in their backgrounds and abilities, but possibly intimidating to working-class parents who have not had access to education. She finds, however, that other parents from varied classes come to read to children and have children read aloud to them and they participate in "open elective" time when a range of activities is offered.

I remember a woman who could tell wonderful stories to kids. If reading and writing were your criteria for literacy, she was illiterate. She had grown up in the Fernald School (a school for developmentally delayed people). But she would tell kids about animals. When her daughter learned to read, she really became interested in learning to read and went to the adult learning center.

When Judy conducted a theme on the local area, all parents could contribute. Some came from families who had lived in the area for generations and could share many stories. Others were recent immigrants who could talk about why they moved to the area. All these contributions were valuable to the children's understanding.

Judy modified her Friday morning problem-solving groups to be more inclusive. Children in heterogeneous groups of five meet weekly to solve non-routine mathematics problems. Her experience had been that her middle-class children perceived themselves as strong problem solvers. They approached these weekly problems as relevant, no matter the context, and even if the problems only included numbers. For them, problem-solving, in and of itself, felt connected to their lives. Her poorer students, on the other hand, believed that this kind of schoolwork was something only for the middle-class kids. For a number of years, Judy had used the following problem: "You go to the stream with a three-liter container and a seven-liter container. You want to come back with exactly five liters of water. How do you do it?" Judy has since "repackaged" this mathematics problem by using a Haitian folktale that the children know in which a girl makes friends with a fish and thus gets clearer water than her brother. Judy uses the names of the girl and boy and their mother and incorporates their personalities when explaining what she wants them to solve in the mathematics problem. By changing the problem in this manner, the middle-class children were no longer the dominant forces in the problem-solving groups. The Haitian children became the "experts" and leaders in their groups. Once they saw the problem *in context,* they could relate to it and were better able to do the mathematics.

By changing the cultural and class bias of the problem, Judy shifted the perceptions about her students' apparent academic abilities. When a group of her students who usually perceive themselves as less academically competent saw a problem connected to their lives, that connection then increased their self-confidence and thus their ability to solve the problem.

Judy also has advice for teachers about grouping children for academic instruction. She encourages teachers to consider carefully when forming small groups. If, when organized by skills, groups are not diverse by class and race, Judy believes this grouping is not acceptable for a classroom. She cautions teachers to look at their groupings and figure out how to make each group diverse. For example, Judy encourages the students to form small book groups that are based on children's interests rather than their reading levels. One group might read horse stories, for example. Some in the group may need more support than others, which can be done by listening to the story on audiotape or practicing reading it aloud. Judy says, "You can't just say, 'It's fate,' or 'It's beyond my control' because this is the situation. Instead, you have to say, 'Well, it's going to make it harder; now, what else can I do?' and then do what you need to do to make these groupings work."

Clothing

Another class issue that comes up repeatedly for both Judy and Alma is clothing, an issue from which two important points emerge. First is the need to approach students without fixed preconceptions and assumptions. The other is to refrain from making value judgments; rather, we should observe and try to understand.

Judy talks of middle-class teachers who "sit back from a haughty place and say, 'You ought not to spend your money on Nike sneakers when money is scarce and you should spread it out. You could get a whole outfit for this price.' " She also points out how teachers relate differently to poor students who are particularly well-dressed compared to those who are poorly dressed.

Alma also comments on clothing:

I find that some of my children who are coming from welfare homes, they're dressing, they're bringing in toys, they're sharing things, they're talking about places they go as well as kids who are coming from middle-class homes. Sometimes they have a lot more because a lot of the young, single-family welfare homes put more emphasis on dressing and making sure they're keeping up. . . .

Alma has found this situation to be true for the more than 30 years she has been at her school. Judy also reports that the working-class and poor children tend to be consistently well dressed. She believes middle-class parents are more able to say, "Hey, they're gonna get dirty, why dress them up?" A middle-class teacher may not be too concerned about a child getting paint on his or her clothes, but this can be, in fact, a big deal to a family that has struggled hard to buy those clothes. She finds that families will not send children back to school in those clothes if they cannot get the paint stains out.

The parent wouldn't say, 'You got it in school, you're going back with it to school.' That's one of the places where I think we set kids up. We set kids up who are not middle-class kids. We say, 'It's okay if you get paint on yourself.' Well, it's not always okay and that's a place where teachers have to be mindful and not to devalue clothes. The parents work very hard to dress their children and have them ready for school and we can't turn around and say it's okay. So you make sure you either have classroom painting clothes for everyone or you have smocks from wrist to knee for everyone. It's important not to sit back and make casual calls.

While quality of clothing may not be as simplistically based on class as we may have thought, economic issues do affect what children have. While many students bring in their own snacks, both Alma and Judy serve a "common snack" in their classrooms. They provide an appealing, reasonably nutritious snack (but not so nutritious that it stands out as being different from what the children bring) that is available to everyone and that they themselves eat. In both classrooms, the children accept and enjoy this practice; it brings about a kind of equality during that portion of the children's day.

School Success

Both Alma and Judy feel certain that achievement in their classes, as defined by standardized tests and other commonly used methods, correlates directly with the socioeconomic class of the students. Alma believes that while the discrepancies in standardized scores in Boston may at first glance seem to be based on race, they actually are based on class and are due to the demographics of Boston public schools. Middle class and a white population are highly correlated. Alma believes her district's teachers often expect less of children from low-income homes. She says that by expecting "utopia" for her children, she makes a major contribution toward their success.

Alma reflects on her own background in order to explain her own understanding of class issues and her teaching style relative to class. Alma grew up in a rural Florida town of 1,500 people with an African American population of 500. Her mother completed 6th grade and her father 8th. Alma credits her own educational and professional success and that of her classmates to the support they received growing up. Her teachers were all African American professionals at an all-black school. They were also all active church members. The students from her small elementary school had to be bused 30 miles to the black high school. The community held high expectations that these students would graduate from college. Although all these children came from homes with parents who had not attended high school, their children did, indeed, all graduate from college and many from graduate school. The community provided ongoing support by giving students needed money, clothing, and equipment, and by sending care packages and checking on grades. Alma remembers, "You had a feeling that if you didn't succeed you failed the whole town. We knew that the teachers liked us and wanted us to succeed." Alma sees role models and supportive teachers, parents, and community members as central to students' academic achievement.

Both Alma and Judy facilitate parental contact in a variety of ways, staying mindful of the realities of lower class parents. This includes phoning and visiting parents at home, showing support for them with their own problems, and being understanding. They try to be firm and clear about parental responsibilities and to provide help when needed. Keeping in mind that some parents do not have the resources or cultural knowledge to strengthen their children's chances for school success, Alma and Judy share information with parents that will enhance their children's educational opportunities. Given that many parents have jobs that do not allow them free time during the day to visit the school, Judy and Alma are careful to schedule parent conferences at times convenient to different families.

Alma feels that her school does well in terms of making all children feel welcome and competent. They begin each school year with an emphasis on self-esteem for all children. She says that her 1st- and 2nd-grade children's aspirations are not based on class or race. When Alma does an activity about "What I Want To Be When I Grow Up," she finds that their goals do not at all correlate with class or race. She presents children with a range of role models, varied by race and class. Even though most of her African American students come from low-income families, she is able to find parents and friends of the parents who model a range of alternatives. She brings into her classroom guest speakers from a variety of occupations and a variety of backgrounds.

Judy discusses how the values of competition and cooperation have a major impact on learning. She says the Haitian children talk of "we," not "I." In classroom discussions in Judy's room, the custom is that after a child has finished talking, he or she calls on another child rather than having the discussion refocus on Judy. This power sharing has a positive effect on the flow of these talks. In the computer lab, the middle-class students tend to talk with each other only in order to compare what lessons they are doing. The Haitian students, on the other hand, are concerned with cooperating with and helping each other, even if it means not "getting as far." Judy notes, "Teachers need to look again at what we value in school. We give lip service to cooperation, but when kids do it naturally, it appears counterproductive to what we want, when we want them to get this much done in this much time." Judy believes that this cultural bias towards cooperation can be used to break the "who's at the top" dynamic. Such an effort requires serious restructuring of our classrooms, yet it would result in important growth in social and academic learning for all children. "You set up situations where there's different leadership. . . . You look at the leadership of kids who are not middle class and say to yourself, 'Let's incorporate that leadership style in our classroom as well.' So 'who's on top' is not always the same."

CONCLUSION

As we become more aware of and concerned about class issues in our classrooms and schools, we can modify our educational work in many ways. We can develop activities that increase students' awareness of class issues, create new methods for sharing resources within the classroom community, structure groups differently, create more inclusive curriculum that reflects people and the values of a variety of class backgrounds, and work toward creating parent involvement programs that respect all parents' skills and needs. In any case, we can reflect on the impact of our actions and classroom culture on children of different socioeconomic classes. In this context, it is important to be conscious of classism in society and how that affects our efforts. For example, since schools are typically funded through property taxes, disproportionately greater resources are available to schools in wealthier communities. We can become involved in our unions, professional associations, and community groups to push for more equitable school funding. We can educate our peers, parents, and students about ways that standardized testing, NCLB, and vouchers actually increase class inequality and we can work together for change.

Most of all, we can expand our vision of the potential for public schools in a democracy. Our classrooms and schools can be places where students and teachers are cared about, where all forms of diversity are appreciated, and where everyone has equitable access to resources and opportunities. The efforts described above to foster class equity can be viewed as part of a broader belief about curriculum and classroom practice that can contribute toward our vision. It fosters work that is: grounded in the lives of children, academically rigorous, multicultural and culturally sensitive, participatory, activist, and joyful.

Our efforts to foster class equality can contribute to a more hopeful future, one posed to us by the editors of *Rethinking Schools*.

The alternative to critical teaching for social justice is to surrender to a system that, left to its own logic, will never serve the common good. . . . A classroom veteran once told younger colleagues that teachers had two choices: 'We can teach for the society we live in, or we can teach for the one we want to see.' (Bigelow, Harvey, Karp, & Miller, 2001, pp. 4)

Join us as we reach together for our dreams!

Notes

[1] Excellent sources for materials for educators on class inequality and teaching strategies to address it are available from: Rethinking Schools, 1001 East Keefe Ave., Milwaukee, WI, 53212; 800-669-4192; www.rethinkingschools.org and United for a Fair Economy, 37 Temple Place, 2nd floor, Boston, MA 02111; 617-423-0191; www.ufenet.org.

[2] Good sources for teaching how poor and working-class people contributed to history and culture can be found, for example, in Zinn (1995) and Lerner (1992). (See "Resources for Teachers.")

[3] For this activity, participants line up as if playing "Mother May I" or "Giant Step." The reader of the list calls out each item and whether to move one or two steps forward or one or two steps back, depending on the answer to the item. Play continues for each of the 10 items.

[4] Davidson, E. (1990, July). Interview with Judy Richards, Graham-Parks School, Cambridge, MA.

[5] Davidson, E. (1990, July). Interview with Alma Wright, The Trotter School, Boston, MA.

References

Barton, P. E. (2003). *Parsing the achievement gap: Baselines for tracking progress.* Princeton, NJ: Educational Testing Service, Policy Information Center.

Caufield, R. L. (2003). Intellectual impairment in children with blood concentrations below 10 g. per deciliter. *The New England Journal of Medicine, 348*(16), 1517-1526.

Delpit, L. (1995). *Other people's children: Cultural conflict in the classroom.* New York: New Press.

deMarrais, K. B., & LeCompte, M. D. (1999). *The ways schools work* (3rd ed.). New York: Longman.

Entwisle, D. R., Alexander, K. L., & Olson, L. S. (2001). Keep the faucet flowing: Summer learning and home environment. *American Educator, 25*(3), 10-15, 47.

Hacker, A. (1992). *Two nations: Black and white, separate, hostile, unequal.* New York: Scribner.

Houston, P. D. (2003). The bigotry of expectations. *The School Administrator* (Web edition). Available at www.aasa.org/publications/sa/2003_01/execper.htm.

Jerald, C. D. (2002). (data analysis by Richard M. Ingersoll). *All talk, no action: Putting an end to out-of-field teaching.* Washington, DC: The Education Trust.

Kellogg, P. (2001). *Ten chairs of inequality.* In B. Bigelow, B. Harvey, S. Karp, & L. Miller (Eds.), *Rethinking our classrooms: Teaching for equity and justice* (Vol. 2, pp. 82-84). Milwaukee, WI: Rethinking Schools.

Knapp, M., & Woolverton, S. (2004). *Handbook of research on multicultural education* (2nd ed.). San Francisco: Jossey-Bass.

Kohn, A. (2004). Test today, privatize tomorrow: Using accountability to "reform" public schools to death. *Phi Delta Kappan, 85*(8), 568-577.

Kostigen, T. (2004). "Inequality Matters" conference puts nations on alert. Available at *CBS.MarketWatch.com.*

Kozol, J. (1992). *Savage inequalities: Children in America's schools.* New York: HarperCollins.

Lee, V. E., & Burkham, D. T. (2002). *Inequality at the starting gate: Social background differences in achievement as children begin school.* Washington, DC: Economic Policy Institute.

Lyman, K. (2001). The trial: How one teacher explores issues of homelessness. In B. Bigelow, B. Harvey, S. Karp, & L. Miller (Eds.), *Rethinking our classrooms: Teaching for equity and social justice* (Vol. 2, pp. 140-142). Milwaukee, WI: Rethinking Schools.

McGill-Franzen, A., & Allington, R. (2001). Lost summers: For some children, few books and few opportunities to read. *Classroom Leadership, 4*(9) [online publication; http://shop.ascd.org]

McKenzie, J. (2003). The cheapening of America: NCLB and the decline of the good job. *No Child Left, 1*(12). Available at nochildleft.com/2003/dec03cheap.html

National Center for Education Statistics. (2001). *The condition of education.* Washington, DC: Author.

Oakes, J. (1994). Tracking: Why schools need to take another route. In B. Bigelow, L. Christensen, & S. Karp (Eds.), *Rethinking our classrooms: Teaching for equity and justice* (pp. 178-181). Milwaukee, WI: Rethinking Schools.

Percell, C. H. (1993). Social class and educational equality. In J. Banks & C. A. M. Banks (Eds.), *Multicultural education: Issues and perspectives* (2nd ed., pp. 71-89). Boston: Allyn and Bacon.

Peterson, B. (2001). Tracking and the project method. In B. Bigelow, B. Harvey, S. Karp, & L. Miller (Eds.), *Rethinking our classrooms: Teaching for equity and social justice* (Vol. 2, pp. 214-218). Milwaukee, WI: Rethinking Schools.

Sanders, B. (2003). The rich get richer, the middle class struggles and the poor suffer. *Sanders Scoop, Fall,* 1.

Schniedewind, N., & Davidson, E. (1998). *Open minds to equality: Learning activities to affirm diversity and promote equity.* Englewood Cliffs, NJ: Prentice-Hall.

Smerdon, B. et al. (2000). *Teachers' tools for the 21st century: A report on teachers' use of technology.* Washington, DC: National Center for Education Statistics.

Wilson, W. J. (1996). *When work disappears: The world of the new urban poor.* New York: Knopf.

RESOURCES
Books for Students

(P) -Primary; (E) -Upper Elementary; (M) -Middle School

Bledsoe, L. J. (1995). *The big bike race.* New York: Holiday House. (P)

Brisson, P. (2000). *Wanda's roses.* Honesdale, PA: Boyds Mills Press. (P)

Bunting, E. (1991). *Fly away home.* New York: Clarion Books. (E)

Bunting, E. (1995). *Smoky night.* San Diego: Harcourt Brace Jovanovich. (P)

Byars, B. (1977). *Pinballs.* New York: Harper and Row. (E)

Crutcher, C. (1993). *Staying fat for Sarah Byrnes.* New York: Greenwillow. (M)

DiSalvo-Ryan, D. (1991). *Uncle Willie and the soup kitchen.* New York: Morrow Junior Books. (P, E)

Donnelly, J. (2003). *A northern light.* New York: Harcourt (M)

Estes, E. (1944). *The hundred dresses.* New York: Harcourt Brace Jovanovich. (M)

Greenfield, E. (1980). *Grandmama's joy.* New York: Philomel Books. (P)

Hakim, J. (1994). *A history of US.* New York: Oxford University Press. (M)

Hamilton, V. (1986). *The planet of Junior Brown.* New York: MacMillan. (M)

Hansen, J. (1980). *The gift giver.* New York: Clarion. (M)

Hansen, J. (1986). *Yellow bird and me.* New York: Clarion. (E, M)

Hazen, B. S. (1983). *Tight times.* New York: Puffin Books. (P)

Jordan, J. (1975). *New life: New room.* New York: Crowell. (P)

Keats, E. J. (1969). *Goggles.* New York: Collier Books. (and many others by this author) (P)

Kingsolver, B. (1988). *The bean trees.* New York: Harper Row. (M)

Levine, A. (1993). *Pearl Moskowitz's last stand.* New York: Tambourine Books. (P)

Mazer, N. F. (1981). *Mrs. Fish, Ape and me, the dump queen.* New York: Avon. (M)

McKissack, P. C., & McKissak, F. (1994). *Christmas in the big house, Christmas in the quarters.* New York: Scholastic. (E)

McPherson, S. (1993). *Peace and bread: The story of Jane Addams.* Minneapolis, MN: Carolrhoda. (E)

Miklowitz, G. (1985). *The war between the classes.* New York: Bantam Doubleday. (M)

Mills, L. (1991). *The rag coat.* Boston: Little, Brown and Company. (E)

Mohr, N. (1989). *El Bronx remembered.* Houston, TX: Arte Publico Press. (and others by this author) (E)

Myers, W. D. (1989). *The young landlords.* New York: Puffin Books. (and many others by this author) (E)

Nolan, M. S. (1978). *My daddy don't go to work.* Minneapolis, MN: Carolrhoda Books. (P)

Patterson, K. (1978). *The great Gilly Hopkins.* New York: Crowell. (E)

Rahaman, V. (1997). *Read for me, mama.* Honesdale, PA: Caroline House. (P, E)

Ringgold, F. (1991). *Tar beach.* New York: Dial Books. (P)

Ryan, P. M. (2000). *Esperanza rising.* New York: Scholastic. (M)

Sachs, M. (1971). *The bears' house.* Garden City, NY: Doubleday. (and others by this author) (E)

Springer, J. (1997). *Listen to the world's working children.* Toronto: Groundwood Books. (M)

Taylor, B. (1994). *The table where rich people sit.* New York: Charles Scribner's Sons Books for Young Readers. (E)

Taylor, M. (1976). *Roll of thunder, hear my cry.* New York: Dial Press. (and many others by this author) (E)

Thomas, L. (1979). *Hi, Mrs. Mallory!* New York: Harper and Row. (P)

Voight, C. (1981). *Homecoming.* New York: Fawcett, Jr. (and others in this series) (E)

Williams, V. (1993). *Scooter.* New York: Greenwillow. (E)

Williams, V. B. (1982). *A chair for my mother/Something special for me.* New York: Greenwillow. (and others in this series) (P)

Wolff, V. (1993). *Make lemonade.* New York: Henry, Holt and Co. (M)

Woodson, J. (1992). *Last summer with Maizon.* New York: Dell Publishing. (and others in this series) (E)

Woodson, J. (2002). *Maizon at Blue Hill.* New York: Delacorte (M)

Woodson, J. (1994). *I hadn't meant to tell you this.* New York: Delacorte. (and others by this author) (M)

Resources for Teachers

Arnow, H. (1954). *The dollmaker.* New York: Avon.

Barlett, D., & Steele, J. (1994). *America: Who really pays taxes.* New York: Simon and Schuster.

Baxandall, R. (1995). *America's working women: A documentary history.* New York: Vintage.

Coalition for Basic Needs. (1990). *Up and out of poverty campaign.* Cambridge, MA: Author.

Collins, C., & Yeskel, F. (2000). *Economic apartheid in America: A primer on economic inequality and insecurity.* New York: New Press.

Cose, E. (1993). *The rage of the privileged class.* New York: HarperCollins.

Dollars and Sense. 1 Summer Street, Somerville, MA 02143.

Dixon, B. (1977). *Catching them young: Sex, race and class in children's fiction.* London: Pluto Press.

Dorsey-Gaines, C., & Taylor, D. (1988). *Growing up literate: Learning from inner city families.* Portsmouth, NH: Heinemann.

Ehrenreich, B. (2001). *Nickel and dimed: On (not) getting by in America.* New York: Henry Holt.

Folbre, N. (2001). *The invisible heart: Economics and family values.* New York: New Press.

Folbre, N., & Heintz, J. (2000). *The ultimate fieldguide to the US economy.* New York: New Press.

hooks, b. (1989). *Keeping close to home: Class and education. Talking back: Thinking feminist, thinking black.* Boston: South End Press.

Kelly, J., & Soto, G. (1993). *The pool party* [video]. 43 The Crescent, Berkeley, CA 94708.

Kowalski, L. (1991). *Rock soup* [video]. New York: First Run/Icarus Films.

Kotlowitz, A. (1991). *There are no children here: The story of two boys growing up in the other America.* New York: Anchor Books.

Kozol, J. (1992). *Savage inequalities: Children in America's schools.* New York: HarperCollins.

Lee, V., & Barkum, D. (2002). *Inequality at the starting gate: Social background differences in achievement as children begin school.* Washington, DC: Economic Policy Institute.

Lerner, G. (1992). *The black woman in white America: A documentary history.* New York: Vintage Books.

Network of Educators on the Americas. P.O. Box 73038 Washington, DC 20056-3038.

Nieto, S. (1995). *Affirming diversity: The sociopolitical context of multicultural education.* New York: Longman.

Parenti, M. (1994). *Democracy for the few.* New York: St. Martin's Press.

Payne, R. (2003). *Framework for understanding poverty* (3rd ed.). Highlands, TX: Process Inc.

Pizzigati, S. (1992). *The maximum wage: A common sense prescription for revitalizing America by taxing the very rich.* New York: Apex Press.

Rose, S. (1992). *Social stratification in the United States.* New York: New Press.

Rothstein, R. (2004). *Class and schools: Using social, economic and education reform to class the black-white achievement gap.* New York: Economic Policy Institute.

Rubin, L. B. (1976). *Worlds of pain: Life in the working class family.* New York: Basic Books.

Ryan, W. (1976). *Blaming the victim.* New York: Vintage Press.

Ryan, W. (1982). *Equality.* New York: Pantheon.

Schniedewind, N., & Davidson, E. (1998). *Open minds to equality: Learning activities to affirm diversity and promote equity.* Englewood Cliffs, NJ: Prentice-Hall.

Schniedewind, N., & Davidson, E. (1987). *Cooperative learning, cooperative lives: A sourcebook of learning activities for building a peaceful world.* Dubuque, IA: W. C. Brown.

Seabrook, J. (2002). *No-nonsense guide to class, caste and hierarchies.* London: Verso.

Sennett, R., & Cobb, J. (1993). *The hidden injuries of class.* New York: Vintage.

Shange, N. (1985). *Betsey Brown.* New York: St. Martins Press.

Shipier, D. (2004). *The working poor: Invisible in America.* New York: Knopf.

Shulman, B. (2003). *Betrayal of work: How low-wage jobs fail 30 million Americans.* New York: New Press.

Sidel, R. (1983). *Women and children last.* New York: Viking Books.

Sleeter, C., & Grant, C. (1994). *Making choices for multicultural education: Five approaches to race, class, and gender.* New York: Macmillan.

Smedley, A. (1973). *Daughter of the earth.* Old Westbury, NY: Feminist Press.

Susskind, R. (1999). *A hope in the unseen: An American odyssey from the inner city to the Ivy League.* New York: Broadway.

Tea, M. (Ed.). (2003). *Without a net: The female experience of growing up working class.* Seattle, WA: Seal Press.

Wolff, E. (2002). *Top heavy: The increasing inequality of wealth in America and what can be done about it.* New York: New Press.

Zinn, H. (1995). *A people's history of the United States.* New York: Harper & Row.

Acknowledgments:

The authors would like to thank Judy Richards and Alma Wright for sharing their experiences as teachers, and Nancy Braus at Everybody's Kids Books, Brattleboro, Vermont, for her help with the Resources section.

Chapter 5
Language Diversity in the Classroom

Deborah A. Byrnes, Lisa Pray, and Diana Cortez

proximately 16.7 percent of school-age chil-
, representing 8.8 million children. This is a
Census Bureau, 2003). These children, many
ltural groups as diverse as Haitians, Afghans,
f these students, approximately 71 percent of
speak Spanish as their native language.
rience or training in working with linguisti-
achers who instruct ELL students possess a
cation. Only 30 percent of all teachers with
pment specific to the needs of ELL students
. In addition, the education of ELL students
teen states have enacted "English only" laws
people who speak English as a second lan-
a, and Massachusetts, enacted initiatives re-
se laws suggest that many ELL students may
eir native language (Crawford, 2000).
d Act of 2001 (NCLB) place increased pres-
ly achieve English language proficiency and
Thus, ELL students come to school with two
ultaneously: they must learn a second lan-

age differences that are relevant to the regu-
erse children in his or her classroom. First,
that classroom teachers need to be aware of
xperiences of linguistic minorities. Second,
the authors make specific suggestions for teaching linguistically diverse students. Third,
ways in which teachers can help English-only students be sensitive to the language differences of others will be addressed. The chapter will conclude with a short case study of one
classroom teacher's work with non-English-language-background students.

UNDERSTANDING LANGUAGE DIFFERENCES AND LANGUAGE LEARNING

A number of important points and misconceptions regarding linguistic differences and second-language learning need to be addressed before discussing specific strategies for working

with linguistic minorities. The following section introduces some basic concepts and issues relevant to language diversity.

English Language Learners—A Diverse Group

Children who do not speak English or who are limited in their knowledge of English are incredibly diverse and have a range of educational needs. Some of the diverse groups included under the label of ELL students are: 1) Immigrant children with a sound educational background, but little or no exposure to English. They need assistance with English and learning to understand the new culture in which they are now living. 2) Immigrant children who have had little or no exposure to English and, due to political or economic turmoil, have little or no education in their native language. These children need to learn English, basic educational concepts, and knowledge of American culture. 3) Immigrant children who come to the United States with a sound education background and some knowledge of English but are not familiar with American culture. Such children have a head start but will still need assistance with the language and culture. 4) U.S.-born children who live in non English-speaking homes. These children may know little English but they have the advantage of being familiar with the culture. All of these children require instruction in English, and some may require more understanding of American culture and the requirements of the American educational system (Myer, 1985).

Acquisition of a Second Language

Typically developing children acquire their native language effortlessly and without instruction (Pinker, 1994; Slobin & Bowerman, 1985). During the most active acquisition period, the preschool years, children learn approximately 10 to 12 new words per day (Gleitman & Landau, 1994). Upon entry into school, children possess verbal grammar skills that are almost indistinguishable from adults' (Bickerton, 1981; Chomsky, 1981). Children learn a language because it meets their needs; they can interact with people from their environment, and learn interesting and relevant information. For many of the same reasons, children are motivated to learn a second language.

An ELL student learns a second language by using his or her first language as a starting point. The first language provides the foundation, and from it an ELL child intuitively understands the general principles of acquiring a second language (Bialystok & Hakuta, 1994). A second language is acquired through a complex process involving the motivation of the child, adequate modeling of the language, and a social setting that brings the child into frequent contact with the second language (Wong-Fillmore, 1990). This process of second-language acquisition is mastered through gradual awareness of, and the ability to effectively use, the grammar rules of the second language. Although formal instruction is an important avenue for providing language models and stimulation, formal instruction alone cannot speed up the natural developmental process needed to acquire a second language (Ovando, Collier, & Combs, 2003). An accessible and stimulating classroom environment provides ELL students with a structure from which to learn and use vocabulary commonly used in academic contexts, and with the skills they need to read and write, using their second language.

Many experts distinguish between children's verbal English ability and their academic use of English in the classroom context. These experts note that reading and writing in a language differs from conversational use of a language. An ELL child's academic success is preceded by his or her success in acquiring English. Other factors that predict academic success of an ELL learner are the child's first-language experience, the child's prior educational background, the educational background of the child's parents, and whether or not the child lives in a print-rich environment (Krashen, 1996).

When native English speakers resent the time it takes to communicate with a person whose knowledge of English is limited or suggest that immigrants should "learn English or leave the country," they might do well to consider their own ancestors. Learning a language and a culture takes time. For many reasons, children take different lengths of time to acquire a second language. A few children take as little as one year to acquire oral English ability, and some take as long as six or more years; the majority of school-age children take between three and four years to learn to speak English (Pray & MacSwan, 2001). Many people are surprised to learn that older children usually learn to speak a second language faster than younger children do (Bialystok & Hakuta, 1994; Pray & MacSwan, 2002). Initially, the child may go through a "silent period" when he or she is actively listening and trying to make sense of the language. Doing this period, the child might say little or nothing until he or she begins creating, experimenting, and developing simple phrases and statements in context. The child makes many errors in grammar and pronunciation at this stage. Eventually, children internalize most of the rules, use more complex structures, and make fewer errors until they are able to express complex ideas in their new language. As this developmental process proceeds, teachers need to provide a supportive classroom environment where children feel comfortable practicing, experimenting with, and taking risks while using their second language. Each lesson must be designed to provide opportunities for the children to express themselves and display their new language in a risk-free environment.

A positive classroom environment encourages second-language learning. Such an environment promotes positive attitudes about the language and motivates children to learn it. A teacher's warmth and interest in the linguistically diverse child will influence a student's attitudes about school, English speakers, and the English language. More specifically, a child needs to know, by the teacher's words and actions, that his or her language and culture are respected. Children also must sense that the teacher has faith in their ability to learn and believes they are worthwhile (Kottler, 1994). A child who feels valued and self-confident is more likely to be a successful second-language learner.

Language and Culture Are Inseparable

Teachers must address the ever-increasing language diversity as part of the cultural diversity within the classroom. They must examine their own attitudes and the attitudes of their students toward speakers of other languages (Adler, 1993). When a teacher and student can communicate through a common language, they gain a sense that they can share their cultures and learn from one another. When the child does not speak English and the teacher does not speak the child's language, both culture and language limit communication. Such limitations and miscommunications often lead to frustration on the part of the teacher, student, or the student's family. Teachers, therefore, must make every effort to extend their knowledge and understanding about the child's cultural and linguistic background.

An intimate relationship exists between language and culture. Through socialization into a culture, language is acquired. Language, in turn, shapes how we view the physical world, the social world, and the spiritual (or metaphysical) world that gives meaning to life (see Farb, 1975, for a discussion on the "Sapir-Whorf hypothesis"; that is, the notion that language shapes our view of reality). For example, many Asian languages have words or word markers to indicate the social status of the speaker and the person being addressed. These words denote a person's relative position in the social order and the rights (e.g., respect and reverence) and obligations (e.g., showing deference) he or she has compared to others. Some languages come from radically different cultures, like English and Hopi. Embedded in the languages are two totally different perceptions of reality (Hall, 1973). The Hopi language, for example, has no nouns and no verb tenses. If one wanted to refer to "a table," the rough translation into English would be "tabling"—in a spiritual sense, the table has always existed, it exists now, and it will exist forever. The metaphysical or spiritual view implied by the Hopi language is one in which time is not linear—a view that may be difficult for English speakers to grasp. Language, then, serves "both as a conveyor of culture and as an extension and expression of culture" (Newmark & Asante, 1976, p. 4).

Consequently, one cannot effectively address linguistic differences without acknowledging and respecting cultural differences. Conversely, one cannot respect cultural differences without acknowledging and understanding the importance of a person's language. A child thinks and constructs understanding about the world in his or her language. Language is intricately tied to a child's identity. Ignoring or devaluing the child's native language is denying an important part of who the child is, including a rich store of past and present cultural experiences. Thus, it is critical for a classroom teacher to acknowledge and respect a child's home language, whether it is a completely different language from English or a variant of it, such as Black English or Appalachian English.

Bilingual/Bicultural Children

A teacher's goal should be to help non-English-language-background children become bilingual so they can have access to two cultures. Unfortunately, many children, when we try to teach them English, lose their primary language in the process (Wong-Fillmore, 1990). Children living in the United States learn that English is the primary language of education, business, mass media, and government. English is associated with success and high status. In an effort to be part of this successful, high-status community, and not stand out or be different, English-language learners may give up speaking their native language. This so-called "subtractive bilingualism" occurs when a child learns a second language (usually English) at the expense of his or her native language. Teachers may foster this loss by not demonstrating respect for a child's language and culture, and by encouraging a child to speak English even while at home (Wong-Fillmore, 1990; Wong-Fillmore & Valadez, 1986).

Subtractive bilingualism may have unanticipated consequences for home life. If a child's parents are not proficient in English, children who begin speaking English at home may lose the ability to communicate with their parents or other family members. Parents lose their ability to communicate important values to their children or pass on important cultural traditions and lessons. Family unity and closeness may be sacrificed when children adopt English as their primary language. Instead of encouraging parents and children to practice English at home, educators should assist parents in helping their children become more proficient speakers of their native language.

Ironically, the advantages of speaking a second language are touted by educators across the nation (see, e.g., Willis, 1996) while the resource of a second language brought to school by many language-minority children is ignored. The advocates of foreign-language study admonish schools to put more emphasis on teaching foreign languages, even as immigrant children are rapidly mainstreamed in such a way that many of them must take foreign-language instruction to relearn their native language (Wyner, 1989). Maintaining and developing students' home languages is an obvious way to enhance individuals' development, helping them to become bilingual/bicultural.

The type of language programs offered in the schools often can determine if children will learn English at the expense of their native language (subtractive bilingualism) or if they will become truly bilingual, biliterate, and bicultural (additive bilingualism). The type of programs a school offers depends on the value the community places on bilingualism. Although there is a substantial range in the types of programs offered, a general outline of the programs include: 1) English as a Second Language (ESL) programs, also called "structured immersion programs," which serve ELL students by providing content area instruction in English, using special methods to assist ELL students in understanding instruction. Very little, if any, of the students' native language is spoken in the classroom. 2) "Transitional-bilingual programs" begin teaching ELL students content area instruction in their native language and introduce English gradually as the students are developmentally prepared to learn the language. 3) Dual-language programs, also called "dual or two-way immersion programs," teach content-area instruction in English and another target language (such as French). Ideally, 50 percent of the children in such a program would be native speakers of French and the other 50 percent would be native speakers of English. Typically, these programs begin in kindergarten and the goals of the program are that upon graduation from elementary school, children would be fully proficient in two languages and have mastery over the curriculum in two languages.

Research demonstrates that ELL students who graduate from ESL and transitional-bilingual programs acquire adequate English skills but may lose their native language. Students who graduate from dual-language programs often add new skills to existing skills in their native language and score higher on yearly standardized tests in English than ESL and transitional-bilingual program students (Thomas & Collier, 2003). Although these research results appear straightforward, there is rancorous debate in many communities about which type of programs should be available to ELL students. Much of this debate and political discourse is directed toward immigrant groups, with one side often insisting that the minority group assimilate to the majority language and culture (Crawford, 2000). Add the short supply of trained bilingual teachers to the equation and it becomes clearer as to why so few dual-language programs exist.

EFFECTIVE STRATEGIES FOR ELL STUDENTS IN THE REGULAR CLASSROOM

Most teachers of ELL students recognize that children learn academic content better when it is taught in their native language (Williams, 1991). It only makes sense that children will learn skills and content more quickly and more easily in the language they know best. We only need to imagine just how much we would learn if we were asked to attend an important lecture that was given in a language in which we were not proficient.

Unfortunately, the United States suffers from a critical lack of certified bilingual teachers. Thus, the responsibility of helping ELL students learn English and academic content while retaining their home language falls upon the regular classroom teacher, who often speaks only English. Extensive research on how the regular classroom teacher can work more effectively with ELL students (see, e.g., Solórzano & Solórzano, 1999) emphasizes that teachers of ELL students must create nurturing, supportive environments where students are engaged in challenging learning experiences, through the use of appropriate strategies.

Creating Nurturing Environments for ELL Students

Teachers can begin creating a nurturing environment on the very first day of class. A "Welcome!" poster written in many languages and inspirational messages written in both English and the students' native languages will help the students and their parents feel comfortable in their new classroom environment. Providing such a classroom will model respect for all languages and cultures to the native-English speakers and encourage appreciation of the linguistic background of their non-English-speaking peers.

Teachers should take the time to learn about the particular cultural and linguistic differences of their students. It is critical that a learning environment recognize and respect such differences, or ELL children will likely feel unaccepted and uncomfortable. For example, some Native American children may find a teacher's normal teaching voice to be loud, and incorrectly interpret it as indicating anger or meanness (Grove, 1976). Children from some cultures may have been taught that it is inappropriate to volunteer information. When a teacher is aware that such cultural differences exist, he or she can explain and bridge the differences so that the child does not feel anxious. Krashen (1981) suggests that lowering children's anxiety level will help them acquire a second language and build their self-confidence and their motivation for learning a second language.

Knowledge of values and beliefs, such as concepts of kinship, family patterns, and appropriate social proximity, are also particularly necessary in order to communicate effectively with ELL students and their parents. Looking at .edu, .gov, and .org Web sites that share cultural norms from around the world can provide quick and easy access to basic cultural information. The Web site online.culturegrams.com also offers such information, while charging a small fee per four-page pamphlet.

If a teacher can learn how to speak some of the child's language, even if only a few words and phrases, this can help to enhance the child's self-image and help other students to recognize that the teacher values and appreciates other languages (Perez, 1979). As with information on cultures generally, an Internet search can provide free, easily accessible information and translations for major languages. Do recognize, however, that these sites create literal translations that do not reflect the way people really speak the language. The child can usually help the teacher correct pronunciation and syntax, and thus may feel accomplished and important for knowing something the teacher doesn't know.

Creating Effective, Functional Learning Environments for ELL Students

Educators can draw upon numerous methods to create an appropriate classroom learning environment for ELL students. We briefly share a few here and encourage all readers to delve deeper into the literature on this topic by consulting the references at the end of this chapter.

Structure. Adding structure to your classroom day may help ELL students. Children in classrooms with teachers who follow distinct patterns day after day, who have established routines and consistency in organization, learn more English than students in less-structured classrooms. In classrooms with patterns, routines, and appropriate labels, children do not have to figure out what is going on every day. They can concentrate on the language and what they are supposed to be learning.

Comprehensible Input. Teachers should ask themselves, "If I did not understand English, would I be able to get some meaning from what is occurring in the classroom?" Krashen (1981) coined the term "comprehensible input" to describe making academic instruction understandable and providing lessons in a coherent and logical structure that is useful for children who speak English as a second language.

Teachers can make their instruction more comprehensible in several ways. Generally, the main requirements of providing comprehensible input are: 1) using authentic materials, 2) modifying the language of instruction, and 3) providing opportunities for students to use language in authentic ways.

Authentic materials are those that have a real purpose in life and allow learners to make direct connections with real-world information and language. Such materials might include visual images, props (sometimes referred to as "realia" if closely tied to the child's world), literature, graphs, newspapers, brochures, diagrams, bus schedules, magazines, and signs. Use of authentic materials enhances a child's motivation to acquire language because the learning is not isolated from his or her own life experiences.

Clearly, modifications in the language of instruction will help ELL students learn more effectively. Whenever possible, support materials in the students' native language should be used as instructional tools for both language development and content-area instruction. Teachers can seek books in the students' native language from libraries, refugee centers, cultural centers, or distributors of children's books. Textbook publishers may offer some foreign-language editions.

Effective teachers of ELL students also should examine the way they use language when they teach, and make efforts to be more comprehensible. Teachers should enunciate clearly and use gestures, demonstrations, and props to focus students on the critical vocabulary and concepts necessary for understanding new ideas. A judicious use of paraphrasing or repetition is helpful. Teachers should be careful in the use of idioms and sayings, such as "I could have died," which can easily so confuse an ELL student that he or she misses the important part of a lesson. Teachers should not assume that ELL students understand what may be new words to them. Teachers should plan many opportunities for the students to apply and clarify new concepts and vocabulary in interactions with adults and peers. Most important, they need to engage students in dialogues that require higher level thinking. For example, if a child states that a character in a book was behaving suspiciously, other students can be asked to describe what may make a character appear "suspicious."

Teachers should develop activities that provide important reasons for ELL students to express themselves. This should be done in a low-stress environment where students feel secure experimenting with their new language and possibly making errors. Teachers should refine their discourse skills to promote discussion and creative expression of complex ideas, rather than asking questions that only require a one- or two-word responses.

Unfortunately, in many classrooms, children who know the language are given more practice and feedback than children who are learning English. This is particularly true in classrooms where only a few children volunteer to participate (i.e., the most assertive students). One way of promoting meaningful communication can be establishing daily tasks that provide structured ways for students to participate. This could involve the teacher presenting questions to groups of students, allowing them to discuss the answers among themselves (encouraging them, as necessary, to discuss the question in their native language), and then requesting a group response. Teachers also can use turn-taking strategies that require every student to contribute in some non-threatening way.

Helpful Programs for Teachers of ELL Students

Engaging ELL students with the content and language necessary to function at their grade-level expectations is challenging. Fortunately, several successful methods have been developed for teachers who do not understand the ELL student's native language. These methods include Specifically Designed Academic Instruction in English (SDAIE) or Sheltered Instruction Observation Protocol (SIOP). For detailed information about these methods, refer to Echevarria, Vogt, and Short (2004) and to Peregoy and Boyle (2005). These programs include such strategies as the use of cooperative groupings where ELL students are paired with English-speaking peers, the involvement of teacher assistants who speak the students' native language, and the use of concrete materials (realia) that engage children linguistically while also teaching concepts. An example of the latter would be bringing in clothing or cooking utensils from different cultures to spark discussions on variations in meeting basic needs.

Many of the instructional strategies emerging from the whole language movement also benefit students for whom English is a second language (Hudelson, 1986). For example, a simple beginning to creating an effective learning environment for ELL students is to label all learning centers and materials in the classroom (e.g., the door, pencils, desks, books, and so forth), using English and all other native languages spoken by your students. Providing this visual information will model respect of all languages and cultures. A print-rich environment for young children also would include daily journal writing and predictable books that help children learn about structural regularities of the language (Hough, Nurss, & Enright, 1986; Moustafa, 1980).

Teachers must avoid "watering-down" the curriculum for ELL students. At every stage of second-language proficiency, teachers should allow students to demonstrate content area knowledge in an academically rigorous manner. At the early stages of second-language acquisition, this may include demonstrations, illustration, displays, modeling, and other methods, so that the child can display knowledge and higher order thinking skills although using little English. Teachers should stay away from age-inappropriate materials. For example, giving a non-English-language-background 4th-grader a kindergarten workbook when he or she was performing at grade level before coming to the United States is not appropriate. Materials that are far below students' grade level are uninteresting, and children often find it embarrassing to be reading them. Consequently, children may lose interest in school and learning English. Inappropriate materials also can lead to students being permanently tracked in lower levels. Whenever possible, therefore, content and supporting activities (adapted for the linguistically diverse child) should be drawn from grade-level curriculum.

Assessment

Teachers of ELL students must pay close attention to the types of assessment they give to their students and modify as necessary. For example, if a teacher were to assess an ELL student's understanding of the scientific method, it may be inappropriate to ask her to complete an essay test or a multiple-choice test, because she may be just developing the language necessary to express her ideas. Teachers can modify their assessment for ELL students by requiring them to demonstrate knowledge in ways that are not focused on their language skills. Under these circumstances, it would be more appropriate to ask the student to demonstrate the method, or perhaps draw pictures of each step of the scientific method. In this respect, teachers must be thoughtful and creative when it comes to assessing the content area knowledge of the ELL student.

Assessment is critical for the appropriate referral and placement of ELL students into special education. Currently, there is an overpopulation of language-minority students placed into special education for such "high incidence" disabilities as mild mental retardation and learning disabilities (Artiles, Rueda, Salazar, & Higareda, 2000). Notably, states (such as Arizona, California, and Massachusetts) that have put strict limitations on bilingual education have seen an increase in special education referrals and placements of ELL students. The reasons behind this problem vary but have much to do with the kind of instruction that ELL students receive in the regular classroom, low teacher expectations, and the use and misinterpretation of results from assessments used in the referral process to measure language and cognitive ability (Artiles et al., 2000). An inappropriate placement can be detrimental to an ELL student. Before referring a child to special education, teachers should collect a portfolio of documentation and observations about the child, critically evaluate their pedagogical approach to teaching ELL students, and try multiple strategies and techniques to assist the child with learning. Teachers should avoid referring an ELL child to special education based on the results of any standardized test alone. Instead, teachers should consider all factors relating to the child's learning environment and make all attempts to ameliorate the conditions relating to the learning difficulty.

Teacher Professionalism

Professional educators with increased knowledge about and experience with ELL students appropriately reject any way of thinking that uses students' cultural or language background as an excuse for student failure. Thus, teachers should take advantage of every opportunity to build the knowledge, skills, and attitudes necessary to be an effective teacher of ELL students.

Central to the idea of professionalism is the need to communicate with colleagues on matters of learning and instruction. Teachers should build professional relationships with colleagues to share teaching insights and to coordinate learning activities for students. New teachers should value and elicit ideas from trained, more experienced teachers in the school to provide appropriate instruction for ELL students. English-only teachers can use the services of a trained bilingual teaching assistant to help fill the language and cultural gap between the teacher's linguistic and cultural background and that of her students. In addition, teachers should engage volunteers and parents to assist in the classroom.

Teachers will find that they have the greatest success with ELL learners when they promote and encourage parental involvement in the classroom. Every effort should be made to communicate with parents in a language they can understand. Many resources are available to assist in communication with parents whose English proficiency is limited, including Web resources (such as www.babblefish.com) that can provide translations for written notes to parents or support staff and other parents who can assist in communication. It is important for teachers to reassure parents that it is appropriate and helpful to read and speak to their child in their native language, to come to school and be involved with their child's education, and to question, rather than simply accept, the education their son or daughter is receiving in school, if they feel they have cause for concern.

Teaching Children About Language Differences

A non-English-language-background child may feel isolated not only because of his inability to communicate with others, but also because other students may see the student as different and inferior and thus may avoid, tease, or exclude him. How someone speaks and what language someone speaks immediately evokes certain reactions in the listener (Adler, 1993; Gardner & Lambert, 1972). Individuals associate certain ways of talking with particular people who use that language. Consequently, social and racial attitudes are linked to these associations. The attitudes that children form about language differences may be based on personal experiences, or a child may have learned such attitudes indirectly from hearing or observing the responses of other people. Some languages and accents are more likely to be stigmatized than others.

Teachers must work to eliminate the stereotypes and misconceptions children hold regarding speakers of other languages or speakers of nonstandard varieties of English. Children must learn that no language or dialect is intrinsically good or bad, correct or incorrect. All languages are tools for communicating ideas within a given speech community (Taylor, 1986; Tiedt & Tiedt, 1990).

Activities To Build Understanding of Language Differences

Teaching children about languages and language differences is one way children can gain insights into culture and increase their understanding and acceptance of cultural and linguistic minorities. Here are some possible activities:

• Have a person who speaks another language give a lesson and assignment to the class in a foreign language. After it is over, have the children share how they felt. Talk with them about how non-English-speaking people feel when they are not able to understand much of what is going on around them. Help the children to understand that people generally do not give much thought to language unless they are put in a position where they cannot understand what someone is saying. You may want to compare it to oxygen. Nobody focuses on the critical need for oxygen until one is put into a situation where it is lacking. Have the children discuss how they can help learners of English as a second language in their own communities.

• Viewing segments of an international movie can be a sensitizing experience. Most large video stores carry subtitled international movies in such languages as French, Spanish, Japanese, and Russian that can be shown to elicit discussion on languages. (Make sure you have previewed the movie before using it as a teaching tool. The segments shown should be acceptable for children and should not create negative attitudes toward the language group.) Because older children will likely read the subtitles, the teacher may want to hold a narrow piece of poster board over them. Students can discuss what they think was being said and how it feels not to understand a language. This activity also can be used to look at nonverbal behavior in other cultures.

• Provide students an opportunity to learn a new language, in the process helping them understand how languages differ and how challenging it is to learn a new language. Learning at least a little of another child's language will promote communication. Additionally, the learner of English will sense that he or she has something important to share.

• Children usually recognize that individuals from different cultures may have differences in clothing, housing, and language. Generally, however, they do not understand that a language and culture may reflect ideas and concepts that do not exist in, or are quite different from, their own culture (Welton, 1990). The idea that others may look at the world quite differently is difficult to understand. Most children believe that one can translate one language directly into another without any loss of meaning.

Have a bilingual person talk about how they deal with conversing in two languages. Children may not realize that a simple English statement such as "I miss you" would be constructed differently in other languages. The literal translation in French, for example, would be: "You are lacking to me." English idioms, such as "I'll be darned," may have no direct translation in another language. The translator must think of a phrase that carries a similar meaning in the other culture to use as a substitute. Even when words have direct counterparts in another language, they may have slightly different meanings. The word "sharp" in English can have a positive connotation, such as being a sharp thinker or sharp dresser. In Chinese, however, it connotes cunning and is considered a negative term. Even among speakers of the same language, words can mean different things. The word "teaspoon" means different things to the British than to Americans. In Canada, the word "serviette" is used in place of "napkin." On the West coast of the United States a "tonic" is a medicinal stimulant; on the East coast, it is a soft drink.

• It is important for children to understand that words alone are not the only conveyor of the message. Sometimes the words play only a small part. A great deal of a message can be shared through culturally specific ways of speaking. For example, while using a different tone of voice and different inflection each time, say the words "It's raining outside" (e.g., make it sound like a question, make it sound exciting, make it sound depressing). Help the children understand how tone, pitch, tempo, and use of pauses in speech convey meaning. Discuss all that a new learner of a language has to learn in addition to vocabulary.

You also can discuss how the use of tone, pitch, tempo, and pauses varies across cultures. Students may find it interesting to know that in many Asian languages, words have only one syllable. Various meanings of the same one-syllable word are determined by its pitch or tone (Welton, 1990). For example, the word "nam" in Vietnamese can mean several different things, depending on pitch. The reason that Asian languages have a singsong quality to Western ears is because of these variations in pitch. This characteristic of Asian languages also influences how one writes them—because variations in pitch would be difficult to represent when writing a language using a phonetic system, many Asian languages use pictographs.

• Share books that involve characters being placed in situations where they have to learn another language and culture. Discuss the role of language in the character's life. Help the children to develop an understanding for what it must be like not to understand what is going on around you. (Some examples of such books are shared in the resource section of this chapter. The resource section also lists a number of interesting children's books that deal directly with language learning and differences.)

• Involve children in exploring the linguistic diversity that exists in their own classroom. What languages are represented in the classroom and in the extended families of the students? For those whose families only speak English, have them find out what languages their ancestors spoke. List the languages that have been found and show the countries of origin. Children will quickly realize that many have family members (past or present) who struggled to learn English when they first came to the United States.

- If children in the class have ever traveled in another country where they did not know the language, have them share their experiences. It is important, however, to realize that English speakers generally have an advantage in world travel. The English language is widely spoken in many countries; English speakers are not likely ever to feel the total sense of helplessness, confusion, and fear that some immigrants entering the United States feel.

- Lessons for older children might focus on the historical evolution of various languages and dialects, regional differences, and similarities and differences among various language systems. It can be an interesting and exciting area of study. For example, many people don't realize how geographical barriers (e.g., mountains, rivers, lakes) have isolated certain groups of people and led to mild to extreme language differences among groups of people, even those who are geographically adjacent to each other.

- Often children do not understand why second-language learners sound different than native speakers. Children are probably not aware that sounds they take for granted, such as the "th" sound, do not exist in many other languages. Speakers of English as a second language will replace the unknown sound with one that is familiar. In the case of the "th" it may be replaced with a "z" or a "d" sound. Children can be helped to understand that we develop a sound system based on the languages we hear as we are learning how to talk. As we grow older, it is difficult to produce those sounds we did not hear as we first learned how to talk. To illustrate your point more effectively, have children try to make sounds that other languages use but that are not present in the English language. Examples are the rolled "r" in Spanish, the nasal vowel sounds in French, or the clicks used in some African languages. If you are unable to model the sounds and do not have access to someone you can record, some libraries offer language-learning tapes.

- It is also appropriate for children to begin understanding and valuing various English dialects and accents. Children should be taught that all varieties of English are valid forms of communication and that dialects and accents reflect cultural and social variations within a broader language group (Taylor, 1986). Children can be exposed to various forms of English through reading stories aloud or perhaps by listening to tapes of dialects. Regional and social dialects also can be identified from television programs and discussed. Throughout such lessons, it is important for the class to reflect a positive attitude of respectful listening and enjoyment of the variety of languages that are heard.

CASE STUDY

Julie Becker[1] has made improving education for ELL children in regular classrooms her professional goal. A classroom teacher in Salt Lake City, Utah, for 12 years, Julie also spent six years as an educational specialist and consultant for other teachers who are addressing the needs of culturally and linguistically different children. Julie's focus on linguistic minorities started many years ago when a boy from Mexico joined her 3rd-grade classroom. Miguel didn't speak any English. As many teachers do, Julie turned to her school district for support and materials, only to find out that she was basically on her own. Miguel would get some tutoring in English, but as far as what happened in her own classroom, that was up to Julie. She took the challenge of teaching Miguel very seriously and, thus, other language-minority children entering 3rd grade at her school were placed in her classroom.

Julie believes it is essential that a teacher's attitude toward receiving an ELL child be one of acceptance, understanding, and compassion. It will be obvious if the teacher shows signs of being upset, indifferent, or frustrated. The entire class will feel the tension and respond negatively. Julie acknowledges that it is normal to feel frustrated, but having English language learners in your classroom can be better than you think.

Creating a loving, caring, supportive, and stimulating environment for every student is important to Julie. For such an environment to exist, she believes that all students must be engaged in the process. When a new student who does not speak English enters her classroom, Julie enlists all of her students' help. She begins by helping her students understand what it is like to come to a different country and a new classroom where nothing is familiar and everything is written and spoken in another language. She encourages her children to empathize with the new child by talking to them in another language and even writing lesson material on the chalkboard in another language. Thus, the students get a sense of what it is like not to understand what is expected of them.

Julie encourages her students to help the child learn English and make an effort to learn some of the child's language. She also finds ways to include the new student in children's play at recess; initially, a buddy is assigned each day to help the new child feel included and to help him or her learn the routines of the playground and classroom. In class, Julie seats the child next to a capable and kind child and, for a limited time, encourages the new child to copy, as needed, from this student's paper. She is pleased with the amount of peer tutoring, albeit nonverbal, that occurs in such situations. She always emphasizes to the other children that the new student is not cheating and that if they did not speak the language, they also would receive this kind of assistance.

Julie always reinforces her students for being helpful and for teaching positive words and behaviors to new ELL students. She finds that if children are not sensitively engaged in helping the new child, they sometimes engage in counterproductive teaching. For example, some students might think it is great fun to teach a child swear words and encourage him or her to act in socially unacceptable ways. She confronts such behavior immediately.

Whenever a teacher receives a child from another culture, Julie thinks it is essential that the teacher gain some information about the child's culture in order to communicate effectively with the child and his or her family. In her class, when a student comes from another country, the whole class spends time learning about that country and discussing cultural differences in an accepting and positive manner. Julie cautions, however, that it is important to know what a child's experience was in the country of origin. For example, some teachers she has worked with have children in their classes who came from refugee camps. Of course, such an experience affected the students deeply. American students need to understand how this can affect someone's perspective and behavior so that they can be more understanding of their new classmate. At all times, the class must show respect and courtesy toward the child's culture.

Julie helps her ELL students to learn English and function easily in her classroom in many ways. She labels items in her classroom in both English and the child's native tongue and makes passes with pictures and words on them. Passes show someone getting a drink of water or going to the restroom, for example; another shows a clock with the time the child is to go to English as a Second Language (ESL) class. This way, the child can get his or her basic needs met without embarrassment during the first days or weeks. Julie encourages and accepts any attempts the student makes to communicate; she recognizes that it can takes months for a student to feel comfortable speaking in a new language. Julie learned, early on, that it is important to use many visual cues and demonstrations with her class, and to repeat or paraphrase important concepts and directions several times for the benefit of her ELL students.

Julie found that ELL children can understandably develop behavior problems if they are asked to sit all day in class without understanding what is going on around them and getting little recognition for what they know. Julie tries to incorporate the child's language into many aspects of the classroom and to challenge her native English-speaking students to learn another language. For example, when children were working in cooperative groups, she would require children to ask for and name colors in Spanish. Her Spanish-speaking students thus became assets to their groups. She would also include bonus spelling words for the whole class in the language of the student. So that other children could feel comfortable engaging the ELL in play and other activities, Julie teaches her class basic verbs, such as "play," "help," "eat," "run," and "work," in the foreign language. Students often ask her for more words as their desire to communicate in the child's language increases. Even if you don't know the language, Julie states, you can look up basic words in a foreign-language dictionary and create picture flash cards. Asking the child to help with pronunciations is always a good idea.

When possible, ELL students are also provided textbooks and storybooks to read in their native language. Julie's district houses a multicultural library that offers Spanish textbooks, foreign-language dictionaries, children's literature in a variety of languages, and sheltered-English instruction materials. Julie has found some excellent, sheltered-English textbooks that she incorporates into her social studies curriculum. These books provide content instruction while making the language easier to understand by limiting vocabulary and the use of idioms. While teachers can design their own sheltered-English materials, they can benefit from a growing number of published programs. Given time constraints, Julie encourages teachers to see what is already available.

Julie also encourages her ELL children who have been schooled in their native language to write stories in their first language while others write in English. The children are asked to share their stories orally in class, just like everyone else. She feels that such efforts communicate to ELL students that she respects their language and that it is important to continue learning in one's home language. Julie believes this method also helps her English-speaking students develop empathy by having the experience of listening to a presentation in a language they do not understand. These experiences also demonstrate to the rest of the class that Julie, as the teacher, values different languages.

Julie admits that some ELL students may not want public attention. This is particularly true if they have been in the United States for a while and have developed the attitude that speaking a language other than English is not prestigious or admired. Such children may feel uncomfortable if they are asked to translate or to speak their native language, for they do not want to appear to be different. Obviously, their desire not to use their native language should be respected. Applying any undue pressure to have ELL students speak their home language in an English environment will simply add to their discomfort.

Julie shares that it was important to regularly adjust the curriculum so that ELL students could participate in challenging, but not overwhelming activities. For example, in spelling, learners of the English language are given a shorter set of words, with additional words added gradually as they prove their mastery. As mentioned earlier, words in the child's native language are also included, and are given as bonus words to the entire class.

Related to adjusting the curriculum is the importance of teachers giving up some of their grading expectations. Julie encourages teachers to reduce some of the stress they feel evaluating ELL children by initially only grading in some areas. As the child gains more facility with English, additional areas can be added. Julie believes that it is senseless to feel you must grade ELL students on the same scale as you do native English speakers. Grades based on assignments in a language that a child does not understand are hardly fair assessments. At this point, they can only serve to discourage a child. With a new ELL student, Julie sometimes grades only in math and handwriting during the first grading session. She accompanies the report card with a handwritten note to the parents so that they will understand why she is not grading in all areas. When she cannot readily get the note translated, Julie sends it in English. Julie has found that many parents' English comprehension is such that they can understand notes written in English; sometimes, they know of someone in their language community who can translate it for them. Julie believes that communicating in English is better than not communicating at all.

Julie also makes an effort to coordinate her work with her non-English-background students with whatever kind of special instruction they are receiving. She finds that it is often possible to integrate and reinforce the learning that is taking place in these other settings. Taking time to find out what the child is being taught by an ESL teacher or tutor can help the teacher create a more consistent and integrated learning environment.

Julie is the kind of teacher who accepts language diversity in her classroom and takes advantage of it. As demonstrated by this short case study, linguistically diverse students do create extra work for the classroom teacher, but they also provide an opportunity for the teacher and English-speaking students to grow in their understanding, knowledge, and acceptance of language and cultural differences. In turn, non-English-background children who have teachers like Julie can learn English and acquire knowledge in a positive and supportive environment that respects their home culture and language.

CONCLUSION

All in all, we can do much to help learners of English as a second language function more effectively in English-speaking classrooms. However, teaching English to language-minority students is only part of what teachers should be striving to do. As educators, we also must work hard to ensure that the price these children pay is not the loss of their mother tongue and their cultural identity. We also must help all students recognize the worth of all languages and to see fluency in another language as an advantage, rather than a stigma.

RESOURCES
Books for Children

These books are about adjustment to American culture by immigrant children, and about language differences generally. Although some of these books are guilty of presenting pat answers to difficult and complex problems, they do raise important issues and can be used to discuss discrimination and help children learn respect for languages other than their own.

Atkinson, M. (1979). *Maria Teresa*. Chapel Hill, NC: Lollipop Power. [Gr. 1 -4]

Borlenghi, P. (1992). *From albatross to zoo: An alphabet book in five languages*. New York: Scholastic. [Gr. K-2]

Bouchard, L. (1969). *The boy who wouldn't talk*. New York: Doubleday. [Gr. 4-7].

Castle, S. (1977). *Face talk, hand talk, body talk*. New York: Doubleday. [Gr. PreK-2]

Feelings, M. (1976). *Moja means one: Swahili counting book*. Garden City, NY: Dial. [Gr. K-3]

Giff, P. R. (1995). *Say hola, Sarah*. New York: Yearling Books. [Gr. 3-6]

Gilson, J. (1985). *Hello, my name is Scrambled Eggs*. Fairfield, NJ: Lothrop. [Gr. 5-7]

Haskins, J. (1982). *The new Americans: Cuban boat people*. Berkeley Heights, NJ: Enslow. [Gr. 6-9]

Herrera, J. F., & Gomez, E. (2000). *The upside down boy*. San Francisco: Children's Book Press. [Gr. 1-4]

Howlett, B. (1993). *I'm new here*. Boston: Houghton Mifflin. [Gr. 3-5]

Levine, E. (1989). *I hate English*. New York: Scholastic. [Gr. 1-3]

Lewiton, M. (1959). *Candita's choice*. New York: Harper & Row. [Gr. 4-6]

Lord, B. B. (1984). *In the year of the boar and Jackie Robinson*. New York: Harper & Row. [Gr. 4-6]

Michels, B., & White, B. (Eds.). (1983). *Apples on a stick: The folklore of black children*. East Rutherford, NJ: Coward-McCann. [Gr. 3-6]

Nagda, A. W. (2000). *Dear whiskers*. New York: Holiday House. [Gr. 3-6]

Nye, N. S. (1994). *Sitti's secret*. New York: Four Winds Press. [Gr. K-3]

Orgel, D. (1996). *West side kids: Don't call me Slob-O*. New York: Hyperion. [Gr. 3-5]

Paek, M. (1988). *Aekyung's dream*. San Francisco: Children's Book Press. [Gr. 2-4]

Rosario, I. (1981). *Idalia's project ABC: An urban alphabet book in English and Spanish*. Orlando, FL: Holt, Rinehart and Winston. [Gr. K-2]

Stanek, M. (1989). *I speak English for my mom*. Niles, IL: Whitman. [Gr. 1-3]

Surat, M. M. (1983). *Angel child, dragon child*. Milwaukee, WI: Raintree. [Gr. 3-5]

Wartski, M. C. (1980). *A long way from home*. Philadelphia: Westminster. [Gr. 6-9]

Notes

[1]Julie Becker was a teacher in the Granite Public School District in Salt Lake City, Utah, at the time this case study was completed She is now an instructional specialist for that district.

References

Adler, S. (1993). *Multicultural communication skills in the classroom.* Boston: Allyn and Bacon.

Artiles, A. J., Rueda, R., Salazar, J. J., & Higareda, I. (2000). Factors associated with English-language learner representation in special education: Evidence from urban school districts in California. In D. Losen & G. Orfield (Eds.), *Minority issues in special education in the public schools* (pp. 117-136). Cambridge, MA: Harvard Publishing Group.

Bialystok, E., & Hakuta, K. (1994). *In other words: The science and psychology of second language acquisition.* New York: Basic Books.

Bickerton, D. (1981). *The roots of language.* Ann Arbor, MI: Karoma.

Chomsky, N. (1981). *Lectures on government and binding.* Dordrecht, Netherlands: Foris.

Crawford, J. (2000). Language politics in the United States: The paradox of bilingual education. In C. Ovando & P. McLaren (Eds.), *The politics of multiculturalism and bilingual education* (pp. 107-125). Boston: McGraw-Hill.

Echevarria, J., Vogt, M., & Short, D. (2004). *Making content comprehensible for English learners: The SIOP model* (2nd ed.). Boston: Pearson.

Farb, P. (1975). *Word play: What happens when people talk.* New York: Knopf.

Gardner, R. C., & Lambert, W. E. (1972). *Attitudes and motivation in second-language learning.* Rowley, MA: Newberry House.

Gleitman, L., & Landau, B. (1994). *The acquisition of the lexicon.* Cambridge, MA: MIT Press.

Grove, C. L. (1976). *Communications across culture.* Washington, DC: National Education Association.

Hall, E. T. (1973). *The silent language.* Garden City, NY: Anchor.

Hough, R. A., Nurss, J. R., & Enright, D. S. (1986). Story reading with limited English speaking children in the regular classroom. *The Reading Teacher, 39*(6), 510-514.

Hudelson, S. (1986). ESL children's writing: What we've learned, what we're learning. In P. Rigg & D. S. Enright (Eds.), *Children and ESL: Integrating perspectives* (pp. 23-54). Washington, DC: Teachers of English to Speakers of Other Languages.

Kottler, E. (1994). *Children with limited English: Teaching strategies for the regular classroom.* Thousand Oaks, CA: Corwin.

Krashen, S. (1981). *Second language acquisition and second language learning.* New York: Pergamon.

Krashen, S. (1996). *Under attack: The case against bilingual education.* Culver City, CA: Language Education Associates.

Moustafa, M. (1980). Picture books for oral language development for non-English speaking children: A bibliography. *The Reading Teacher, 33,* 914-919.

Myer, L. (1985). *Excellence in leadership and implementation: Programs for limited English proficient students.* San Francisco: San Francisco Unified School District.

National Center for Education Statistics. (1997). *1993-94 schools and staffing survey: A profile of policies and practices for limited English proficient students: Screening methods, program support, and teacher training.* Washington, DC: U.S. Department of Education, Office of Educational Research and Improvement.

Newmark, E., & Asante, M. K. (1976). *Intercultural communication.* Urbana, IL: ERIC Clearinghouse on Reading and Communications Skills.

Ovando, C. J., Collier V. P., & Combs, M. C. (2003). *Bilingual & ESL classrooms: Teaching in multicultural contexts* (3rd ed.). Boston: McGraw Hill.

Peregoy, S. F., & Boyle, O. F. (2005). *Reading, writing, and learning in ESL* (4th ed.). Boston: Allyn & Bacon.

Perez, S. A. (1979). How to effectively teach Spanish-speaking children, even if you're not bilingual. *Language Arts, 56,* 159-162.

Pinker, S. (1994). *The language instinct: How the mind creates languages.* New York: William Morrow and Company.

Pray, L., & MacSwan, J. (2002, April). *Different question, same answer: How long does it take for English learners to attain proficiency?* Paper presented at the annual meeting of the American Educational Research Association, New Orleans, LA. Available at www.public.asu.edu/~macswan/rate.pdf.

Slobin, D., & Bowerman, M. (1985). *Crosslinguistic evidence for the language making capacity: What shapes children's grammar?* Hillsdale, NJ: Erlbaum.

Solórzano, R. W., & Solórzano, D. G. (1999). Beginning teacher standards: Impact on second-language learners and implications for teacher preparation. *Teacher Education Quarterly, 26,* 37-70.

Taylor, O. L. (1986). A cultural and communicative approach to teaching standard English as a second dialect. In O. L. Taylor (Ed.), *Treatment of communication disorders in culturally and linguistically diverse populations* (pp. 153-178). San Diego, CA: College-Hill.

Thomas, W. P., & Collier, V. P. (2003). The multiple benefits of dual language. *Educational Leadership, 61*(2), 61-64.

Tiedt, P. L., & Tiedt, I. M. (1990). *Multicultural teaching: A handbook of activities, information and resources.* Boston: Allyn & Bacon.

United States Census Bureau. (2003). *Statistical Abstracts of the United States.* Education, 4, 145-194.

Welton, D. A. (1990, Fall). Language as a mirror of culture. *Educators' Forum,* p. 7.

Williams, S. W. (1991). Classroom use of African American language: Educational tool or social weapon? In C. E. Sleeter (Ed.), *Empowerment through multicultural education* (pp. 199-215). Albany, NY: State University of New York Press.

Willis, S. (1996). Foreign languages: Learning to communicate in the real world. *Association for Supervision and Curriculum Development: Curriculum Update,* Winter.

Wong-Fillmore, L. (1990). Now or later? Issues related to the early education of minority-group children. In C. Harris (Ed.), *Children at risk* (pp. 110-133). New York: Harcourt, Brace & Jovanovich.

Wong-Fillmore, L., & Valadez, C. (1986). Teaching bilingual learners. In M. Wittrock (Ed.), *Handbook on research in teaching* (pp. 648-684). New York: Macmillan.

Wyner, N. B. (1989). Educating linguistic minorities: Public education and the search for unity. *Educational Horizons, 67*(4), 172-176.

Chapter 6
Creating Gender-Equitable Classroom Environments

Janice Koch

What comes to mind when you hear the phrase "gender equity"? Most teachers take the phrase to mean "treating boys and girls equally." That notion of equality addresses most teachers' strong desires not to show favoritism. What research tells us, however, is that girls and boys come to school with different sets of needs, due to the ways in which they are socialized in their families and in contemporary culture. Hence, meeting those needs in *different* ways is appropriate and can ensure equality of outcomes.

Consider a recent newspaper cartoon that shows Cinderella talking to her Fairy Godmother. The caption reads, "Forget the royal ball; can you send me to Harvard?" The message is that the Cinderella social stereotype for females probably does not ring as true today as it may have in the past. Girls and boys alike seek achievement in the public sphere as a means to prepare themselves for the broader adult world of earning a living and caring for oneself. This chapter will explore the field of gender equity in education and will address possibilities for creating gender-equitable environments in our own classrooms.

Gender equity is defined as parity between males and females, as measured in the quality of life, academic, and work outcomes valued by our society. The purpose of the field of gender equity is to develop, implement, and evaluate the success of strategies, programs, and policies designed to promote those outcomes. Klein, Ortman, and Friedman (2002) explain that

Although there is no one legislatively mandated or commonly accepted definition, most would agree with the following. To be *equitable* is to be fair and just, free from bias or favoritism. The term *gender equity* means just that: to be fair and just toward both men and women, to show preference to neither, and concern for both. (p. 4)

Attaining gender equity in and through education means achieving equitable outcomes for females and males in all that is of value to individuals and society, as well as rethinking what we value to include frequently neglected strengths and roles traditionally associated with women. Gender-equity outcomes are attained when:

91

- Both females and males acquire, or are given the opportunity to acquire, the most socially valued characteristics and skills (even if they have been generally attributed to only one gender), so that fewer jobs, roles, activities, expectations, and achievements are differentiated by gender;
- There is decreased use of gender stereotyping in decision making by or about individuals;
- Sex segregation in education and society caused by gender stereotyping and other inappropriate discriminatory factors is reduced and eventually eliminated. (Klein & Ortman, 1994, p. 13)

The term "gender equity" has replaced "sex equity." "Gender" is the preferred term because it is a social, rather than a biological, construct. From their earliest experiences as infants, people are socialized to assume behaviors appropriate to males and females. Hence, gender refers to societal expectations that differ for females and males, not to differences in biology. While important data may be gained by understanding sex-linked traits that can be inherited, this chapter addresses cultural expectations for behavior, attitudes, and achievement, and how they differ for girls and boys. Gender equity in education is one of many aspects of social justice that include topics addressed by chapters in this book: race, ethnicity, and culture; ability differences; religious diversity; social class; sexual orientation; and language diversity.

COMMON PATTERNS OF GENDER BIAS IN THE CLASSROOM

Schools' and teachers' expectations of males and females influence students' development, behavior, and academic success. Classroom interactions and school curriculum socially construct what it means to be female and male and can limit possibilities for girls and boys in schools. A gender issue refers to a practice or policy that differentiates the learning experience in ways that limit opportunities for females and males in the classroom. Each gender issue addresses educationally relevant processes and skills (Koch, 2002).

Teacher Beliefs

It is important to remember that all teachers have been raised in particular cultures and environments that have sent messages about what it means to be female or male. Often, these messages become part of an individual's tacit biases and beliefs. Because "we teach WHO we are" (Koch, 2005) as much as what we know, we often reveal our own beliefs to our students through the ways in which we interact with and respond to them. Simple exchanges, seemingly harmless, can be problematic. Consistently praising the girls in your class for the way they look or how their hair is arranged, for example, reinforces the message that girls should be judged more strongly by their appearance. I visited an elementary school in the northeast region of the United States recently. As the principal was showing me around the building, a young girl, her hair in a very long braid, handed him a message. He thanked her and remarked about her hair. A few moments later, the principal stopped a 5th-grade boy from running down the hall and commented about the home run the boy had hit in a Little League game the day before. While this may not have been a recurring pattern, research has demonstrated that in many elementary schools, girls are much more frequently praised for what they look like while boys are praised for what they can do (Sadker & Sadker, 1994).

What Research Says About Gender Issues and Classrooms

Over the past 25 years, education researchers have gained insight into coeducational environments by observing and documenting teacher-student interactions and peer interactions in classrooms, hallways, cafeterias, and school grounds. These studies compiled data about the nature of teacher-student, and student-student, interactions—in the classroom and in more informal school environments. Field researchers took notes and made extensive ethnographic reports; survey researchers reported on quantitative measures of the gendered character of interactions in schools (see, e.g., Chapman, 1997; Koch, 1996; Sadker & Sadker, 1994). A significant, consistent finding in this gender-equity research is that girls' under-achievement in the sciences is a response to teaching environments, rather than lack of ability. The deficit model, which infers that we need to "fix" the girls to make them better achievers in science, is simply not accurate (Boaler, 2002).

One private school study (Koch, 1996) explored how the school and classroom environments contributed to setting expectations for male and female achievement. In this study, analysis of the gender surveys revealed, among other things, that girls in the high school physics class were receiving preferential treatment (e.g., being allowed to rewrite labs and retake exams). The boys were not given these allowances and were angry about the different treatment. It turned out that the teacher was trying to "help" the girls. Teachers need to hold out the expectation that both females and males can accomplish a task or solve a problem. It is important not to perform a task for a female student, while expecting a male student to do it on his own. This can lead to "learned helplessness" (Eccles-Parsons, Meece, Adler, & Kaczala, 1982), a behavioral phenomenon that describes, for example, females acting "helpless" in order to get things done for them. In the middle school science classes in the study, teachers were observed focusing the microscope for the girls while allowing the boys to focus it on their own (Sanders, Koch, & Urso, 1997). This is an example of encouraging a type of female dependency on the teacher, even as we hold out the expectation that the boys can do the task. This runs counter to the primary goals of education: knowledge, understanding, and personal empowerment.

When looking at classroom interactions through the lens of gender, gender-equity researchers repeatedly saw similar gendered patterns of student-teacher interactions. The repetition of these patterns in research studies from the 1970s, as well as those documented by the end of the 1990s, revealed the pervasiveness of gender bias in the classroom (Marshall & Reinhartz, 1997). Classrooms continue to be microcosms of society, mirroring the gender roles that teachers and students develop through their socialization. Gender roles, which are both in-grained in our individual identity and mediated by social class and ethnicity, inform much of classroom behavior. Instances of gender bias in teacher-student interactions are often subtle, and not usually intentional. Several researchers have noted that consistent gender-biased practices can contribute to lowered self-esteem for girls. However, these patterns can be remedied by intervention strategies (Chapman, 1997; Sadker & Sadker, 1994).

Gender bias in student-teacher interactions has been documented in classrooms from kindergarten through high school. Areas of gender-differentiated instruction include:

- Teacher questions/student responses
- Types of teacher questions/sanctions
- Student voice or "air time"
- Teacher attention to student appearance
- Amount of wait time
- Teacher-student coaching
- Teacher-assigned "jobs"
- Teacher attention to discipline.

A prevalent finding has been that classroom teachers engage boys in question-and-answer periods more frequently than they engage girls. Involving boys more actively in classroom dialogue has been used as a way to control male behavior in the classroom, often in response to male aggressiveness. Studies found that in classroom discourse, boys frequently raised their hands, sometimes impulsively, sometimes without even knowing the answer. Conversely, studies found that girls tended not to raise their hand as often and were overlooked frequently when they did, with preference given to a male student. Teachers tend to reprimand boys more frequently and with longer duration than the girls, thus reinforcing "bad boy-good girl" stereotypes. Teachers, when asked to monitor their interactions with students, consciously changed this pattern (Koch, 1994).

A related finding revealed that teachers tended to ask boys more open-ended, thought-provoking questions than they asked girls, holding out the expectation that boys were capable of more abstract thinking. These findings become exaggerated in different subject area classes in middle and high school, especially mathematics, science, and technology. For example, boys are more likely to demonstrate and use technical equipment and actively engage with materials during experiments (American Association of University Women [AAUW], 1995; Sadker & Sadker, 1994).

Furthermore, boys are routinely overdisciplined; yet when girls exhibited boisterous behavior or impulsively called out a response, they were reprimanded in different ways than how the boys exhibiting the same behaviors were. One study described 3rd-grade girls as suffering from "over-control," a term used to indicate the silencing of girls and their reticence to ask questions even when they did not understand a concept ("Girls: Drawbacks of Early Success," 1985).

Positive change has occurred. There are many more instances of confident girls who are able to dominate the discourse in elementary school than there were 20 years ago. This has occurred over time due to intervention programs on behalf of female students that have been implemented as early as elementary school. Such programs (e.g., the Teacher Education Equity Project, funded by the National Science Foundation) have influenced the achievement of girls and young women as well as the classroom behaviors of many teachers (Sanders, Koch, & Urso, 1997).

Nevertheless, research studies affirm repeatedly that males receive more of all types of the teachers' attention in classrooms and are given more time to talk in class, beginning in preschool and continuing through high school. Teachers tend to offer more praise, criticism, remediation, and acceptance to boys than to girls. Many teachers are often invested in the silence of the girls. Girls tend not to call attention to themselves in classrooms, preferring to be quiet and well-behaved. Even when they are sure of an answer, they are not apt to volunteer. Teachers often sanction this "good girl" behavior in elementary classrooms as a way of maintaining their vision of proper classroom management. As well, girls learn early on that their appearance matters in ways that are not valid for the boys. Being "pretty," "cute," "thin," "charming," "alluring," "well-dressed," and "sexy" are attributes that girls aspire to because they are valued by adults—as is communicated through media messages. Classrooms reinforce those values when girls consistently are praised for their appearance and dress.

When asking the class questions, teachers tend to exhibit longer wait times for boys than for girls. Wait time refers to the period of time between asking a question and calling on a student for a response. Research indicates that wait time is an important teacher technique for encouraging full participation of all students and promoting higher order thinking, rather than simple recall (Rowe, 1987). While some researchers assert that teachers give males longer wait time than females in order to keep their interest and manage classroom behavior, other researchers believe that teachers expect more abstract or higher order thinking from the males, and that those expectations are manifested in longer wait times. Studies reveal that teachers tend to coach boys for the correct answers through prodding and cajoling, but go on to the next student when a girl has an incorrect response (Sadker & Sadker, 1994; Sandler, Silverberg, & Hall, 1996).

Teachers also need to encourage both boys and girls to express themselves with words and appropriate actions. Many boys, as well as some girls, will try to physically intimidate or bully classmates; teachers must intervene and ask them to express their feelings and share their thoughts. Believing the notion that "boys will be boys" and thereby condoning inappropriate physical behavior in the early grades can lead to serious problems in later grades. Girls, compared to boys, tend to be shy and quiet in group discussions, while boys' hands fly up to answer questions. Boys' communication is frequently dominated by body movements. Teachers must encourage girls to participate and speak so they can be heard. Expressing our feelings and thoughts in a public sphere begins in school. Both "bad boys" and "silent girls" (Gallas, 1995) are lost to the learning community in the early grades, and that isolation discourages appropriate development of communication skills.

Teachers also have been found to reward girls' passive and compliant behaviors. Through courses on gender and teaching, elementary school teachers are being made aware of the importance of participation by both genders, expressing their opinions and sharing the classroom discourse. "Good girls" in classrooms are often rewarded by teacher praise and by being the "teacher's pet." This does not encourage the development of so-called refusal skills and other traits related to being assertive. In this way, seemingly positive behaviors toward girls have a strong negative effect on development. Similarly, being overly harsh when boys exhibit inappropriate behaviors only reinforces tacit hostilities and does not encourage boys to express their feelings. Boys need to be encouraged to express their emotions constructively, including anger, from the earliest grades.

Research on gender and play reveals that girls and boys differ in decisions about whether a game or activity can continue after the players have had a conflict. Both conflict-resolution and decision-making skills need to be addressed, regardless of whether the game or activity resumes. Boys tend to ignore fights for the sake of the game. Psychologists argue, however, that ignoring the conflict only causes undesirable behaviors to surface at another time. Conflict resolution and decision-making skills need to be examined through the lens of gender, and each group needs to work on appropriate resolutions. At play time, teachers tend to leave early childhood students to their own devices; those occasions, however, offer ample opportunities to teach girls skills that will help them to continue with the game, and to teach boys skills to resolve the conflict, rather than bury it.

Boys may be quiet and shy, but they are rarely silent. By contrast, it is not uncommon for girls to be silent or speak in voices so low they are barely audible. An oversimplification of this phenomenon includes the belief that girls are silenced by the boys and that if the teacher would intervene the girls will no longer be so quiet. Another oversimplification describes the gendered dichotomies of classroom discourse as originating in the classroom, as though the gender relations suppress the girls' voices. There is a lack of research on girls' silences, however, and their silence in the early grades is accepted. As a result, early childhood teachers see the need to "manage" the boys while the girls remain compliant and quiet. Teachers make no attempt to examine the possible causes of the girls' silences, because the silences are not considered problematic (Koch, 2002).

Boys, however, are more likely than girls to be labeled in need of assistance, to fail a course, or to repeat a grade. Boys are more likely to be identified for special education programs and are more likely than girls to be labeled for their entire school career. Boys are more likely to gain social status through disruptive classroom behavior, which can lead to school failure (AAUW, 1998).

Science Education and Girls

Research has documented that elementary school teachers tend to avoid teaching science because it is the subject area with which they are least comfortable. This attitude often gets communicated to the students and can result in disenfranchising females in science. Fortunately, this mindset is changing; more elementary school teachers are becoming skilled science teachers as they engage students in inquiry activities—the open-ended investigation of a problem. Teachers—both male and female—need to help students feel confident in exploring and investigating natural phenomena, as this is a direct way in which youngsters can learn about their world. It is crucial that elementary school science be a springboard for middle school science, as many students decide by 8th grade whether or not to pursue scientific study (AAUW, 1998).

For example, in high school, a marked gender gap persists in physics and in computer science classes, where girls' enrollments lag behind boys'. In math and science, a larger portion of boys than girls receive top scores on the National Assessment of Education Progress (NAEP), a nationally representative test of specific subject matter given to students in the 4th, 8th, and 12th grades. The gender gap increases with grade level. The exception is African American girls, who outscore African American boys at every assessment point (AAUW, 1998; National Center for Education Statistics [NCES], n.d.). There are many reasons for this gender difference in African American communities; one of the most significant factors may be intervention programs that target girls all over the United States, encouraging them to study science, mathematics, and engineering. Many of these programs, funded by such agencies as the National Science Foundation, have targeted minority girls (Clewell, Anderson, & Thorpe, 1992).

LOOKING AT SOLUTIONS

Changing teachers' gender-stereotyped behavior requires prior knowledge of gender issues in the classroom. Teachers who participate in gender workshops, which are designed to create an awareness of, and an agenda for, gender issues in the classroom, tend to promote more equitable classroom settings than do their peers who have had little or no exposure to the topic. For example, Ms. Slater is a 4th-grade teacher who consistently called upon the students whose hands were waving the wildest; after examining who were raising their hands so enthusiastically, she observed that the boys were being called on far more frequently than the girls. It was common practice for her to use "calling on the boys" as a type of classroom-management technique. After taking a course on gender issues in the classroom, Ms. Slater was able to implement a practice whereby her students placed their thumbs up on their desks if they wanted to respond. Thereafter, she actively and consciously called on boys and girls alternately, whenever possible.

These teacher behaviors are components of what researchers have termed the "hidden" curriculum, the tacit messages students receive from the daily practices, routines, and behaviors that occur in the classroom. The hidden curriculum of the school's climate comprise "things not deliberately taught or instituted, but which are the cumulative result of many unconscious or unexamined behaviors that add to a palpable style or atmosphere" (Chapman, 1997, p. iii). An example of these type of behaviors can be seen in elementary school environments, when teachers assign girls the task of recording information on the board during a demonstration lesson in science, for example, while boys are required to set up or assemble the accompanying materials. This fine motor/gross motor skills distinction is one of many types of gendered expectations that can lead to differentiated outcomes.

Extracurricular computer clubs in middle school are often dominated by boys. No one questions the absence of girls. This lack of taking notice is another example of the ways schools communicate a hidden curriculum. In many high schools, advanced-placement science courses in chemistry and physics have larger male than female enrollments. When school administrators or teachers are not asking "Where are the girls?," the implied message is that girls are not expected to enroll. Similarly, when boys are under-represented in advanced-placement language arts courses, school officials should examine the issue. In short, the hidden curriculum constitutes the unstated lessons that students learn in school. It is the running subtext through which teachers communicate behavioral norms and individual status in the school culture, the process of socialization that cues children into their place in the hierarchy of larger society (Orenstein, 1995).

An awareness of the role of gender in learning and behavior can help teachers avoid the trap of limiting children's growth by making and acting upon stereotypic assumptions about individual students' abilities and development. Consider the following checklist. It can help you understand your own belief systems about the role of gender in your life and in society at large. The checklist is meant as a springboard for discussion, not as a tool for judging your beliefs. Most teachers really want to be equitable and fair, and often that begins with self-examination. If you are observing in an elementary or middle school classroom, you may ask some questions about the gender dynamic in that room. After you list the responses to these questions, analyze them by gender—are the students you named boys or girls? Where are the silences in the room? Who are the students who never contribute? Consider the questions below:

- Who are the brightest students in your classroom?
- Which students are the most talkative?
- Which students respond to classroom discussions most frequently?
- Who is the smartest student in science? math?
- Who are the quietest students during class discussions?
- Who are your most undisciplined students?
- Which students do homework most regularly?
- Which students are the best test performers?
- Which students are your favorites?
- Who helps around the classroom with physical work?

While most teachers believe that they treat girls and boys the same, research reveals that they frequently do not. The teacher's gender has little bearing on the outcome; it is the gender of the student that determines the differential behavior (Sadker & Sadker, 1994).

In teacher-training courses that address gender issues, teachers are asked to examine their classroom interactions and to tape themselves. Often, they notice that they call on boys more frequently for responses and coach boys for correct responses more frequently than they do with girls. When made aware of such practices, teachers tend to change their interactions (Koch, 1994).

Encouraging Girls' Interest in Science

Classroom teachers can use several intervention strategies to explore who does science and why. The following activities are helpful in creating a more inclusive classroom climate around the study of science.

Draw a Scientist. Not long ago, two 3rd-grade teachers in a local elementary school were interested in exploring their students' beliefs about scientists. Distributing crayons and drawing paper, they asked each student (39 in all) to draw a picture of a scientist and describe what the scientist was doing. The students produced drawings of 31 male scientists; only eight were women. Further, of the 31 male scientists, 25 had beards and messy hairstyles.

One boy added a bubble quote for his scientist that said, "I'm crazy." Another 3rd-grade boy described his scientist as follows: "He is inventing a monster. He painted his face green." Still another boy wrote, "My scientist makes all kinds of poisons. He is a weird person." Another caption at the bottom of a drawing read, "Dr. Strangemind." On the back, the student explained, "He does strange things like blow up things and other crazy stuff." Many of the children described their scientists as "blowing things up," acting "crazy" or "goofy," or working with "a lot of potions." You can see that most of these 3rd-graders, young as they were, had already internalized the stereotyped image of the scientist. To understand why this is important, ask yourself the following questions:

- Who is omitted in this stereotype?
- Does the type of person represented in the stereotype reflect the makeup of any class you have recently seen?
- If the students in a typical classroom were omitted by the stereotype, how would that make them feel about science?

You may suppose that stereotypes about scientists diminish as children mature. In fact, however, a study of over 1,500 students in grades K-8 revealed that the students' drawings of scientists became more stereotypical as the students got older. These students drew mostly white male scientists, suggesting that the stereotype persists despite recent changes in curriculum materials (Barman, 1997).

The scientist stereotype can discourage individuals who are not white and male from seeing themselves as truly scientific. Some of the consequences are obvious. For example, substantially fewer females enroll in advanced science courses, except for advanced biology courses, than do males, beginning in high school and continuing through college. This is most noticeable in physical science, computer science, and engineering. This gender gap persists despite many types of interventions designed to encourage the participation of girls and young women in science and technology.

It is a complex issue, but the way in which we conceptualize "who does science" certainly contributes to the problem. One primary school teacher holds a gigantic mirror up to her students when the question of who can be a scientist emerges. This helps the students envisage themselves in the role of the scientist, ensuring that they will feel entitled to be scientists as they explore natural phenomena in their own classrooms (excerpted from Koch, 2005).

The Checks Lab. Many researchers in both science education and professional science, as well as philosophers and historians of science, talk about the unique "nature of science." This refers to the ways in which scientists gather evidence, analyze their data, and draw tentative conclusions. Understanding the nature of science would reveal to many students that, contrary to the stereotype they draw upon, scientists work collaboratively, in teams, and as part of a much more social enterprise than typically portrayed.

Consider the following activity, aimed at promoting gender-equitable and collaborative learning environments in a university science methods course. A class of 20 college students is divided into five groups. Each group of four students receives an identical set of 16 cancelled checks from the same family. The checks are in sealed envelopes, and each group is allowed to randomly select four checks at a time. After each round of check selection, group members are asked to record ideas about the family that they have developed as a result of exploring these cancelled checks. After all 16 checks have been analyzed in relation to the others, the group recorder writes down—on a large piece of poster paper for all to see—the tentative conclusions the group has reached about this family's life.

When the students review all of the information, they find that while each group's story varies in some ways from the others, they have three or four main ideas about the family in common. The class members decide that these three or four ideas are ones they can begin to call their *theories* about this family. They suggest ways to explore their family theories further.

How does this story relate to gender issues and the nature of science? The cancelled check activity is an excellent metaphor for the way scientists work:

- Just like the student groups, several scientists often work together to explore the same problem, with identical evidence, in different sequences.
- The order in which the students select their checks from the envelopes influences their story. Similarly, scientists often find that the sequence of evidence they encounter influences their developing ideas.

- The discussion each student group has about the evidence also influences the outcomes. Scientists, too, work in groups and confer about their evidence regularly.
- The students developed theories based on how they saw the evidence and what their own experiences told them. They did not pursue pre-existing "right" or "wrong" answers. Real science proceeds to find answers where no previous answers exist.

It is significant that conversations among diverse student groups usually yield more accurate data. We do not see things as they are; we see things as WE are. The greater the diversity of people working in science, the more complete the observations and subsequent interpretations of data.

Who Are These Women? The list below represents Nobel Prize winners in science and medicine over the last 100 years. More information about these remarkable women may be found at http://almaz.com/nobel/women.html.

Marie Curie	1903 Nobel Prize for Physics
	1911 Nobel Prize for Chemistry
Irene Joliot-Curie	1935 Nobel Prize for Chemistry
Gerty Radnitz-Cory	1947 Nobel Prize in Physiology & Medicine
Maria Goeppert Mayer	1963 Nobel Prize for Physics
Dorothy Crowfoot Hodgkin	1964 Nobel Prize for Chemistry
Rosalyn Yalow	1977 Nobel Prize in Physiology & Medicine
Barbara McClintock	1983 Nobel Prize in Physiology & Medicine
Rita Levi-Montalcini	1986 Nobel Prize in Physiology & Medicine
Gertrude Elion	1988 Nobel Prize in Physiology & Medicine
Christianne Nusslein-Volhard	1995 Nobel Prize in Physiology & Medicine

Inviting the students to explore the lives and work of these women is one way to dispel the stereotype of the weird, white, male scientist. Having a history also enables students to see themselves as potential scientists. African American women scientists have made extraordinary contributions in the last century and their stories have the power to influence your students. Consider the following scientists, two of whom went on to become college presidents.

Dr. Reatha Clark King—Chemist
 www.hill.af.mil/fwp/kingbio.html
Dr. Jewel Plummer Cobb—Biologist
 www.princeton.edu/~mcbrown/display/cobb.html
Dr. Shirley Ann Jackson—Physicist
 www.princeton.edu/~mcbrown/display/jackson.html
Dr. Mae Jemison—Astronaut
 http://starchild.gsfc.nasa.gov/docs/StarChild/whos_who_level2/jemison.html
Madame C.J. Walker—Inventor
 www.princeton.edu/~mcbrown/display/walker.html

Classroom teachers also can become powerful mentors for their students by modeling their own enthusiasm for science and technology and overtly encouraging students in these areas. Coaching and caring go a long way with students who are unsure of their talents in these areas. Research shows that mentors of both genders who take a personal interest in their students, helping individual students to pursue their science or technology goals, make an important contribution to the future careers of these students (Warren-Sams, 2001).

If You Were a Boy...a Girl... Making a conscious decision to be gender equitable in your classroom often requires the use of intervention strategies, such as the activities above describing women and science and the collaborative nature of science. The activity that follows is used frequently in grades 4 through high school as a way to talk about gender stereotypes in the classroom. Ask the students to clear everything off their desks, except for a pen or pencil and a piece of blank paper. Ask them to put their heads down and close their eyes and take a journey back through time in their imagination.

To begin, step out of your body and see yourself at your desk with your head down. Now, travel back in time until you are in 5th grade, then 3rd grade. What are you wearing? Who is your teacher? What are you doing? See yourself at home; what does your room look like? Who are your friends? What do you do after school? Now, see yourself as a kindergartner; see how you are playing. What do you love to do? Travel back again until you are a baby. Look around your room. Notice things around you. Now travel back again and here you are—ready to be born! Everyone is so excited, so happy, waiting for your birth—and here you are. But this time . . . imagine you are born as the opposite sex. Hence, if you are boy, pretend you were born a girl. If you are a girl, pretend you were born a boy. See yourself as a baby, coming home, learning to walk, starting school, going through elementary school. Look at your room and your friends and your activities. Without talking to anybody, create a list of how your life seems different since you were born a person of the opposite sex.

After students describe their images in writing, the teacher tapes large sheets of paper, labeled "MALES" and "FEMALES," onto the blackboard, and students write one thing from their list on to the large sheets of paper. In this way, they come up and share their thoughts about the opposite sex. The important ground rule is that neither girls nor boys can judge what is being placed on the list even when it doesn't feel true for their gender. This activity is about getting to know what boys think being female is about and what girls think being male is about. When the lists are complete, the teacher facilitates discussion of the items. When girls and boys in class have the opportunity to state what is true for them about being female and male, the students come to see that they are more alike than different. Very few pink and blue bedrooms abound; most are white, for example. Sometimes, however, troubling items may emerge, like, "If I were born a girl, I'd kill myself" or "If I were a boy, I would have more freedom." Help the class to analyze their beliefs and evaluate the causes for the extreme stereotyping (Logan, 1997, pp. 34-36). We know that there are more differences *within* each gender group than between the two, and this activity highlights that observation. It is important to respond to students' lists respectfully, recognizing that students' experiences differ from each other and, often, from the teacher's experience as well. Accepting responses, exploring reactions, and drawing conclusions requires a suspension of judgment. The goal is to articulate frequently held stereotypes and seek common ground.

GENDER EQUITY, COEDUCATION, AND SINGLE-SEX CLASSROOMS

I have often used the term "gender agenda" to refer to classrooms where gender equitable practices are commonplace. When teachers exhibit deliberate and planned gender-fair practices in classrooms, the result is a more equitable learning environment.

Significantly, people tend to assert that "boys will be boys" or "girls will be girls" only in moments when boys' or girls' behavior matches a traditional stereotype about masculinity or femininity—for example, when a girl plays with dolls or a boy roughhouses. People rarely invoke the phrase in response to the myriad and most typical moments when girls and boys act more alike than dissimilar in their basic human qualities or when boys or girls behave in ways that transgress the narrow cliché about their gender. (AAUW, 2001, p. 26)

This quote is significant in order to understand that the consideration of gender equity in schools is both informed by, and seeks to mitigate, the socialized ways in which young girls and boys become women and men. One day, when a boy consoles a friend, or expresses his emotions or feelings, "boys will be boys" will apply.

Recently, the U.S. Department of Education released guidelines that could expand flexibility for schools and districts interested in providing single-sex schools or classes. These guidelines, spurred by amendments within the No Child Left Behind Act (Section 5131, Part C), have reignited a debate in the United States between supporters of single-sex instruction and supporters of coeducational classrooms and schools. Similar debates have been going on in England over the last decade, and researchers in many countries have explored the issue. Although the body of research into single-sex classes and schools is inconclusive, some research suggests an academic benefit for girls, particularly in mathematics and science achievement, as well as increased self-confidence. However, these effects are often attenuated when background variables (such as wealth and prior achievement) are held constant. For example, in single-sex private schools that can be afforded only by the wealthy, females' achievement is not higher than the same group's achievement at a coeducational private school. Although the focus of single sex education is generally on academic achievement, some educators worry that separate education will complicate the transition of students to a gender-integrated society and that equity issues will be exacerbated (Klein et al., 2002). Other activists worry that gender-equity issues focus primarily on supporting girls in subjects where boys have traditionally excelled, rather than helping both boys and girls overcome gender-oriented stereotypes (Shapka & Keating, 2003).

Title IX

Title IX of the Education Amendments of 1972, which prohibits discrimination on the basis of sex in education programs or activities receiving federal financial assistance, is a key civil rights statute. It was modeled on Title VI of the Civil Rights Act of 1964, which prohibits discrimination based on race, color, and national origin. However, unlike Title VI, which applied to *all* programs that receive federal financial assistance, Title IX is limited to education programs or activities that receive such assistance. It was Title IX that mandated that schools' all-female sports teams be on a par with the men's teams. The current push for single-sex education environments flies in the face of Title IX as it separates the students by gender rather than creating meaningful coeducational environments. The challenge is to learn from experiments in single-sex education and determine what attributes of that environment support females and males, and then incorporate those attributes in the coeducational environment.

Equity Is Not Equality

Gender *equity* differs from gender *equality*. Gender equity poses an important question for the classroom dynamic: Do students receive the *right* education to achieve a shared standard of excellence (AAUW, 1998)? Gender equity asserts that males and females do NOT need the same things to achieve shared outcomes. Gender equity is NOT sameness or equality; equity focuses on outcomes—equal access to achievement and opportunity. Hence, equitable education addresses the needs of girls and boys, rather than questioning whether each receives the same thing (AAUW, 1998).

The field of gender equity in education generally acknowledges that equitable classroom environments have the following attributes in common (AAUW, 1992, 1995, 1998; McIntosh, 2000):

- Classrooms are caring communities where individuals feel safe and where understanding is promoted among peers
- Classrooms are free from violence and peer or adult harassment
- Classrooms have routines and procedures that ensure equal access to instructional materials and extracurricular activities

- Classrooms have a "gender agenda," referring to the understanding of stereotyped gendered expectations for students and encouraging full participation of each student, including the expression of non-stereotyped behaviors
- Classrooms address the experiences of students by providing assignments or projects that develop all students' capacity to see their life experiences as part of knowledge, whereby students are authorities of their own experience and contribute to the classroom textbooks by creating "textbooks of their lives" (McIntosh & Style, 1999).

Both in and outside of a schooling context, a substantial focus has been placed on many aspects of the well-being of girls and women, as well as on that of boys and men. Because women, rather than men, traditionally have experienced inequitable treatment and outcomes, and because women's studies is a well-developed field in its own right, most of the gender-equity topics and organizations inside and outside of education focus on females (Klein et al., 2002). However, men's studies and gender studies organizations that focus on men's or boys' issues do exist:

NOMAS (National Organization for Men Against Sexism)
  www.nomas.org
The Society for the Psychological Study of Men and Masculinity, Division 51 of the American Psychological Association
  www.apa.org/about/division/div51 or http://web.indstate.edu/spsmm
The UN Men's Group for Gender Equality
  www.undp.org/gender/programmes/men/men_ge.html

Examining the gender issues in your classroom requires that:

- You explore your students' socialization by observing how they are communicating with each other.
- You evaluate your students' achievement in all subject areas through the lens of gender.
- You ask yourself, "Are the females and males in my classroom limited by the gendered expectations of the school, the society or the particular culture to which they belong?" Asking this question and seeking authentic answers is part of the journey to create a gender-equitable classroom environment.

GENDER EQUITY RESOURCES FOR TEACHERS

American Association of University Women
www.aauw.org
AAUW supports gender equity in numerous ways, and their Web site includes information about educational programs designed to help girls achieve in school.

Campbell-Kibler Associates
www.campbell-kibler.com
This group strives to increase gender and race equity in math, science, and technology education; contact the group about obtaining brochures highlighting their research.

Center for National Origin, Race and Sex Equity
www.nwrel.org/cnorse/
CNORSE, a federally funded educational equity project at the Northwest Regional Education Laboratory, has many resources, including equity-related publications, its own online newsletter, and several equity-related Web site links.

DiversityWeb
www.diversityweb.org/
The Association of American Colleges and Universities and the University of Maryland have designed DiversityWeb, with support from the Ford Foundation, to connect, amplify, and multiply campus diversity efforts through a central location on the Web.

Equity Online
www2.edc.org/WomensEquity/
The national Women's Educational Equity Act (WEEA) Equity Resource Center works to improve educational, social, and economic outcomes for women and girls.

National Women's History Project
www.nwhp.org/
This organization initiated National Women's History Month, now observed each March throughout the United States. Throughout the year, the office serves as a clearinghouse for women's history information, resources, activities, and programming ideas.

References

American Association of University Women Educational Foundation. (1998). *Gender Gaps executive summary*. Washington, DC: Author.

American Association of University Women Educational Foundation. (1995). *How schools shortchange girls: The AAUW report*. Washington, DC: Author.

American Association of University Women Educational Foundation. (1992). *How schools shortchange girls: A study of major findings on girls and education*. Researched by the Wellesley College Center for Research on Women. Washington, DC: Author.

American Association of University Women Educational Foundation. (2001). *Beyond the "gender wars": A conversation about girls, boys, and education*. Washington, DC: Author.

Barman, C. (1997). Students' views of scientists and science: Results from a national study. *Science and Children, 35*(1), 18-24.

Boaler, J. (2002). Paying the price for sugar and spice: Shifting the analytical lens in equity research. *Mathematical Thinking and Learning, 4*, 127-144.

Chapman, A. (1997). *A great balancing act: Equitable education for girls and boys*. Washington, DC: National Association of Independent Schools.

Clewell, B. C., Anderson, B. T., & Thorpe, M. (1992). *Breaking the barriers: Helping female and minority students succeed in mathematics and science*. San Francisco: Jossey-Bass.

Eccles-Parsons, J., Meece, J., Adler, T. F., & Kaczala, C. M. (1982). Sex differences in attributions and learned helplessness. *Sex Roles, 8*, 421-432.

Gallas, K. (1995). *Talking their way into science*. New York: Teachers College Press.

Girls: Drawbacks of early success? (1985, Feb.). *Harvard Education Newsletter*, p. 1.

Klein, S., Ortman, P., with others (1994, Nov.). Continuing the journey toward gender equity. *Educational Researcher, 10*, 13-23.

Klein, S., Ortman, P., & Friedman, B. (2002). What is the field of gender equity in education? Questions & answers. In J. Koch & B. Irby (Eds.), *Defining and redefining gender equity in education* (pp. 3-27). Greenwich, CT: Infoage Publishing.

Koch, J. (1994, October). *Implications of a course on gender and education for changing teacher behavior*. Paper presented at the annual fall conference of the Special Interest Group on Research on Women in Education of the American Educational Research Association, St. Paul, MN.

Koch, J. (1996, April). *A gender study of private school students' attitudes and beliefs about school life*. Paper presented at the annual meeting of the American Educational Research Association, New York.

Koch, J. (2002). Gender issues in the classroom. In I. B. Weiner (Series Ed.) & W. R. Reynolds & G. E. Miller (Vol. Eds.), *Comprehensive handbook of psychology: Vol. 7. Educational psychology* (pp. 259-281). New York: Wiley.

Koch, J. (2005). *Science stories: Science methods for elementary and middle-school teachers* (3rd ed.). Boston: Houghton Mifflin.

Logan, J. (1997). *Teaching stories.* New York: Kodansha Press.

Marshall, C. S., & Reinhartz, J. (1997). Gender issues in the classroom. *Clearing House, 70*(6), 333-337.

McIntosh, P. (2000, May 25). *A learning community with feminist values.* Address at Ewha Womans University, Seoul, South Korea.

McIntosh, P., & Style, E. (1999). Social, emotional and political learning. In J. Cohen (Ed.), *Educations, minds and hearts* (pp. 137-157). New York: Teachers College Press.

National Center for Education Statistics. (n.d.). *Digest of education statistics tables and figures.* Table 125, Table 139. Retrieved August 4, 2004, from http://nces.ed.gov/ programs/digest/d02/ list_tables2.asp#c2_6

Orenstein, P. (1995). *Schoolgirls: Young women, self-esteem and the confidence gap.* New York: Doubleday.

Rowe, M. B. (1987). Wait-time: Slowing down may be a way of speeding up. *American Educator, 11*(1), 38-47.

Sadker, M., & Sadker, D. (1994). *Failing at fairness: How America's schools cheat girls.* New York: Charles Scribner's Sons.

Sanders, J., Koch, J., & Urso, J. (1997). *Gender equity right from the start: Instructional activities for teacher educators in mathematics, science and technology.* Hillsdale, NJ: Lawrence Erlbaum Associates.

Sandler, B., Silverberg, R., & Hall, R. (1996). The chilly classroom climate: A guide to improve the education of women. *AWIS Magazine, 25*(5), 10-11.

Shapka, J. D., & Keating, D. P. (2003). Effects of a girls-only curriculum during adolescence: Performance, persistence, and engagement in mathematics and science. *American Educational Research Journal, 40*(4), 929–960.

Warren-Sams, B. (2001). *Mentors confirm and enhance girls' lives.* Newton, MA: WEEA Equity Resources Center.

Chapter 7
Sexual Diversity Issues in Schools

Deborah A. Byrnes

*I*n a time when educators freely talk about diversity based on a range of characteristics, sexual orientation as a diversity issue is often ignored. Many people operate under the assumption that all people can and should be heterosexual, and thus they do not see sexual orientation as being in the same category as other types of diversity. This assumption that heterosexuality is the only normal, morally acceptable way to be and that anyone who is not heterosexual is deviant, wrong, or immoral is called "heterosexism." A related term, "homophobia," is used to describe the fear and hatred of homosexuality. Homophobia also includes the fear of being perceived as gay or lesbian oneself, often leading to rigid adherence to expected gender-role behavior.

Even in elementary and middle schools, educators cannot ignore the hostility expressed toward homosexuals and people perceived to be homosexual in our communities. Children hear people being called "fags," "homos," "queers," "dykes," and "lesbos." Even if children do not clearly understand the full meaning of these words, they know the terms are meant to be degrading. For example, one commonly heard phrase is "That's so gay," meant to show displeasure and disgust with a situation. Children are quick to pick up on the messages that being gay is a bad thing, particularly if respected adults do not offer counter messages. As vividly shown in Chasnoff and Cohen's 1996 documentary film *It's Elementary: Talking About Gay Issues in School*, elementary students are quite aware of negative societal attitudes toward homosexuals. In Chasnoff and Cohen's documentary, a group of children were asked to create a web of words connected to the term "gay." The children were shockingly aware of the stereotypes and prejudices that abound regarding gay men and lesbians.

The major medical and mental health organizations of the United States have made it clear that variations in sexual orientation are natural and that we should accept this form of diversity, not punish people, seek to change them, or ignore them (Human Rights Watch, 2001). However, sexual orientation prejudice has been particularly difficult to address because not only is it deeply rooted in some people's religious beliefs, but sexuality is also a very personal and private issue. In the past, the issue has been so controversial that many educators have simply chosen not to address it at all (Lipkin, 1999). Discomfort with addressing religious beliefs as well as sexuality has stifled open discussions in school settings. However, society is changing, and as different gay, lesbian, bisexual, and transgender (GLBT) groups fight for fair treatment, equal rights, and the end of harassment and violence, educators are increasingly called upon to help create a more understanding and accepting world for persons who are sexual minorities.

Community standards vary greatly with respect to how openly educators can address issues of sexual orientation in elementary and middle school classrooms. In politically conservative districts, teachers may experience a great deal of uncertainty about how to address homophobia. Some states have laws that prohibit school officials and teachers from doing anything that would be construed as teaching about homosexuality, particularly saying anything about homosexuality that could be perceived as either positive or even neutral (Human Rights Watch, 2001). Some conservative leaders argue that if children are taught to treat homosexuals with respect, it is tantamount to saying it is acceptable to be gay (Macgillivray, 2004). Their solution is to not deal with the topic at all, hoping that GLBT students will stay silent and hidden and that conflict will be avoided. Thus, intolerance prevails.

Even where such conditions exist, educators can take discrete steps to increase tolerance for sexuality differences. A beginning for all teachers, regardless of where they teach, is to become better informed about GLBT issues and what can be done to promote the safety and healthy development of all students. It is hard to imagine a school, even in very conservative areas, where administrators and school board members do not believe that teachers have an obligation to create psychologically and physically safe learning environments for each and every student. Being a support person for youth who are struggling with issues of sexual diversity and confronting harassment and discrimination in schools whenever it occurs is something we all can do.

In this chapter, the acronym GLBT is used interchangeably with the term homosexual. While homosexual is often used as a catch-all term for people who do not identify as strictly heterosexual, the acronym GLBT (gay, lesbian, bisexual, or transgendered) is increasingly being used, as it is more explicitly inclusive of the range of sexual orientations present in the human population. (GLBT is also interchangeable with LGBT; the words making up the acronym are simply reordered.) This chapter will address basic information about sexual diversity issues, debunk common myths regarding sexual orientation, and offer suggestions for how educators can appropriately address heterosexism and homophobia in their schools and community.

The author recognizes that people reading this chapter will bring a range of personal views and attitudes to bear on the topic. Each reader is encouraged to work at distinguishing between his or her own private moral views regarding homosexuality and his or her professional obligation to protect children from prejudice, discrimination, violence, and attacks on their self-esteem. Regardless of personal religious beliefs and opinions, a teacher's primary role in the classroom is to ensure that all students are emotionally and physically safe, and that they are able to learn. If students are made to feel bad, different, or unacceptable, they will not be able to learn in your classroom.

LEARNING ABOUT SEXUAL DIVERSITY

Many prejudices are based on incorrect assumptions about the groups in question. For educators to speak knowledgeably about and respond appropriately to heterosexism and homophobia, they must have an understanding of sexual diversity issues. Hopefully, the information below will serve as a beginning in every reader's search to better understand issues related to sexual orientation.

What Percent of the Population Is GLBT?

Researchers have conducted many studies to determine what percent of the population is GLBT. Estimates of youth in the United States range from a conservative two percent to over 10 percent. The reason for such disparity in estimates has much to do with how homosexuality is defined by the researchers conducting the studies. In some studies, youth are asked to self-identify. Some researchers ask about same-sex romantic attraction, some measure same-sex sexual behavior. In some studies, being unsure about one's sexual orientation (usually labeled as "questioning") may be counted by researchers as same-sex romantic attraction; in others, it is not. Because youth may have little experience to draw upon, and because early adolescence is a time when sexual identity is just beginning to develop, these figures are quite unreliable.

It is also important to understand that when psychologists study sexual orientation, heterosexuality and homosexuality are usually measured on a graduated scale. For example, on the well-known Kinsey scale of sexuality, a score of "0" means one is exclusively heterosexual with no same-sex attraction. A person with a "3" means that person has romantic attractions equally to both same-sex and opposite-sex individuals. A score of "6" means one is exclusively homosexual with no romantic attractions to the opposite sex. An analogy might be the concept of "handedness." Most people are right-handed. They use their right hand for everything (e.g., writing, sports, work). There are, however, a few people who are ambidextrous; they naturally switch from their left to their right hand quite easily, depending upon the activity in which they are engaged. And a small minority of individuals are completely left-handed. As with the right-handed person, these left-handed individuals fail abysmally if asked to use their non-dominant hand for any kind of skilled work or play.

It is important to note that this analogy with handedness is only appropriate with respect to understanding that homosexuality is a naturally occurring human difference. Being forced to use the "wrong" hand may be awkward and annoying, but it does not require the painful rejection of who you are as a person. The effects of being forced to act like someone you are not are devastating.

Research on sexual orientation that seeks a truly representative picture of the population also is hindered by the difficulty in collecting data from randomly selected individuals who are comfortable being totally frank about issues of sexuality. Researchers in this area recognize the problems inherent in data collection on sexual diversity issues. Nevertheless, even the most conservative research groups place the prevalence of homosexuality or bisexuality among sexually active adults in the human population at 2-3 percent for males and 2 percent for females (Cameron, 1993). It is important to note, however, that GLBT support groups adamantly disagree with such low estimates, believing them to be minimizing and misleading. Regardless of the number of GLBT individuals in the general population, it is important to remember that prejudice and discrimination toward individuals who have diverse sexual orientations is still unwarranted.

When Do Youth Begin To Question Their Sexuality?

The sexual messages that youth receive from fashion, music, movies, television, and the Internet encourage them to focus on sexuality and sexual behavior at a fairly young age. Perhaps for this reason, youth in the United States appear to become interested in expressing their own sexuality at a younger age than was true of their parents. With this change, thoughts about sexual orientation and gender identity appear to be occurring earlier as well (Human Rights Watch, 2001). At the same age that some heterosexual youth are engaged in lighthearted teasing about liking a person of the opposite sex, it is not unusual for homosexual youth to become aware that they are attracted to same-sex peers in a way that is different from the majority of their friends (Baker, 2002). On average, same-sex attraction is first remembered as occurring around age 9 for boys and age 10 for girls (Human Rights Watch, 2001). This research has clear implications for teachers, even for those in elementary schools. If you will be teaching children age 9 and above, you will most assuredly, at some time, have students in your classroom for whom sexual orientation is a concern.

What Is It Like in School for Gay and Lesbian Youth?

Children who have different interests and do not meet cultural expectations for gender-specific behavior may experience extreme social pressure. However, many of these children will not grow up to be gay or lesbian. Conversely, some gay and lesbian children feel very similar to their peers while they are growing up, and only as they mature do they realize that they are emotionally and physically attracted to same-sex peers. Overall, however, the research suggests that adults who are gay or lesbian are much more likely than heterosexual adults to report feeling like outsiders even when they were in grade school (Baker, 2002).

Savin-Williams (1996) interviewed young gay males about their early childhood memories. A majority of these young men seemed to be aware of having a strong attraction toward other males even at an early age, although they reported having no sexual connotation to these feelings until puberty. A smaller group were considered effeminate by others and were attracted to activities typically preferred by girls. A third small group seemed unaware of any attraction to same-sex peers until puberty and were often surprised when these feeling emerged.

Boys who early on are identified as being different, and who are in fact homosexual, have the greatest risk of suicide, depression, and other psychological problems (Baker, 2002). The more "femme" a boy is, the tougher it is to be accepted by peers, and the harder it is to escape the aggression of males who see such behavior as a sign of weakness and vulnerability. Unfortunately, little outside help is given to these youth, at school or elsewhere.

Girls are given a little more latitude in their behavior than boys. The girl who likes football and enjoys trucks experiences fewer social sanctions than the boy who enjoys dolls and ballet. Even as adults, lesbians appear to be more accepted than gay males, perhaps because many heterosexual people do not see lesbians as a threat to the male dominance in our society. Still, it is very difficult to be different. How does a 13-year-old girl tell her family that, unlike her peers, she is attracted to girls instead of boys? This is especially difficult if her family members have made derogatory and hurtful comments towards homosexuals in the past.

Learning you are different, that you are part of a minority group to which your family members and friends do not belong, is often frightening and traumatic—especially when you know that this group is disdained by others. GLBT youth are members of a stigmatized group, often with no access to people who can or will provide support, understanding, or a sense of community. Adolescence is already difficult for most children; add the additional stressor of struggling with sexual identity and it is no wonder that these youth may withdraw, isolate themselves, suffer from depression, become suicidal, or use drugs and alcohol to escape from knowing they are different from and offensive to others (Harris, 1997).

The American Academy of Pediatrics, American Counseling Association, American Association of School Administrators, American Federation of Teachers, American Psychological Association, American School Health Association, Interfaith Alliance Foundation, National Association of School Psychologists, National Association of Social Workers, and National Education Association (1999) argue that if others understood that homosexuality is a natural variation in human sexuality, children who exhibit this variation would experience less harm. As educators, it is important that we teach tolerance so that the lives of young gays and lesbians are less stressful, painful, and dangerous.

Sexual Orientation Harassment

In a study that included data from 14 cities, 80 percent of gay, lesbian, and bisexual students reported being victims of anti-gay slurs, 44 percent were threatened, 33 percent were targets of objects thrown at them, and 30 percent were forced to flee to avoid harassment (Checkley, 2001). There is clearly a serious failure on the part of schools to protect students who are homosexual and those who are presumed to be homosexual but are not. While gay bashing escalates as children get older, clear evidence exists that harassment and bullying of children who do not conform to typical gender roles begins in the elementary years (Baker, 2002). Some of the children who are victims of this harassment will grow up to be heterosexuals, others will not. Regardless of their future sexual orientation, all children come away from such events, whether they are victims, victimizers, or observers, with the clear message that if you do not conform to gender expectations, you will pay a heavy price. Some individuals (both heterosexuals and homosexuals) get this message so loud and clear that they repress healthy interests in activities typically associated with the opposite gender for fear that they will be labeled homosexual (Harper, 1992). For example, a boy might shy away from such interests as ballet or clothing design for fear of being considered gay. Some youth have so internalized negative feelings toward homosexuality that the self-hatred and guilt they feel when they realize their own attraction to same-sex peers leads to severe depression, and even suicide (Baker, 2002). Compelling medical evidence links youth suicidality with homosexuality (Remafedi, 1999).

Codes of conduct for males and females tend to be rigid. Girls are expected to be interested in getting boys' attention, attentive to their appearance, and less strong (physically and emotionally). Girls who avoid stereotypically feminine behaviors (such as grooming and fashion concerns) in favor of sports or other stereotypically male interests, especially during the adolescent years, are breaking the "girl" rules and often are teased and excluded by peers and even some adults.

Boys are expected to be athletic, unemotional, and strong. Boys who cry easily, prefer not to engage in sports, or enjoy stereotypically female interests are often taunted. The message for boys is: You are not acting like other boys or you are acting like a girl; therefore, you must be homosexual. The most disparaging name-calling that boys report is references to their sexual orientation, such as "homo," "fag," and "queer" (Crocco, 2002). Such taunting often leads to fighting or becoming sexually active at a young age to prove one isn't homosexual. Unfortunately, adults also model disparaging behaviors. Imagine the message even young boys get when a coach yells out, "If you can't kick that ball harder than that, you better go home and play with your sister's dolls." Such interactions tell all who are present that boys must live up to certain male expectations or risk being labeled as inferior (because they are now acting like girls).

The National Association of School Psychologists (1999) gives a clear message to schools that harassment and discrimination against sexual-minority students are unacceptable and must be met with consequences and education for the perpetrator, and support and protection for the victim. Many schools have clear policies prohibiting any form of harassment toward sexual-minority students. Unfortunately, when underlying attitudes that lead to overt harassment are not addressed, the harassing behaviors may simply become more covert.

While boys are likely to physically threaten peers perceived as homosexuals, girls are more likely to engage in social aggression when they seek to reject a peer (Simmons, 2002). Such behaviors include whispering (name-calling in secret), rumor spreading, alliance building, note passing with the intent to create anxiety for someone else, humor at someone else's expense, or nonverbal gesturing. Simmons contends that teachers are likely to miss this type of socially aggressive behavior because it is almost invisible and generally undisruptive. It takes incredible courage for a lesbian student experiencing such aggression to either confront or ignore it. Being excluded and isolated in subtle but clear ways is a deeply humiliating experience. Unfortunately, gay and lesbian students often sense that there are no rules against this type of social cruelty and that teachers are either clueless about its occurrence or do not care. An apathetic attitude can easily be interpreted by victims and victimizers as support for discrimination.

You may or may not have a student in your classroom at this time who has or will eventually self-identify as GLBT; however, statistically, it is highly likely that you will have a student in your classroom who has a close relative or family friend who is GLBT. The Human Rights Watch (2001) estimates the United States has somewhere between two and eight million lesbian or gay parents. Add GLBT siblings to the equation, and it becomes clear that many students have close caring relationships with people who are homosexual. Heterosexual children in such families are often vulnerable to the same hostilities that homosexuals themselves receive. Blumenfeld (1992) tells the poignant story of a young heterosexual girl who was continuously teased throughout her school years about having a "faggot" brother and taunted with questions about whether she was "like her brother." Peer pressure and fear of becoming a target herself led her to openly reject her brother. No child should be asked to choose between caring about family members and being accepted at school.

Homophobia can put children in the position of being secretive about family members. Teachers and/or parents, because they know that peers and adults will be cruel if they know the truth, may even ask children to lie about family members who are GLBT. A child might be told not to talk about certain family members to anyone or to tell a lie (e.g., "I live with mom and my aunt"). Thus, homophobia can encourage deception and create anxiety not only for GLBT individuals but also for their loved ones.

Religion and Homosexuality

Homosexuality is an incredibly divisive and controversial issue within many institutions of religion today. Some religious groups believe that their holy writings are clear on the issue of homosexuality, viewing homosexuality as a sin and condemning it. Other religious groups believe that homosexuality is not a sin unless it is acted upon. Thus, homosexuals are shown acceptance, but they are counseled to make a commitment to lifelong celibacy. Still other religious groups have accepted homosexuals into their church and some even have allowed them to be ordained into leadership positions (Gollnick & Chinn, 2004).

Religious leaders who are more accepting of homosexuality suggest that while scriptures exist that have been interpreted to support attacks on homosexuality, the overwhelming religious message of sacred writings, such as the Bible, is one of acceptance and love for one another. Other religious leaders teach that their church's holy writings are clear with regards to homosexuality and must be interpreted literally. As teachers, it is important to recognize that children will come to school with varying religious views on homosexuality. While religious viewpoints cannot be banned from discussion, teachers need to situate these discussions within the core democratic values of liberty, tolerance, and equality (Lipkin, 1999). Stated more simply, in a democratic nation, it is not okay to create an uncomfortable, discriminatory environment for other students, even if your actions are based on religious convictions.

It is important to recognize that this is not the first time in the history of the United States when religious leaders have weighed in with divergent views on human rights and civil rights issues. Past conflicts concerned slavery, women's suffrage, racial segregation, and interracial marriage (Haynes, 2002). Both sides quoted extensively from the Bible to support their positions. For example, many Christians honestly believed that slavery was morally right and that to oppose slavery was a sin. Slavery was considered to be the natural order of things and scripture from the Bible was used to support the practice. In contrast, abolitionist ministers used different scripture readings as they worked hard to encourage their congregations to rise up against slavery. They chose religious scriptures that supported their efforts to gain greater human and civil rights for all.

MYTHS ABOUT HOMOSEXUALITY

Many myths continue to influence public views on homosexuality. Becoming informed about these myths helps reduce heterosexism and homophobia. Some of the most persistent myths are explored on the following pages.

Myth 1: Homosexuality Is a Choice

The causes of homosexuality are not completely understood. However, what is known scientifically suggests that sexual orientation (for the vast majority of people) is not something a person chooses; it is something that develops over time. Just as you do not choose to be heterosexual, you do not choose to be homosexual (Hewitt, 2002). That is why the term "sexual orientation" is greatly preferred to the term "sexual preference." We cannot point to a single cause for homosexuality. It appears to result from such varied factors as prenatal or postnatal hormonal influences, brain differences, genetics, early socialization experiences, temperament, as well as other yet unknown factors (Baker, 2002, p. 23).

Sexual orientation is sometimes compared to handedness. The biological basis for hand-edness is also poorly understood and, like sexual orientation, a number of developmental influences have been proposed, in addition to social and cultural factors (Coren, 1993). Interestingly, it was not that long ago that some teachers and parents insisted that children use only their right hands for certain activities, like writing. Many senior citizens can still re-count stories of left-handers having their left hands tied behind their backs to force them to become right-handed. Left-handedness was considered to be an inferior trait and some reli-gious persons believed it to be a sign that the person would work as a servant of the devil. Fortunately, science validated the normalcy of left-handedness and the idea of "hand-switch-ing" therapy is no longer considered healthful or reasonable. The more serious and damag-ing rejection of GLBT persons—rejection that prevents many persons from loving and living openly and honestly in their families and communities—continues to occur in society on a regular basis.

Myth 2: People Who Are Homosexual Are Mentally Ill

The American Medical Association, American Academy of Pediatrics, American Psychiatric Association, and American Psychological Association have all taken stands in proclaiming that homosexuality is not an illness (Baker, 2002). They also have stated that reparative therapy (therapy that attempts to change a person's sexual orientation) can be harmful and is not supported by the medical and psychiatric literature (American Academy of Pediatrics et al., 1999). Unfortunately, even after the most prestigious psychological and psychiatric organizations in the United States have taken a clear stand that homosexuality is a natural variation in human sexuality, and is not an indicator that a person is sick or mentally devi-ant, many people persist in calling homosexuals sick.

Myth 3: People Who Are Gay or Lesbian Will Molest Children

The vast majority of homosexuals, as with heterosexuals, believe that sexual contact be-tween children and adults is horrifying. Pedophilia, the desire to have sexual contact with children, has no relationship to sexual orientation.

Myth 4: Homosexuals Will Convert Others to Their "Ways"

No scientifically valid evidence suggests that one person can change another person's sexual orientation. Sexual orientation does not appear to be amenable to change. If it were, reparative therapy would be effective for homosexuals. Despite claims by some individuals who have profited greatly from endorsing such therapy for homosexuals, when objective, highly qualified scientists conduct objective research studies on repara-tive therapy, long-term healthy change is not supported (American Academy of Pediat-rics et al., 1999). Given that medical researchers have concluded that reparative therapy is not effective in changing homosexuals into heterosexuals, the reverse is probably also true; namely, that homosexuals would be unsuccessful at converting heterosexuals to homosexuality.

Myth 5: More People Are Becoming Homosexual

Homosexuals constitute a small portion of all societies. There will always be people who fall in love with members of the same gender. There will always be children who will grow up to be lesbian or gay. They do not grow up to be homosexual because some person has perverted or converted them, nor will they disappear because some people in our communities want them to disappear. The *visibility* of homosexuals in any given society, however, does change. In societies and communities where homosexuals are not discriminated against, homosexuals feel freer to live their lives in the open. As the presence of gay and lesbian rights groups grows, in the same way as other civil rights groups have grown in the past, more homosexual people will feel comfortable "coming out" and not hiding their sexual orientation. Homosexuals and heterosexuals share a desire for the freedom to be authentic, go places with their partners, make commitments to a special person, and plan for a life of safety, happiness, and well-being. Research (Lipkin, 1999) also suggests that as more homosexuals "come out" to people who already know and care about them, tolerance for homosexuality grows.

Myth 6: Homosexuality Is Just About Sex

Many people think only about the sexual aspects of homosexuality. It is important to realize that homosexual attraction, like heterosexual attraction, is generally about much more than meeting one's physical/sexual needs. Homosexual attraction is just as much about meeting needs for intimacy, connectedness, closeness, commitment, self-revelations, and bonding as heterosexual attraction is (Holben, 1999).

Myth 7: Out of Respect for Religious Beliefs, Schools Should Avoid Addressing the Topic of Homosexuality

As Haynes outlines in his chapter on religious diversity in this book, respect for religious diversity is critical and attacks on religious theology do not belong in the classroom. People have a right to their religious beliefs. This does not mean, however, that a teacher should sanction or tolerate actions that show disrespect for, or violate the rights of, others (Brandt, 1994). Diverse religious beliefs need to be respected, but this does not mean that religious views outweigh a teacher's civic responsibility to protect the rights of all students. Discriminatory comments and actions, whether they have their roots in religious beliefs or not, are unacceptable. Educating about homophobia in a way that focuses on the democratic values of liberty, equality, and tolerance for diversity is critical.

Myth 8: I've Never Known a GLBT Person

Never knowing a GLBT person is highly unlikely, given even the most conservative statistics on the prevalence of homosexuality within the human population. One's sexual orientation is totally different from other forms of minority status because sexual orientation can be hidden. And, unless one does something to call attention to one's sexual orientation, one is generally assumed to be heterosexual. Many people, including some very famous individuals, have lived their lives as GLBTs in relative secrecy. Sexual orientation can be invisible to the general public. Given the social stigma attached to being homosexual, gay men and lesbians often maintain a public image of heterosexuality, even creating fake heterosexual relationships to keep others from knowing their sexual orientation.

MAKING A DIFFERENCE

Baker (2002) contends that what one person says or does about homophobia over time will make a difference in all of our lives. As parents, teachers, and community members, we can each help lessen homophobia and make the world a safer and kinder place for GLBT youth and their families. We all need to take steps, even if these steps push our comfort levels at times, to educate others about how our treatment of sexual-minority members reflects our overall humanity.

Beginning Steps

Below are several suggestions for ways educators can begin to take action. These are just a beginning. Many resources are available to extend your thinking in this area. See, for example, *Beyond Diversity Day: A Q&A on Gay and Lesbian Issues in Schools* (Lipkin, 2003) and *Sexual Orientation and School Policy: A Practical Guide for Teachers, Administrators, and Community Activists* (Macgillivray, 2004).

- Check state and district policies regarding how sexual orientation issues may be addressed in your school. As needed, inquire as to how such policies can be improved. Work to establish policies that protect children from anti-gay/lesbian harassment, violence, and discrimination.
- Help to educate others. Help people connect the positive values they hold regarding compassion, fairness, equality, and tolerance to people who have different sexual orientations.
- Work on negative attitudes you might hold by becoming informed about gay/lesbian/bisexual people in your community. Consider attending a gay/lesbian organization meeting or an ally meeting such as PFLAG (Parents, Families and Friends of Lesbians and Gays). Prejudices are often broken down through getting to know each other in a positive environment.
- Speak out against homophobia. Challenge homophobic name-calling and nonverbal gestures and expressions, as well as other forms of harassment. Discourage jokes about people who are GLBT and refrain from telling them yourself.
- Help promote sensitivity and training programs for school-district personnel at all levels of schooling.
- Don't assume everyone is heterosexual unless they tell you otherwise. Start being aware of how you can use inclusive language. Use "parent" instead of "mother" or "father," "partner" instead of "wife" or "husband," "date" instead of "boyfriend" or "girlfriend."
- Provide support for youth who have experienced gender-orientation stereotyping and harassment. Let them know that you will not judge them negatively and that you will work to ensure their psychological and social well-being, and their physical safety.

Working With Lesbian- and Gay-Parented Families

A growing number of gay- and lesbian-headed families are choosing to be open about their family composition. Thus, a growing number of children in our school are living in openly alternative families (Casper & Shultz, 1999). Because it is important for all children to feel that their parents are involved in their education and are welcome at school, teachers must consider how inclusive their schools appear to all families.

Teachers can help gay and lesbian parents feel comfortable about being involved at school by examining their parent involvement activities and classroom practices for instances of "heteronormativity." In other words, the teacher must move beyond previously held assumptions that all parents are heterosexual. Simple changes can help alternative family parents and children feel more included. For example, using the term "parents" when talking with children is much more inclusive than referring to "moms" and "dads." Volunteer forms that only seek information for "mother" and "father" make it difficult for gay- or lesbian-headed families to respond. Providing blanks for "parents" or "guardians" to fill in is more inclusive for all kinds of families.

Teachers who have children from alternative families in their classroom need to recognize that assignments that include the sharing of family events and pictures can create excellent opportunities to illustrate how much diversity exists in family composition. However, the wishes of each child regarding what will be shared and how should always be honored. Members of alternative families do not necessarily want to be used as examples of family diversity.

The only way to know how best to work with each and every alternative family is to communicate with them openly and honestly. Gay and lesbian parents have typically given a great deal of thought as to how to interact as a family with a world that is, all too often, prejudiced against them. An excellent resource for teachers to gain more insights into these issues is Casper and Shultz's (1999) book *Gay Parents/Straight Schools: Building Communication and Trust.*

Enforcing the Law

The scope of anti-discrimination law is currently having some bearing on how schools address issues of sexual-orientation harassment. A number of school districts and officials have had to pay large settlements for failure to protect youth from harassment that is based on sexual orientation. Lipkin (1999) cites several legal cases that involved the sexual-orientation harassment of children even as young as 11 and 12. In these cases, teachers, administrators, and school systems were cited for failure to protect students from repeated acts of aggressive, homophobic behavior. While some school officials would like to blame only the harassers for these problems, the courts are increasingly implicating schools as partners in the offense when school officials have demonstrated "indifference" by not taking clear action to prevent such behavior. A recent harassment case in San José, California, resulted in a $1.1-million settlement that also required the school district to implement mandatory annual training regarding sexual-orientation and gender-identity discrimination for all school personnel, as well as for middle school and high school students (Romney, 2004).

Schools also have been chastised for having anti-harassment policies in place, but failing to sensitize teachers and staff regarding the "spirit" of these policies. In some schools, perpetrators of harassment are punished, but no guidance is given to assist faculty and staff in how to educate all students about basic human rights that apply to all individuals, regardless of sexual orientation.

While legal cases can act as an impetus for change, we all have a responsibility to support fair and just treatment in schools so that such cases are unnecessary. Stopping prejudice is not easy and we must all give a great deal of thought to how we can work with students whose homophobic actions are often supported by peers and the larger community.

What Can I Say?

Many well-meaning adults have felt that they should have said something when a homophobic remark was shared (by a peer, parent, or student), but they just weren't sure what to say. Before they knew it, the time to intervene had passed. Below are examples of frequently heard comments and possible responses. Many of the ideas and responses for these dialogues were adapted from Berzon's (1996) book, *Setting Them Straight: You Can Do Something About Bigotry and Homophobia in Your Life.* While reading this section, remember the responses are just possibilities to get you thinking about how you might respond. The Gay, Lesbian and Straight Education Network (GLSEN) suggests that challenging inappropriate remarks openly and sensitively, as opposed to pulling an individual aside, can be important. If other people heard the offensive remark, then it is also important that they hear a response intended to educate and encourage tolerance.

"That's so gay" (meant as a derogatory assessment of a given event). "Excuse me, but your comment really disturbs me. When you say something is 'gay' to make the point that you find it bad, distasteful, or disgusting, you are not only offending people who are gay or lesbian, but also those people who have friends and loved ones who are homosexual."

"Well, if people are homosexual, they should keep it to themselves. There's no need for the rest of us to even know." "When you ask gays and lesbians not to be seen or heard, you are asking them to see themselves as abnormal, sick human beings, who should be hidden from view. This simply isn't fair."

"There seems like there are more and more homosexuals these days." "There aren't more gay people around, it's just that there are gay and lesbian people who feel comfortable not hiding who they are. They want to be able to live normal lives."

"I don't want anything to do with them. I'll probably get AIDS if I spend time around them." "AIDS is a virus that is not carried in the air. It is transmitted by unprotected sexual activity with a person who has AIDS or by sharing needles or getting infected blood transfusions with such a person."

"Discussions about homosexuality don't belong in school." "Homosexuality is already being talked about in schools by children. Teachers have a responsibility to respond to their students' comments by presenting age-appropriate information that discourages the development of homophobic thinking and actions."

"Talking about homosexuality in school will turn kids into homosexuals." "Education about homosexuality cannot cause a change in sexual orientation. It may, however, help students who are struggling with their sexual identities and help eliminate the stereotyping and bullying they often encounter."

"I don't know anyone who is homosexual." "Chances are that you know people who you think are heterosexual but are not. They simply haven't been comfortable in telling you of their orientation. Some GLBT individuals hide their sexual orientation from others, even their friends, co-workers, and family members, because they fear they will be rejected."

"Homosexuals are sick." "Being homosexual is not a choice. It's a natural and normal way for some people to be. Every major mental health organization has agreed that gays and lesbians are just as mentally healthy as heterosexuals. What is normal for a homosexual person is to be emotionally and physically attracted to a same-sex partner. Homosexuality is not a psychological disturbance."

"Homosexuals are a threat to family values." "Homosexuals are members of families and, like heterosexuals, they care about such values as loyalty, trust, love, and commitment."

"It might be best if kids who are openly GLBT went to alternative schools of some kind." "Sending GLBT kids away gives everyone in the school the message that they don't belong. They have a right to feel as comfortable in our community as anyone else. We aren't helping GLBT youth when we reject them in our schools."

"What does it mean to be homosexual?" (Asked by a young child.) *"Sometimes people of the same sex choose to make a life together. A person who is homosexual is a man who falls in love with another man or a woman who falls in love with another woman."*

"Stop acting so gay." (Stated by a child.) "It sounds like you are using the word 'gay' to make someone else feel bad. When you use the word 'gay' in that way, you are using it as a put-down. Not only is it meant to be hurtful to your friend, it is hurtful and disrespectful to people who are gay or lesbian. Just like other name calling, using the word 'gay' as a put-down is not allowed."

When responding to homophobic or heterosexist comments, try to respond in ways that show what you are *for,* instead of what you are *against.* Endeavor to appeal to people's higher principles whenever possible. Pluralism is a great challenge. The people in our communities must learn to be comfortable with heterogeneity, whether it be racial, ethnic, religious, linguistic, income, or sexual orientation. Becoming comfortable with differences takes time and effort. Developing a capacity in our youth to work and live in a pluralistic community, and a strengthening commitment to the civil and human rights of all citizens, should be central to every educator's purpose.

RESOURCES

A growing number of online resources can assist teachers in better understanding the issues that GLBT youth confront as they mature. Below are several well-known ones.

GLAAD (Gay & Lesbian Alliance Against Defamation). This organization promotes accurate and inclusive media images that can help shatter stereotypes about homosexuality. www.glaad.org

GLSEN (The Gay, Lesbian and Straight Education Network). GLSEN is the leading national organization fighting to end anti-gay bias in K-12 schools. Excellent resources for teachers. www.glsen.org

HRC (Human Rights Campaign). This large national organization focuses its efforts on gay, lesbian, bisexual, and transgender equal rights. www.hrc.org

PFLAG (Parents, Families and Friends of Lesbians and Gays). PFLAG works to create a society that is healthy and respectful of human diversity. Its project "Safe Schools for Our Children" was developed specifically to help teachers and school administrators with issues confronting gay and lesbian youth. www.pflag.org

References

American Academy of Pediatrics, American Counseling Association, American Association of School Administrators, American Federation of Teachers, American Psychological Association, American School Health Association, Interfaith Alliance Foundation, National Association of School Psychologists, National Association of Social Workers, & National Education Association. (1999). *Just the facts about sexual orientation and youth: A primer for principals, educators and school personnel.* Washington, DC: Authors.

Baker, J. M. (2002). *How homophobia hurts children: Nurturing diversity at home, at school, and in the community.* New York: Harrington Park.

Berzon, B. (1996). *Setting them straight: You can do something about bigotry and homophobia in your life.* New York: Plume.

Brandt, R. (1994). On educating for diversity: A conversation with James A. Banks. *Educational Leadership, 51*(8), 28-31.

Blumenfeld, W. J. (1992). Introduction. In W. J. Blumenfeld (Ed.), *Homophobia: How we all pay the price* (pp. 1-19). Boston: Beacon.

Cameron, K. (1993). *The numbers game: What percentage of the population is gay? Family Research Group.* Accessed online on June 1, 2004, from www.familyresearchinst.org/FRI_AIM_Talk.html

Casper, V., & Schultz, S. (1999). *Gay parents/straight schools: Building communication and trust.* New York: Teachers College.

Chasnoff, D., & Cohen, H. S. (1996). *It's elementary: Talking about gay issues in school [Film].* San Francisco: Women's Educational Media.

Checkley, K. (2001). A persistent intolerance. *Education Update, 43*(2), 5.

Coren, S. (1993). *Left-hander syndrome: The causes and consequences of left-handedness.* New York: Vintage.

Crocco, M. S. (2002). Homophobic hallways: Is anyone listening? *Theory and Research in Social Education, 30*(2), 217-232.

Gollnick, D. M., & Chinn, P. C. (2004). *Multicultural education in a pluralistic society* (6th ed.). Upper Saddle River, NJ: Pearson.

Harper, P. B. (1992). Racism and homophobia as reflections on their perpetrators. In W. J. Blumenfeld (Ed.), *Homophobia: How we all pay the price* (pp. 57-66). Boston: Beacon.

Harris, M. B. (Ed.) (1997). *School experiences of gay and lesbian youth: The invisible minority.* New York: Haworth.

Haynes, S. R. (2002). *Noah's curse: The biblical justification of American slavery.* New York: Oxford University.

Hewitt, J. A. (2002). *The architecture of thought: A new look at human evolution.* London: Holmhurst House.

Holben, L. R. (1999). *What Christians think about homosexuality.* Richland Hills, TX: Bibal Press.

Human Rights Watch. (2001). *Hatred in the hallways: Violence and discrimination against lesbian, gay, bisexual, and transgender students in U.S. schools.* Accessed on June 1, 2004, from www.hrw.org/reports/2001/uslgbt/Final-04.htm#P558_78365

Lipkin, A. (1999). *Understanding homosexuality, changing schools: A text for teachers, counselors, and administrators.* Boulder, CO: Westview.

Lipkin, A. (2003). *Beyond diversity day: A Q&A on gay and lesbian issues in schools.* Lanham, MD: Rowman & Littlefield.

Macgillivray, I. K. (2004). *Sexual orientation and school policy: A practical guide for teachers, administrators, and community activists.* Lanham, MD: Rowman & Littlefield.

National Association of School Psychologists. (1999). *Position statement on gay, lesbian, and bisexual youth.* Accessed on July 23, 2004, from www.nasponline.org/information/pospaper_glb.html

Remafedi, G. (1999). Sexual orientation and youth suicide. *msJAMA, 282*, 1291-1292.

Romney, L. (2004, January 7). Ex-students settle harassment suit. *Los Angeles Times*, p. B1.

Savin-Williams, R. C. (1996). Memories of childhood and early adolescent sexual feelings among gay and bisexual boys: A narrative approach. In R. C. Savin-Williams & K. M. Cohen (Eds.), *The lives of lesbians, gays, and bisexuals: Children to adults* (pp. 94-109). Fort Worth, TX: Harcourt Brace.

Simmons, R. (2002). *Odd girl out: The hidden culture of aggression in girls.* New York: Harcourt.

Chapter 8
Integrating Anti-Bias Education

James J. Barta and Corinne Mount Pleasant-Jetté

Simple lessons last a lifetime! By inviting children to explore and understand the cultural heritage and traditions of their neighbors, classmates, and friends, the teacher opens a window of opportunity to instill respect and denounce prejudice and discrimination. Anti-bias educators play a crucial role in the formation of nonprejudicial attitudes and in supporting respectful behaviors among schoolchildren. Children's perception of difference, as well as their capacity to accept it as a positive element of society, is heavily influenced by the messages they receive at home, through mass media, and, particularly, within the school community. As they interact daily with teachers, children should experience learning opportunities that will shape their future abilities to appreciate diversity, acknowledge difference, and respect the multicultural fabric of society.

These learning opportunities can be provided directly by integrating anti-bias learning across the curriculum. Or, they can be provided through specific learning activities focused on cultural differences. Moreover, by weaving a thread of multicultural awareness into lessons of math, science, music, social studies, art, and language arts, the teacher broadens and enriches critical thinking around the issue of difference, which will grow in complexity as the child matures. Whether the exposure to diversity comes in the form of integrated science lessons or through the study of a speech by Martin Luther King, Jr., children can gain crucial insights into respect for difference within either context. Simple lessons last a lifetime.

While the suggested approach of cross-curricular, anti-bias learning offers a pedagogically sound means of sensitizing young minds to diversity, teachers also can adopt specific lessons and activities that promote respect for difference among their students. Appreciation of difference can become a topic for conversation while varied species of plants grow and thrive together in a terrarium, multi-colored threads compose a tapestry, or brilliant mosaic tiles reveal an intricate and beautiful design. For some teachers, placing a two-quart jar of multi-colored jelly beans on a classroom shelf can prompt a simple discussion of what life would be like in the absence of difference or diversity. Every child, particularly those from ethnic-minority groups or those who possess different levels of ability, can identify with the concept of not belonging to some larger group. If the teacher stresses the advantage and desirability of variety and difference, the concept of a monocultural, singular, and non-differentiated community can easily be understood as undesirable. After all, who wants a jar exclusively filled with green jelly beans?

While the multicultural emphasis in contemporary education is well-intentioned, it too often fails to address people's prejudiced and discriminatory behavior when responding to group differences. For example, teachers often select literature for their classrooms that describes a number of diverse populations. Stories about children of many racial/ethnic groups and of children with disabilities may be commonly used. Current textbooks show boys and girls of color involved in meaningful daily activities and free of stereotypic gender-related job roles. Is the presentation of these differences enough? People saying or doing things differently are not the real issues. If group variations were viewed as merely different ways that people do the same things, then inequity and prejudice would not exist. It is the biased responses to variations that pose problems. Judgments about diversity, not diversity itself, are the cause of the turmoil (Derman-Sparks & Phillips, 1997).

The goal of the anti-bias educator is to help all children learn to respect differences and work to identify and reduce oppressive attitudes and behaviors (Derman-Sparks, 1991). Educators may be concerned that anti-bias instruction is just one more element to add to an already overloaded schedule. Teachers must know, however, that anti-bias teaching is the right thing to do. Rather than being additive, anti-bias education must become seamlessly infused with the ongoing class curriculum as it becomes integrated into other critical academic content. Rather than minimizing other educational goals, the integration of anti-bias curriculum can enrich the content. Through anti-bias curriculum, children can develop the knowledge, attitudes, and skills that are vital for a smoothly functioning society of diverse citizenry (Banks et al., 2001).

LESSONS IN ANTI-BIAS EDUCATION

The authors of the preceding chapters have described ways teachers can help illuminate our common bonds, validate the experiences of all children, and empower the learner to question and challenge prejudice and discrimination. The anti-bias integration lessons and activities for elementary and middle school children described in this chapter will help teachers explore the interrelations between subject areas and an anti-bias perspective (Pappas, Kiefer, & Levstik, 1999).

Mathematics

All humans have the potential for developing ways (consistent with their culture and environment) to understand and apply their mathematical reasoning as they tackle the problems of daily living. In most elementary math curricula, however, mathematics is presented as an enterprise removed from everyday life. Moreover, the significant contributions of women and non-Europeans are seldom discussed. Mathematicians mentioned in textbooks are usually male and European (e.g., Pythagoras, Thales, Euclid), and this has the effect of distorting children's knowledge about how math has evolved and who contributed to this evolution (Barta et al., 2001). Students who harbor such misconceptions may develop the perception that since people of their cultural communities are not recognized for their mathematical intelligence and achievements, then they may be excused for having a limited mathematical understanding. Many of these children do not believe that they are mathematically capable because they are continually exposed to subtle curricular messages that tell them otherwise. Teachers seldom describe the rich mathematical heritage of many cultures (Cajete, 1999). Children learn about only one system of mathematical knowledge and consequently dismiss mathematics developed and used by minority cultures (Joseph, 2000).

Children need to understand that each group's mathematical contributions reflect a link between the need for and the use of the mathematical technique within the context of the culture that developed it (Ascher, 2002; D'Ambrosio, 2001). Several "real world" examples can be used to make this point. Masingila (1994), for example, describes the mathematical inventiveness of carpet layers who develop their own techniques for accurately carpeting irregularly shaped areas of floors. Brazilian street children who struggle to earn a living selling gum and candy have also developed nonstandard, yet sophisticated and reliable, procedures for mentally computing change for their customers (Saxe, 1988).

Culturally Relevant Problems. Educators can help children understand the cultural context of mathematics by challenging them to develop mathematical problems that reflect their own experiences. Students may create culturally specific problems around games or sports, the production and harvesting of local crops, handicrafts, cooking, or shopping. Teachers can help children understand that all people use mathematics, but may use it in different ways and for different purposes.

For exceptional students, who often learn math in resource rooms removed from the regular classroom and curriculum, this problem-focused, culturally relevant instruction has important implications. It has been the author's experience that special needs children begin to realize greater success when the remedial instruction is less skills-directed and more process-oriented, using situations the children find meaningful. They learn that they are already problem solvers; thus, their individual approaches, experiences, and understandings are validated.

Math With a Message. Mathematics, when seen from a culturally relevant perspective, becomes something all people do in everyday life. Rather than portray math as a subject the Greeks invented only for the sophisticated, mathematics becomes an endeavor in which all human beings have always participated (Zaslavsky, 1996). This perspective shows that all humans have the potential to develop ways (consistent with their culture and environment) to understand and apply mathematical reasoning as they tackle the problems of daily living. When this is understood, students begin to see how bias plays an important role in maintaining a misinformed perspective of what math is and who is capable of doing it. Educators can create anti-bias mathematics curriculum by developing mathematical activities about virtually any aspect of culture related to an ethnic group.

Dancing Numbers. Elmer Ghostkeeper, a Metis educator from Alberta, Canada, suggests that some "native kids struggle with mathematics because for them, the numbers don't dance" (E. Ghostkeeper, personal communication, February 14, 2001). Some children feel disconnected from the learning and use of mathematics because they develop no relationship to what is being studied. They do not hear stories of the mathematical accomplishments of people like themselves and may come to believe that they also lack mathematical competence. Ironically, it seems that sometimes children learn as much from what we do not say as from what is discussed.

"Dancing Numbers" (Barta & Shockey, in review) is an approach to teaching mathematics that makes specific, overt connections to Native traditions, activities, beliefs, and values, and incorporates aspects of an indigenous world view. Mathematics as typically taught in our classrooms carries subtle yet powerful cultural "lessons" illustrating a Western way of looking at the world. In such a world (Ka'a, 1976), thinking is valued for its ability to be "objective" and "measurable." Topics are dissected into isolated lessons where the parts become more important than the whole. Indigenous worldviews tend to focus on relationships between the learner(s) and what is being learned and the development of individual understanding and meaning. While Native students may think in "native ways," the mathematical instruction they receive often does not include connections to their lived experience or ways of knowing (Barta, 1999). Bias in believing that we all "see" the world similarly or that a Western way of knowing is somehow best only places these students and others like them at a significant disadvantage. If these students are to succeed in such instructional environments, they often must give up who they are. Rather than helping to foster increased student competence and confidence, such a narrow instructional perspective can undermine students' progress and achievement.

Native American beadwork is an activity many Native students have seen or experienced. The dance regalia often seen at powwows are typically adorned with brilliantly colored beads in a myriad of patterns. Beadwork has a long history and is a craft practiced by most Native American groups. Historically, items for daily or for ceremonial use were decorated with colors and patterns that told a story or denoted significance.

The bead patterns used by various tribal members can help distinguish tribal affiliations. Even within the same tribe, variations occur as the artists illustrate their own individuality and intentions through the color of beads they select and the geometry of the patterns they create. For many, beadworking is a spiritual activity.

Sometimes you dream the designs you are beading. The designs sometimes will come to you in your dreaming and you get up [and] write it down. Some people see the dream as a gift that was given to them. Beautiful beadwork symbolizes your respect to God, your Creator. We believe the Creator is a colorful person and is good. Everything He makes is colorful, and that is why we also like to express ourselves that way. (F. Jenks, personal communication, January 15, 2001)

Beadworking requires one to think mathematically. Beadwork provides a hands-on demonstration of math in action and can be used as an effective vehicle for teaching mathematics. The mathematical connections to Native American beadwork are many and incorporate lessons involving all five of the content standards of the National Council of Teachers of Mathematics (2000): numbers and operations, algebra, geometry, measurement, and data analysis and probability. Students can learn about the basic operations of addition, subtraction, multiplication, and division. They can explore concepts involving shapes and symmetry. Fractions, percentages, perimeter, and area concepts also can be studied. There is virtually no mathematical concept appropriate for elementary students that cannot be illustrated using beadwork. In the example below, young children begin creating a beadwork pattern by coloring in squares representing beads on the grid. They consider the story they are "telling" through their pattern, count and calculate the numbers of each color of beads, and later represent the numbers in a graph. Suggested directions to students are:

1. Native American beadwork uses designs and colors to tell a story that was in the mind of the beadworker who made it. Think of a story you want to tell by using colors you select and patterns you create. Color in the grid to create your story and design. Keep this design handy, because you will use it for a number of other math activities.

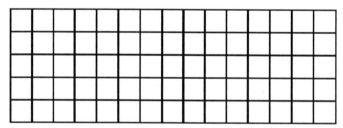

2. Write about the story your beadwork tells.

3. Place a bead in each grid square to match the color of the square in your design. After the design has been filled, sort the beads used into groups according to color.

4. Count the number of beads of each color you have used and write that number next to the color name below:

Red_____   White_____   Black_____   Yellow_____
Dark Blue_____   Light Blue _____   Dark Green_____   Light Green_____
Other Color_____   Other Color _____

This activity can be extended through children's literature to examine additional Native American cultural practices and values. In the book *Rainy's Powwow* (Raczek, 1999), for example, Rainy, a young Native girl, is attending her first powwow. This is the story of a young dancer who learns more about the powwow and her traditional ways as she faces the challenges of self-discovery and family responsibility. Students who may not previously have understood that Native cultures incorporate a variety of mathematical concepts and applications in their lives can gain new appreciation for the many uses of mathematics by Native peoples.

Art

Jane Rhoades-Hudak grew up in Appalachia among people for whom art was not just a subject or an activity, but also an expression of their mountain culture. The wooden and metal artifacts they created, today considered collectibles, primarily served a utilitarian purpose, yet were also pleasing to behold. They were crafted of materials indigenous to the region, using skills that had been handed down over generations.

An examination of any culture shows that the creation of art is an important aspect in helping to convey a sense of the people, their traditions, and their values; an understanding that words alone may fail to adequately communicate. Although all cultures produce art, not all art is valued by mainstream society as being worthy of the same distinction or praise. The works may represent equally high degree of skill, but the culture(s) they represent may be viewed through a biased lens.

The ballet, the symphony, and expensively framed oil portraits in major art museums all denote an air of high culture and good taste. Creators of such art were formally trained in a particular style that is reflective of a European history and people. To enjoy this art, one often must pay to view it and dress and behave in a manner that is considered cultured and dignified. Powerful organizations use their political and social influence to promote "their art" and they deny funds when the art deviates too far from what they consider to be socially acceptable and enriching.

On the other hand, art of the "people," often referred to as "folk art" or "arts and crafts," is often found close to where it was produced, is accessible for little or no cost, and requires no specific dress or manners to enjoy it. Wherever one travels, one can find art that reflects the local flair and culture(s). While many enjoy this art, the formal art community often judges it to be less sophisticated or valuable.

In today's classrooms, children seldom learn of this bias toward certain styles of art and even more infrequently study ways to minimize its influence. It is unrealistic to expect everyone to like every painting, drawing, or sculpture created, and this should not be the intent of the art teacher. It is reasonable, however, to teach children to base their opinions on the attributes of the art itself, rather than on its acceptance as "true" art. Students should learn to appreciate how each piece of art provides them a greater awareness of the artist and his or her culture. Rhoades-Hudak (1995) recommends that teachers in anti-bias classrooms use a series of specific questions to help children think more deeply about the cultural context of art and the existence of bias. A few such questions are:

- What emotions, values, and/or qualities are being communicated?
- What does the artwork (techniques and materials used) tell us about the artist and his or her culture?
- Is the art "pleasing" or "not pleasing," and what are your reasons for such a consideration?

Whose Art? How Do We Judge It? An art activity for older children uses a variety of examples of "formal" art (pictures of European classics) and folk art. Pictures of both formal and folk art are available in reference books, multimedia, or on the Internet. The teacher presents the students with a variety of artistic examples and applies the questions described by Rhoades-Hudak (1995) to promote a discussion. Students are encouraged to express their perceptions of each piece's value. As students carefully consider the art, it becomes necessary to consider the artist and the cultural context in which it was developed. Bias, which causes one to value the class or culture of one artist over another, is replaced with a deeper and more objective understanding of the role of art in culture. Teachers and their students may want to create their own "museums of art" that inclusively reflect the variety of art present in today's world.

Science, Technology, and Society

Science, technology, and society (STS) lessons differ from traditional science lessons, because STS allows us to see how bias in science may be used to rationalize the things people do and the decisions they make that benefit the interests of the majority—often at the expense of the less powerful. A sample lesson may involve plant growth, propagation, and harvesting. These processes cannot occur without some sort of effect on human beings and the environment. Teaching about plants (or any science topic) without discussing its context or impact does little to develop student scientists who can see beyond their own cultural and personal experiences.

In the plant growth lesson, STS would include an anti-bias focus that guides students to consider more deeply the implications of science. In examining how plants grow (or are grown) in many places, other than where they indigenously began, a teacher may lead students to question how this is done and why. When plants are farmed where they do not naturally occur, how must their requirements be met, and at what cost? What is the impact on their new environment and its ecology? How is their propagation sustained? Because the new ecosystem of the farmed plant almost assuredly will be different from the one in which the plant originated, what artificial supports for survival are necessary, and what are the consequences? If irrigation is required, from where will the water come, and how does this affect people living nearby and the environment downstream? If chemicals, pesticides, and fertilizers are used to sustain the orchard or farm, what will happen to the groundwater as a result of runoff? How toxic are these chemicals to those who harvest the crop? Are the workers who harvest the crop paid a living wage?

Through such explorations, children often come to realize that many products they take for granted are acquired at great cost to other individuals. The individuals who pay the greatest cost are often people of color who are economically disadvantaged. Our actions as consumers may inadvertently support practices that perpetuate inequalities in society.

Birds of a Feather. Diversity in nature is a topic that seems to intrigue students. Hence, the topic of "birds" is ideal for an integrated curriculum activity. Students should have access to a variety of resources they can use to investigate a range of birds, including each one's particular characteristics. For instance, shore birds may have scooping bills to collect and filter plants and organisms living in the water. Birds of prey have talons for catching and holding their victims and sharp beaks for ripping and tearing meat. Discuss with students the characteristics that all birds have in common and some that are different.

As students grasp the concept of diversity in nature, this same concept can be used to discuss human beings. Read the book *People,* by Peter Spier (1988), to the students. This book illustrates the variety of physical and cultural characteristics found in humans around the globe. After discussing the range of physical and cultural characteristics found among human beings, have each student draw or paint a picture of him- or herself. ("Multicultural" crayons or paints allow students to more clearly match the variety of shades and hues of human skin colors.) Pictures can be mounted on a bulletin board with a title along the lines of "Human Beings: There Is Beauty in Diversity."

Language Arts

In language arts lessons, children learn about the power of words, which are often used to express bias. Many thoughtful stories and poems (many of them listed in previous chapters of this book) can help children to explore a range of cultures, understand the damaging effects of bias, and develop empathy.

Poems With a Purpose. The following poem is an excellent tool for discussing how words develop social meaning. In the poem "Me" (*Salt Lake Tribune*, 1994, p. B1), the author uses the term "colored" in an ironic way.

Me
(author unknown)

When I was born—I was black
When I grew up—I was black
When I am sick—I am black
When I go out in the sun—I am black
When I am cold—I am black
When I die—I am black
But you . . .
When you were born—you were pink
When you grew up—you were white
When you are sick—you turn green
When you go out in the sun—you turn tan
When you are cold—you turn blue
When you die—you turn gray
And you have the nerve to call me "colored"?

After sharing this poem, ask students to research the historical meaning of the term "colored." Why is this term considered offensive to African Americans today? If a term is offensive to the group of people to whom it refers (e.g., "colored," "chick," "Indian"), what can and should we do?

Understanding and Appreciating Dialects. An area that naturally lends itself to anti-bias teaching is the study of dialects. Dialects abound in our classrooms. A dialect is a variation of a language associated with a particular regional or social group (Dandy, 1991). With our families at home, we may use a dialect that is entirely different from the one we learn at school. With our friends, we may use slang and syntax not used in other contexts. When teachers address students or parents, they adopt the standard code—matching the demands of the situation with the grammar and vocabulary that is deemed appropriate. In schools, children seldom learn of their multilingual capabilities and, therefore, fail to comprehend the real power of language, which is not just to convey a message but also to share a culture.

Reactions to dialects vary. Southern and African American dialects, for example, both stem from similar linguistic roots. Yet those who speak them are perceived differently. Southern dialect spoken by whites is often thought of as genteel and charming, while African American English is typically perceived as ignorant or low class. It is not enough in an anti-bias classroom merely to note that differences exist, particularly when societal responses to these culturally based variations are not equal. Educators must guide their students to develop accurate knowledge of and positive attitudes toward linguistic diversity.

Many children's books allow extensive study of cultural variation. A good example is *Flossie and the Fox* (McKissack, 1986), a southern "Little Red Riding Hood" story written in African American rural dialect. A five-step procedure is suggested for exploring linguistic bias when using a book such as this one (Barta & Grindler, 1996). Step one entails children reading or listening to the story. In step two, the teacher helps her or his students identify cultural aspects of character(s) and language that are different from those of the dominant culture. To explore bias and extend the learning, students could identify, list, or chart ways in which the writer uses his or her dialect to express thoughts and feelings. Specific words or phrases could be listed and their meanings interpreted into "standard" English. Discussions of the ways that some individuals or society may perceive, evaluate, and respond negatively to these linguistic differences will make up step three. During step four, students describe the literal message the speaker is trying to convey. When the intent of the speaker is analyzed, students realize they probably have communicated the same message. The difference this time is that a minority dialect is being used to best reflect the speaker's experience and perspective.

During the final step, students trace the history and development of the dialect. The culturally based vocabulary, grammar, and syntax used to describe their experience and perspective typically follow sophisticated and systematic grammatical conventions. They usually find that the dialect, previously devalued, is as rule-bound and grammatically systematic as the "standard" language they study. Children helped to this realization can marvel at the complexity and diversity of the multiple dialects of various languages.

Ugly Adjectives. "Sticks and stones may break my bones, but words will never hurt me" is a common children's chant. As children increase their vocabulary, however, it is important that they learn how words can be used either to uplift and inspire or diminish and hurt. Often, children use words to describe others without considering what effect those words may have on people. Show students a list of adjectives that includes words such as "smart," "friendly," "compassionate," and "helpful," as well as "lazy," "dirty," "stupid," "dishonest," and "irresponsible." Have students read each adjective and discuss its meaning. Give students three sticky labels and have them randomly select three words from the list and write each one on a label. Collect all the labels, place them face-down on a desktop, and shuffle them around. Ask students to come and collect three labels without looking at what has been written on them. When students are seated, have them place their labels on the back of the nearest student (someone who has not yet been "labeled"). Give students time to circulate and read each other's labels. Next, with the help of a friend, students should remove their labels. Ask students to express how it felt to be labeled even when the act was entirely random. Help students to understand that negative labels can cause pain and that people's perceptions of themselves and others are influenced by the use of such labels. This activity can be extended by having students look for labels that are used in everyday life. A study of a newspaper's letters to the editor, particularly when controversial topics such as affirmative action or immigration quotas are being discussed, is a great place to start.

Storytelling. Storytelling is a time-honored tradition used in many cultures to teach important lessons to children. The Native American legend "Look at the Trees of the Forest" illustrates the importance of demonstrating tolerance, understanding, kindness, and compassion to all we meet, as it points out the negative effects of discriminatory behavior. While this story legend is told among members of Algonquin communities (the most populous and widespread of North American Native groups), similar stories can be found among many other Native Nations. This legend involves one of the tales of Grey Wolf, an honored elder who teaches practical lessons, and Little Mouse Sister, an energetic, inquisitive child who follows Grey Wolf along different paths through the forest.

When young children encounter strangers, or react with hostility toward someone different from themselves, their fears and mistrust can easily give way to anger. The following story illustrates the calming wisdom of Grey Wolf as he tries to help Little Mouse Sister overcome her misplaced feelings of impatience, anger, and intolerance. For even the youngest child, uncontrolled outbursts based on negative perceptions need to be acknowledged, discussed, and dealt with in simple terms. Racism flows from fear; fear from ignorance. By seizing an opportunity to educate Little Mouse Sister, Grey Wolf dispels her fears, counters her intolerant attitude, and helps her turn unacceptable behavior into actions that are caring and respectful.

Look at the Trees of the Forest: An Algonquin Legend
(author unknown)

Late one afternoon in the season following the snows, Little Mouse Sister walked with Grey Wolf along a narrow path at the rocky edge of the forest. Melting waters from the hillside had turned the sides of the path into a slippery mixture of mud and ice patches, so the two were forced to walk in single file, Little Mouse Sister leading the way as the grandfather followed behind. The day had turned cold as the sun began to sink low in the sky, and both felt hungry as they followed the winding path toward their home fire. With each careful step, Little Mouse Sister moved quickly, turning frequently to see that Grey Wolf was not too far behind her. She waited occasionally so the gap between them could close and to be sure that the grandfather could see her through the heavy branches that overhung their path. Few words were spoken as they walked except for brief exchanges in their tribal language, and the comforting songs the child sang as they made their way home.

The path became steep as it turned toward a particularly tricky, rock-covered section, and Little Mouse Sister was forced to hold on to some small twigs at the side of the path in order to keep her balance. She had moved a good distance ahead of Grey Wolf and didn't notice that he had fallen farther behind. Suddenly, as she stepped carefully along the narrow path, a young man who was coming toward her from the opposite direction met her. Startled, she saw that his clothing was different from any of her tribal members, and that he carried tools she had never seen before. She called out to him to step aside so she wouldn't fall off the path, but he said nothing. She shouted at him to make room for her, but he obviously didn't understand her language. His eyes were wide, and his leg was wrapped in soft buckskin, like her mother used whenever someone had sustained an injury. He was leaning on a strong stick, and seemed to be moving even more slowly than the grandfather.

Because Little Mouse Sister couldn't step around him, and was unable to make him understand that he should get out of her way, she began to shout at him in a most unfriendly way. The young man stood still and seemed puzzled by the noises she was making. Then, Little Mouse Sister grabbed a large rock from the edge of the path, hurled it with all of her might and, with a good aim, struck the stranger on the side of his head. The blow caused him to lose his balance, drop the strong stick, and fall to the ground. As he lay across the path, holding a hand to the bloodied mark on his forehead, he was unable to get up without the stick he had been leaning on. At that moment, Grey Wolf slowly stepped up behind Little Mouse Sister and asked her what she had done.

"I asked him to let me pass, Grandfather, and he didn't say anything. I told him that we needed to get home before dark, and he didn't move. I've never seen someone with eyes like that before, and he was leaning on a stick, so I thought he might use it to hurt me. I called for you, but you didn't hear me. I didn't know who he was, Grandfather, so I threw a rock at him and he fell down."

With that, Grey Wolf picked up the injured man's crutch, helped him to his feet, and offered his hand in friendship. The young man carefully made his way around the two, and stood in silence at the side of the path. Because the stranger was in pain, Grey Wolf reached out to him, led him to a large rock, and helped him to sit down and rest. Then he turned to Little Mouse Sister and asked her to come closer and sit beside them for a moment. Grey Wolf spoke slowly and softly as he began his lesson.

"Little Mouse Sister, your words and your actions have caused pain for this young man. He was already wounded and you didn't try to help him. I understand that he is a stranger

to you since he belongs to a different tribe. Your words were unknown to him, just as his ways were unknown to you. It was wrong to tell him to move over. His weakness should have caused you to help him. Just because he is not of our tribe was not a good reason to hurt him. Instead, you should have made room on the path for him. This man meant you no harm; he simply didn't understand you. There is room for everyone on this path and we must all travel it together.

"Look at the trees of the forest, Little Mouse Sister. The oak, the birch, the pine, and the spruce live together in harmony. The beauty of our forest comes from the Creator, and all of the trees share the gifts from Mother Earth. They share the water and the sunlight so they can all grow tall and strong. They provide their branches so the birds can build their nests and their leaves so we can be sheltered from the heat of the sun. Each of the trees in the forest is different: some are tall, and others grow close to the ground so we can pick berries. Some are straight and green, while others change their colors in the time of the frost. Together, they make up the forest, and each one carries out its duties without complaining. The oak tree doesn't tell the pine tree to move over. The spruce tree doesn't tell the birch to move over. The pine tree doesn't drink all of the water and the birch tree doesn't keep the sunlight all for itself. Together with the bird creatures and the four-legged creatures, the trees live in harmony with each other so we can walk along our path. This young man meant you no harm. He and his people are here to share the gifts of the Creator with us. Like the trees of the forest, we are all different; but we must live in harmony together.

"We have rested now. Offer your hand in friendship to this young man and help him to his feet so he can continue on his way." Little Mouse Sister moved closer to Grey Wolf and then did as he had instructed her. She helped the stranger stand up and watched as he continued on his way along the path. As the sun faded slowly beneath the hills, Grey Wolf and Little Mouse Sister resumed their journey to their home fire.

"Look at the Trees of the Forest" is a story that teaches children the wisdom of co-existence, the importance of sharing, and the value of respect for others. By borrowing from the storytelling methodology of teaching, anti-bias educators can offer their students memorable lessons that will help them understand and value diversity, and help them develop a good level of respect for difference.

Social Studies

A major goal of social studies education is the development of citizens who can function successfully within a culturally diverse and democratic society (Martorella, 1994). Thus, anti-bias education is a central component of the social studies curriculum. Here are some sample activities.

Heroes and Sheroes. Historically, notable women and minorities have been relatively absent from curriculum materials presented to children (Lewis, 2004; Martorella, 1994). The effects of this curricular bias can be seen when children discuss their heroes. To redress this, teachers need to point out the absence of information regarding the contributions and achievements of women and people of color. This activity will help students to recognize and discuss the significant social contributions made by diverse groups of women and men. Ask students individually to list "heroes" and "sheroes" from each of these groups:

European American
Native American
Hispanic or Latino
Asian American
African American
People with disabilities
Gay/Lesbian

Create a large master list from the names contributed by individual students. As a group, discuss characteristics that contribute to someone being considered a "hero." (They usually say a hero is someone who has done something courageous for other people.) Analyze the list with your class. What conclusions can be made? Are there biases or stereotypes evident in the names listed? What do the names on the list reveal about people we think of as heroes? Review names to determine which people are current heroes and which are historical. What are the people known for? Is there agreement about the names that are on the list? (Do entertainers and sports stars qualify as heroes? Are some of the people on the list personal heroes, but not famous?) How can we account for the names that are on the list? How do people become known as heroes?

Teachers may want to continue this discussion by having students research notable people from categories that are underrepresented on the board. Some examples may be Rosa Parks, Harriet Tubman, Amelia Earhart, and Chief Joseph, to name only a few.

Where on Earth? On the typical classroom world map, Europe is in the center. While all maps distort parts of the world in order to portray a spherical object as flat, the projections used in most classroom maps significantly distort (showing them larger than they actually are) the countries in the northern hemisphere. Greenland appears to be the size of South America, for example, when in reality it is about the size of Mexico. Some world maps may even bisect the continent of Asia and place half of it on one side of the map and half on the other. Various map projections send out subtle messages that may distort our understanding and reinforce biased perceptions of our place in the world (e.g., countries where Caucasians live appear to be larger on the maps than they actually are).

Children can develop new insights into their perspectives of the planet and the global community. First, have students explore and describe their ethnic ancestry. Use a map of the world to place pins where their ancestors lived. Stories (real or imaginative) can be composed describing the journey of their ancestors to the United States. Teachers and students also may research how many cultural groups (Jews, Latinos, Japanese, Irish, and Mormons, to name a few) encountered discrimination and prejudice after they migrated. The findings can be related to the experiences of immigrants today.

Next, look at a traditional world map. Discuss how it is presented and briefly discuss how all maps distort the physical world. Teachers can provide older children with a copy of a world map that has no writing on it. Turn the map upside down, so Antarctica is at the top, and label the continents. Have children identify their ancestral country of origin and the place where they currently live. How do continents and specific countries look when viewed from this perspective? How does looking at the map from a different perspective change our view of our place in the world?

First Thoughts. As students study people and society, they benefit from recognizing the stereotypes that they and others may hold about various groups of people. Stereotypes limit our thinking and always inaccurately portray some individuals because individual differences exist, even within the same population. Create a large chart with a variety of people (e.g., boys, girls, homeless people, people in wheelchairs, gay men, and lesbians) listed at the top. Ask students to anonymously write on a paper strip the "first thought" that comes to mind when thinking of each type of person listed. For each category of people, sort the first thoughts into positive, negative, or neutral piles. Attach the strips of papers to the chart. Ask your students to analyze the results. How many of the first thoughts were negative? How many were positive? Where did these first thoughts come from? Help students to understand that these first thoughts may be stereotypical and that if we do not take care, they can influence our interactions with individuals. Encourage students to monitor their first thoughts and recognize that actions should not be based on stereotypes, but rather on reasoned assessments of an individual person's behavior and interactions.

Banners and Slogans. Students can apply art and/or computer-drawing skills within an anti-bias context when they design posters and T-shirt slogans promoting non-discriminatory and anti-prejudice messages. Some slogan ideas might be: "ONE WORLD, ONE PEOPLE" and "CELEBRATE DIVERSITY!" These banners and slogans can be used to kick off a series of preplanned activities in schools with a pledge to dedicate a week, a month, or a year to decreasing prejudice and discrimination.

"Teacher, They Called Me a Qu....!" It seems that society, in general, provides little support for boys and girls who enjoy games, clothing, and activities typically "reserved" for the opposite gender. When a girl eschews dresses and can throw a ball, run as fast, or climb trees as well as a boy, she is considered to be a "tomboy." Boys are called "sissies" if they cry, play with dolls, or take ballet. As children grow older, terms like "tomboy" and "sissy" may be replaced with more damaging words like "queer," "fag," "homo," or "dyke." Children sometimes adopt these words to degrade peers who do not meet stereotyped notions of gender-appropriate dressing, thinking, or behavior. These words also are used as powerful verbal weapons to provoke, anger, or hurt people, regardless if they are gay or straight. No matter the context, such words carry a strong message to people of all ages that being gay or lesbian—or not following strict gender scripts—is something bad. An anti-bias curriculum teaches children to examine stereotypes and discriminatory actions, including those related to sexual orientation.

Just as a teacher would not allow students to use racist terms, the use of homophobic words requires an immediate response. Children must learn that name-calling of any kind is unacceptable. Byrnes (1995) describes several actions a teacher can take in response. First, teachers should discuss with students what instigated the name-calling and what the student was really trying to communicate. (Many times children do not even understand what the terms mean, only that they are powerful and hurtful.) Students should be helped to understand that because such name calling is intended to deprecate someone, it is hurtful not only to the individual to whom it was directed, but also to all individuals who are gay or lesbian and to all the friends and loved ones of such individuals. While a student may find a person's sexual orientation to be unacceptable (for religious reasons, perhaps), it is not acceptable to engage in hateful and discriminatory actions against that person. Children should be given opportunities to think about and develop more appropriate ways to act and react when becoming angry or frustrated with someone.

Whose Job Is It? In a social studies unit on "community helpers," students could work cooperatively to cut out pictures of people from magazines and newspapers (select from many sources: *Ebony, Ms., Hispanic Lifestyle Magazine, Native Peoples, Newsweek*). Children then assign "jobs" to the people in the pictures. The jobs might include firefighter, police officer, nurse, doctor, teacher, cab driver, cleaning person, chef, or president of a company. Make sure to stretch students' thinking by including job titles that traditionally have been considered gender- or ability-specific. Use discussion time to expose any bias when the students are finished assigning their jobs. Tabulate the number of men and women doing the various jobs. Are people of color equally distributed across the occupations? Do students have a person in a wheelchair doing an important job, portray a woman as an executive, or show a man caring for children? After analyzing the data, discuss the social implications of this activity.

Music

In teaching music, as with other subjects, teachers must do more than present different music and styles. In the anti-bias classroom, society's response and reaction to music, and to the diverse people making the music, must be examined. Children can be helped to understand that we tend to enjoy most the music that we have heard most frequently and that we connect to positive cultural experiences. Children's enjoyment of music can be used as a tool for teaching important anti-bias messages.

Different Notes for Different Folks. Children can bring in examples of their favorite music (provided it is age-appropriate and its lyrics are not derogatory toward other groups), and the teacher can lead discussions about what music they like and do not like. By modeling acceptance of a range of music styles, the teacher can help children to understand that having different tastes does not mean that one group's or another's preference is wrong.

As children share their music, they can be helped to understand that as cultures have come in proximity to one another, their musical traditions often have blended to create new forms of music. Much of today's popular music (e.g., rap, reggae, country) represents a combination of various cultural contributions. Encourage children to explore the cultural roots of the music they enjoy. Through such research, children can come to understand that by sharing and enjoying each other's cultural traditions, we can create something new that may be greater than the sum of its parts.

Celebrating Diversity. Bill Schmid (personal communication, December 20, 2004), music professor at Georgia Southern University, says that jazz is a perfect example of what can occur when diversity is validated. He observes,

A jazz performance is like a multilayered conversation among the players, with everyone accepting what the soloist of the moment is saying, and then validating it by emphasizing, repeating, using it as a jumping-off point for further exploration of the song.

Wynton Marsalis, the internationally acclaimed trumpet player, supports this view and states,

Jazz means working things out musically with other people. You have to listen to other musicians and play with them even if you don't agree with what they're playing. It teaches you the very opposite of racism and anti-Semitism. It teaches you that the world is big enough to accommodate us all. (Smith, 1994, p. 17)

One anti-bias music activity that celebrates diversity models the importance of each note or instrument maintaining its own identity when accompanying others. Each different type of instrument within a group (e.g., stringed, percussion) shares similar characteristics, yet they are distinct. A teacher with a collection of instruments can model for the students their particular sounds.

Multicultural Harmony. Any instrument can be substituted for the guitar in this suggested activity. The students can be seated around the teacher, who begins by explaining that he or she will be playing a song. The teacher plucks one and only one string, thus reproducing the sound repeatedly. Initially, the students will listen intently, but will soon tire of hearing the monotonous repetition and will look quizzically at the teacher. The teacher then asks the students if they like the "music." Generally, students reply that it is not music, because music has more varied sounds. A short discussion of how people are like instruments, each making a particular note or sound, can ensue. In a band, no one instrument is more important than another. At times, some may be played more loudly or more continuously than others. Change songs, however, and each instrument has a different role. Students can be asked to consider how interesting life would be if we were all the same and remark how wonderful it is that so many different people exist.

It's in the Words. Music can bring us together in ways few other subject areas can. Certain songs, such as "One Light, One Sun" (by Raffi) and "In Harmony" (by Alan Menken and Howard Ashman), convey strong messages of peace and acceptance. The Teaching Tolerance Project offers a CD of music promoting appreciation of diversity, caring, and courage through a variety of musical styles and traditions.

When selecting music, consider incorporating songs that include strong anti-bias messages. As children learn these songs, discuss the messages conveyed by the lyrics. Having children share such songs with parents at school programs and meetings is also an excellent way to let parents know what the school values.

IMPLEMENTING ANTI-BIAS CURRICULUM: CASE REPORTS

All these activities demonstrate how anti-bias messages can be integrated easily into teaching mathematics, science, art, social studies, music, and language arts. Once a teacher starts thinking about all the ways anti-bias concepts can be integrated into the curriculum, it is hard to stop. The following two case reports illustrate this point.

That's Diversity!

For the young students in Carol Ellis's preschool class at the Family Life Center, located on the campus of Georgia Southern University in Statesboro, Georgia, the year-long theme of "diversity" helped them make sense of differences they saw and experienced in the world. Carol's main objective was to make children aware that diversity exists everywhere. Diversity is a common occurrence not only among human beings, but also among all living things. She incorporated the concept of diversity into virtually every aspect of her curriculum (e.g., the environment, pets).

Carol proceeded by asking the students, "How would you like it if everyone looked like me?" She noted that she has never had a single student reply in favor of such a world! She explains, "If everything were the same, it would get pretty boring and that is why diversity is important!" Without diversity, there would be only one flavor of ice cream or one kind of dog. "Diversity means different and that is good," Carol contends.

Carol does not shy away from addressing sensitive issues, because she believes such discussions, if handled appropriately, help children feel secure about sharing their insights or asking their questions. Children's literature plays a big role in her diversity theme. *Be Good to Eddie Lee* (Fleming, 1993), for example, is an excellent book to begin a discussion about people who have a disability. Carol makes use of persons in the community to teach children about the purposes of wheelchair ramps, hearing aids, and signs printed in Braille.

Carol seizes opportunities to replace stereotypical and erroneous information with more accurate descriptions. When a book was shared that described all the heads of animal families as male, for example, she pointed out that lionesses catch most of the food for the pride and also care for the young cubs. By the spring of the academic year, Carol's students had substantial experience reflecting on the theme of diversity. As she modeled her own wonder, excitement, and respect, her students grew to perceive diversity just as positively.

Perhaps the most telling indication of the effect anti-bias education has on children is in the way that they respond to diversity. Jacob, one of Carol's 4-year-old students, was walking through a mall with his father when they both spotted a man with a mane of dreadlocks. Jacob stopped in his tracks and stared at the man and the man stared back. After silently watching for a few seconds, Jacob said to his father, "That's diversity!" and went on his way.

Lightening the Load

Chris Bowen, a 1st-grade teacher at Mattie Lively Elementary School (also located in Statesboro, Georgia), personifies many of the characteristics of an anti-bias educator. According to Chris, many of his children come to him already loaded down with "baggage." The baggage he refers to is the prejudice and discrimination that they and their families have experienced.

Chris's community is probably not that much different from many other places in the United States. What is different about Chris's situation is that he has dedicated himself to helping his students develop positive attitudes toward diversity and to confronting prejudice and discrimination. He wants his students to consider many points of view and to learn the reasons why people have certain perceptions. The following several scenarios shared by Chris (personal communication, October 21, 1995) typify how deeply rooted prejudice is and how clearly aware young children are of race.

During our study of community helpers, the class took a walking tour of the downtown area to view the various businesses located there. Since our class was traveling independently from the other classes participating, we took a special trip to see businesses operated by African Americans. I did not tell students of my agenda, but after going into several businesses, one black student said, "Hey, Mr. Bowen, blacks work here." I replied to the student, "Not only do blacks work here, black people own the businesses." The student simply returned, "Well, I'm going to do that!" (The field trip was a success, reported Chris.)

The second situation shared occurred during a cooperative activity.

As the students were working on the class assignment, Chris overheard a conversation between a black girl and a white boy. The girl stated that her grandma cleans houses after she gets off work. The boy replied in eagerness, "Oh yeah, well my mom cleans houses and a big hospital." The girl innocently remarked that she "didn't know white people could clean."

The theme central to daily activities in "Mr. Bowen's room" is how we treat each other and why. Chris finds many "teachable moments" that fit into this theme. During Thanksgiving, students discuss sharing and community needs, the hardships faced by the Pilgrims, and the openness of the native peoples who met and helped them. The students learn to understand the needs, cultures, and perspectives of both parties. Stereotypes and misinformation about the natives who met and helped the pilgrims are countered with hands-on activities. To counter the common misconception that all Native Americans lived in teepees, for example, Chris and his students used the jungle gym on the playground to construct a life-size model of a house used by the native people who met the Pilgrims. They covered the equipment (virtually a perfect dome) with brown sacks to resemble the bark used in making wigwams.

Chris once talked about the time his class spent examining the life of Martin Luther King, Jr. The discussion turned to how some people are considered less worthy because they are a certain color. Chris supported his African American students as they shared their feelings about being black in America. The white children were awestruck. They had never heard race talked about so openly before. According to Chris, it was a solemn and cathartic event.

In this classroom, students are never considered too young to discuss and learn about complex social issues. Rather, they are respected for their wisdom, which seems to surpass their youthful years. Racism, inequality, and oppression may not be topics we find suggested for discussion in the core curriculum, yet many children live the effects of these social conditions daily. Chris does not ignore the reality of his students' lives. He willingly and enthusiastically helps his students to question and challenge prejudice and discrimination.

CONCLUSION

Classroom teachers who consciously integrate anti-bias activities into their curriculum can offer their students multiple opportunities to deal with, and overcome, prejudice and discrimination. Math, music, language, science, art, and social studies are all reflections of what people do. They are the vehicles for helping us learn more about ourselves and others. As such, it is important to approach them from a position of inclusivity. Teachers must continue to seek ways to make their classrooms places where all are welcome and can succeed. By doing so, we emphasize our common bonds and come to understand and appreciate our differences.

References

Ascher, M. (2002). *Mathematics elsewhere: An exploration of ideas across cultures.* Princeton, NJ: Princeton University Press.

Banks, J., Cookson, P., Gay, G., Hawley, W., Irvine, J., Nieto, S., Schofield, J., & Stephan, W. (2001). Diversity within unity: Essential principles for teaching and learning in a multicultural society. *Phi Delta Kappan, 83*(3), 196-203.

Barta, J. (1999). Mathematics and beadwork. *Winds of Change, 14*(2), 36-41.

Barta, J., Abeyta, A., Gould, D., Galindo, E., Matt, G., Seaman, D., & Voggesser, G. (2001). The mathematical ecology of the Shoshoni: Implications for elementary mathematics education. *Journal of American Indian Education, 40*(2), 1-27.

Barta, J., & Grindler, M. (1996). Exploring bias using children's multicultural literature. *Reading Teacher, 50*(3), 269-270.

Barta, J., & Shockey, T. (2005). *Dancing numbers: Inclusive mathematics education for aboriginal students.* Manuscript submitted for publication.

Byrnes, D. A. (1995). *"Teacher, they called me a____!": Confronting prejudice and discrimination in the classroom.* New York: Anti-Defamation League of B'nai B'rith.

Cajete, G. A. (1999). *Igniting the sparkle: An indigenous science education model.* Skyland, NC: Kivaki Press.

D'Ambrosio, U. (2001). What is ethnomathematics, and how can it help children in schools? *Teaching Children Mathematics, 7*(6), 308-312.

Dandy, E. (1991). *Black communication: Breaking down the barriers.* Chicago: African American Images.

Derman-Sparks, L. (1991). *Anti-bias curriculum: Tools for empowering young children.* Washington, DC: National Association for the Education of Young Children.

Derman-Sparks, L., & Phillips, C. (1997). *Teaching/learning anti-racism: A developmental approach.* New York: Teachers College Press.

Fleming, V. (1993). *Be good to Eddie Lee.* New York: Philomel Books.

Joseph, G. (2000). *The crest of the peacock: Non-European roots of mathematics.* Princeton, NJ: Princeton University Press.

Ka'a, M. (1976). The logic of non-European linguistic categories. In R. Pinxten (Ed.), *Universalism versus relativism in language and thought: Proceedings of a colloquium on the Sapir-Whorf hypotheses* (pp. 85-96). The Hague, The Netherlands: Mouton.

Lewis, A. C. (2004). Schools that engage children. *Phi Delta Kappan, 85*(7), 483-484.

Martorella, P. H. (1994). *Social studies for elementary school children: Developing young citizens.* New York: Merrill.

Masingila, J. O. (1994). Mathematics practice in carpet laying. *Anthropology and Education Quarterly, 25*(4), 430-462.

National Council of Teachers of Mathematics. (2000). *Principles and standards.* Reston, VA: Author.

Me. (1994, June 8). *The Salt Lake Tribune,* p. B1.

McKissack, P. (1986). *Flossie and the fox.* New York: Dial Books for Young Readers.

Pappas, C., Kiefer, B., & Levstik, L. (1999). *An integrated language perspective in the elementary school: Theory into action* (3rd ed.). White Plains, NY: Longman Publishing.

Raczek, L. (1999). *Rainy's powwow.* Flagstaff, AZ: Rising Moon Books.

Rhoades-Hudak, J. (1995). Recognizing the importance of cultural diversity in an art program. In R. Ragans (Ed.), *Art talk: Teacher's wraparound edition* (pp. 14-15). Mission Hills, CA: Glencoe, Macmillan/McGraw-Hill.

Saxe, G. (1988). Candy selling and math learning. *Educational Researcher, 17*(6), 14-21.

Smith, J. (1994, December 18). Wynton blows his horn for jazz. *San Francisco Examiner and Chronicle,* p. C-17.

Spier, P. (1988). *People.* New York: Doubleday.

Zaslavsky, C. (1996). *The multicultural math classroom: Bringing in the world.* Portsmouth, NH: Heinemann Publishing.

Chapter 9
Tooling the Toolbox: Checklist of Skills for Teaching in Diverse Classrooms and Communities

Judith Puncochar

We live in a fast-paced world, where human interaction occurs within increasingly diverse communities. In a rapidly changing world, people need competencies for creating successful and sustainable human interactions. The Chinese proverb "talk does not cook rice" is an apt warning that information alone is not enough to guarantee success when interacting with people of different cultural backgrounds. Misunderstandings and conflicts can arise in quickly transforming multicultural and global communities. People must develop the necessary skills for resolving conflicts and creating thriving human interactions in classrooms and communities.

Learning groups in classrooms with members from diverse backgrounds tend to experience more controversy than those in homogeneous classrooms (Johnson & Johnson, 2006). When problems arise in diverse classrooms, teachers may look for instructional solutions, which are short-term fixes that usually require continuous teacher monitoring (see Terry, 1993, 2001). Teachers and students need to create more self-sustaining solutions whereby everyone strives towards the mutual goal of maintaining respectful, inclusive, and culturally diverse learning environments (Puncochar, Choi, Khan, & Strom, 2003; Puncochar & Roehrich, 2005). Creating successful learning environments in diverse classrooms is attainable with the right tools.

The following checklist is a toolbox of practical actions that teachers can take to create successful learning in diverse classrooms. Teachers can use this checklist as a guide for how to establish successful anti-bias learning environments. The checklist contains the three main tools for: Self-inquiry and Reflection, Productive Pedagogies, and Building Partnerships. Teachers and students who use all three tools will have a better chance at developing the necessary skills for living responsibly in a rapidly changing, multicultural world.

The first tool—Self-inquiry and Reflection—consists of questions for considering the influence of teachers' personal beliefs and expectations on interactions with people from diverse backgrounds. An important task for all teachers is to develop the skill of reflective contemplation. The ancient Greek philosopher Heraclitus argued that we never step in the same river twice. The water where we place our first footstep has already moved downstream before we can make our next footstep; thus, the river changes and we change. Likewise, teachers and students live in changing cultural contexts. Teachers' beliefs in the importance of human diversity and of interacting with people from different backgrounds may vary considerably due to their personal experiences and values. Values are not static. Teachers need to show evidence of an evolving personal understanding of self, personal values, and teaching practices. Teachers' skills in teaching students from diverse backgrounds may vary a great deal with their abilities to reflect on personal experiences and the experiences provided by their teacher-training programs. Nevertheless, even beginning teachers make high-quality decisions about multicultural resources and instruction in diverse classrooms when they are provided with tools for analyzing educational experiences (Puncochar et al., 2003).

The second tool—Productive Pedagogies—includes curricular and instructional strategies for diverse classrooms. Productive pedagogies provide the necessary structures, lesson plans, materials, and information for realizing the positive potential of students' diverse backgrounds and cultures. These strategies are usually sufficient for creating successful classrooms, but insufficient for advancing cultural diversity as a valuable and vital component of communities and democratic societies. Creating prosperous communities requires establishing partnerships with people from diverse backgrounds and cultures.

The final tool—Building Partnerships—frames human and cultural diversity as an essential asset for creating sustainable communities in a changing world. An increasingly diverse society with vibrant and respectful communities is attainable when people collectively uphold the shared values for cultural diversity and human dignity in every individual.

After reading the many chapters of this book and becoming aware of how to be engaged in anti-bias teaching, readers may use the "Checklist of Skills for Teaching in Diverse Classrooms and Communities" to assess their performance. Answer the questions below by assigning a self-rating from the following scale.

1 – Awareness only
2 – Beginning to take steps
3 – Good solid performance
4 – A definite strength

The focus in the questions shifts from "I" to "We" as teachers move from their personal beliefs and expectations to interacting with others in productive pedagogies and building partnerships. Human development and learning are changing processes, so revisit the checklist as needed. Consider making copies of the checklist to display in various locations in your school, which will encourage you and others to continue developing core competencies for successful interactions in dynamic multicultural settings.

1. Self-Inquiry and Reflection
— Do I refrain from using labels or generalizations when describing individuals or their families, communities, and cultures?
— Do I avoid mentally prejudging people based on religion, gender orientation, cultural differences, race, language acquisition and accents, immigrant status, socioeconomic status, or rumor?
— Do I recognize each student as a unique member of the student's cultural group?
— Do I consider *each* student and reflect: "How would I feel in this classroom?"
— Do I demonstrate warmth and empathy in my interactions with all students?
— Do I use language that indicates positive expectations for the growth of all students?
— Do I avoid giving profuse praise and unsolicited help when students are engaged in doable tasks?
— Do I seek out opportunities for broadening my knowledge of cultural diversity in my community?
— Do I accept divergent viewpoints as opportunities for personal and professional development?
— Do I examine myself as a bearer of culture, cultural expectations, and biases?

— Do I seek to understand how my cultural beliefs, values, expectations, and traditions affect the students and families in my community?
— Do I keep up with the research on how culture, cultural expectations, and background experiences influence student learning?
— Do I communicate in ways that demonstrate respect for the feelings, ideas, and contributions of others?
— Do I demonstrate a willingness to listen to and receive constructive feedback?
— Do I build strong collaborative relationships with colleagues from diverse backgrounds?

2. Productive Pedagogies in My School
a) Anti-Bias Curriculum
— Do we discuss how the dominant culture often influences what knowledge is shared and valued in schools?
— Do we examine how our curricular materials portray religion, socioeconomic status, ability, race, gender, gender orientation, culture, history, and language differences?
— Do we adapt and supplement curricula materials, as needed, to correct inequities and biases?
— Do we utilize multiple assessment processes that are designed to ensure the fair evaluation of student learning?
— Do we monitor all forms of communication—inside and outside of the classroom—for signs of prejudice and discrimination (e.g., gender-biased language, Eurocentric bulletin boards)?
— Do we structure activities and projects so that they do not favor socioeconomically advantaged students?
— Do we reduce our reliance on tracking and homogeneous ability groups?
— Do we encourage and empower all students and staff to take appropriate action to reduce prejudice and discrimination?

b) Promoting Diversity
— Do we acknowledge the diversity in our backgrounds and treat the diversity as informative, distinctive, and valuable?
— Do we incorporate students' cultural beliefs, values, and traditions in the classroom and learning activities to help create culturally relevant and inclusive classrooms?
— Do we thoughtfully present the perspectives and contributions of members from diverse cultures, socioeconomic classes, gender orientations, and religions, even when such groups are not represented in our classroom or school?
— Do we take advantage of teachable moments by discussing current events from the perspectives of different cultures and groups?
— Do we include resources written in learners' native languages?
— Do we demonstrate and encourage democratic interaction in the classroom and other learning environments?
— Do we support and encourage the hiring of minority-status teachers and staff?

c) Inclusion
— Do we teach and reinforce the value of understanding and respecting the feelings and ideas of others?
— Do we teach children the skills of conflict resolution and cooperation for use both inside and outside of the classroom?
— Do we create opportunities for diverse groups of students to work collaboratively and cooperatively together?
— Do we ensure that all faculty and staff take responsibility for maintaining a respectful, positive learning environment?
— Do we take responsibility for including and accommodating persons with disabilities?

— Do we demonstrate that we value all learners and languages by finding ways to communicate with students in their home languages?
— Do we use a variety of teaching styles to address the needs of students with varying learning styles?
— Do we provide students with equitable access to teachers' attention?
— Do we persist in seeking out the most effective strategies for students who have difficulty learning?
— Do we act as advocates for all students?

3. Building Partnerships in My Community
— Do we create a school environment where all parents and community guests feel welcome and valued?
— Do we develop productive working relationships with community members and organizations to help support the many diverse groups represented in our school?
— Do we help educate community members about the importance of strengthening community cohesion by modeling a commitment to diversity?
— Do we work with others to create, develop, and maintain a school climate that reflects and respects the ever-changing family, community, and cultural contexts in which students live?
— Do we specifically involve parents and community members with our multicultural, anti-bias curriculum?
— Do we promote the interaction of parents, staff, community members, support professionals, and students across socioeconomic, religious, gender, gender orientation, age, ethnic, and racial lines?
— Do we empower others to seek social justice within the school structure by involving them in discussions of educational and social issues, such as achievement gaps among diverse groups?
— Do we address unfair and biased media portrayals of religious, cultural, historical, socioeconomic, racial, gender, gender orientation, and language differences in our communities?
— Do we engage with community members in critically examining the laws and ethical codes governing diversity in our schools, communities, states, and nation, with an eye toward improving equity, diversity, and justice for everyone?

References
Johnson, D. W., & Johnson, F. P. (2006). *Joining together: Group therapy and group skills* (9th ed.). Boston: Allyn & Bacon.
Puncochar, J., Choi, J., Khan, L., & Strom, T. (2003, April). *Development of a diversity checklist based on a model for authentic leadership.* Paper presented at the Annual Meeting of the American Educational Research Association, Chicago, Illinois.
Puncochar, J., & Roehrich, S. (2005, April). *Who has it tougher? Postsecondary students' attitude certainty concerning gender socialization during structured controversy.* Paper presented at the Annual Meeting of the American Educational Research Association, Montreal, Canada.
Terry, R. (1993). *Authentic leadership: Courage in action.* San Francisco: Jossey-Bass.
Terry, R. (2001). *Seven zones for leadership: Acting authentically in stability and chaos.* Palo Alto, CA: Davies-Black Publishers.

Contributors

JAMES J. BARTA, Associate Professor, Department of Elementary Education, Utah State University, Logan, Utah.

DEBORAH A. BYRNES, Professor, Department of Elementary Education, Utah State University, Logan, Utah.

DIANA CORTEZ, Educational Consultant, Bilingual and Multicultural Education, San Luis, Colorado.

ELLEN DAVIDSON, Assistant Professor, Department of Education and Human Services, Simmons College, Boston, Massachusetts. Teaching Associate, Education Development Center, Newton, Massachusetts.

CHARLES C. HAYNES, Scholar in Residence, Freedom Forum First Amendment Center, Vanderbilt University, Nashville, Tennessee.

GARY KIGER, Dean, College of Humanities, Arts, and Social Sciences, Utah State University, Logan, Utah.

JANICE KOCH, Professor, Science Education, Hofstra University, Hempstead, New York.

CORINNE MOUNT PLEASANT-JETTÉ, Assistant Professor, Engineering and Computer Science, Concordia University, Montreal, Quebec, Canada.

LISA PRAY, Assistant Professor, Department of Elementary Education, Utah State University, Logan, Utah.

JUDITH PUNCOCHAR, Assistant Professor, School of Education, Northern Michigan University, Marquette, Michigan.

MARA SAPON-SHEVIN, Professor, Teaching and Leadership Programs, Syracuse University, Syracuse, New York.

NANCY SCHNIEDEWIND, Professor, Humanistic Education Program, State University of New York, New Paltz, New York.

84844

84844